COLLEGE OF MARIN LIBRARY
KENTFIELD, CALIFORNIA

HISTORY
OF AFRICA
Volume II
From 1800
to 1945

HISTORY
OF AFRICA
Volume II
From 1800
to 1945

HARRY A. GAILEY, JR.
San Jose State University

ROBERT E. KRIEGER PUBLISHING COMPANY
MALABAR, FLORIDA
1989

Original Edition 1970
Second Edition 1989

Printed and Published by
ROBERT E. KRIEGER PUBLISHING COMPANY, INC.
KRIEGER DRIVE
MALABAR, FLORIDA 32950

Copyright © (original material) 1970 by Holt, Rinehart and Winston, Inc.
Transferred to Harry A. Gailey November 28, 1979
Copyright © (new material) 1981, 1989 by Robert E. Krieger Publishing Co., Inc.

All rights reserved. No part of this book may be reproduced
in any form or by any means, electronic or mechanical,
including information storage and retrieval systems without
permission in writing from the publisher. *No liability is
assumed with respect to the use of the information contained
herein.*

Printed in the United States of America.

Library of Congress Cataloging-in-Publication Data

Gailey, Harry A.
    History of Africa.

    Vol. 1 originally published: New York: Holt, Rinehart,
and Winston, 1970. It was reprinted by Krieger in 1981 as
part of the 2 v. Krieger ed. of History of Africa. The 1981
issue of v. 1 is now part of this 1981–1989 3 v. work.
    Vol. 2: 2nd ed.
    Vols. 2–3 have imprint: Malabar, Fla.: R.E. Krieger.
    Includes bibliographies and indexes.
    Contents: v. 1. From earliest times to 1800—
v. 2. From 1800 to 1945—v. 3 From 1945 to present.
    1. Africa—History.   I. Title.
DT20.G3 1981b   960   88-9114

ISBN 0-89464-295-2 (v. 2)

10   9   8   7   6   5   4   3   2

for

LAUREL, KAREN, NANCY, RICHARD, and JENNIFER

Preface

Three years ago when planning this history, I conceived it in terms of a single volume. It soon became obvious that such a book would be overly long unless I wanted to ignore large portions of the continent and treat other segments in a very cursory fashion. The decision was then made to issue the work in two separate but complementary volumes. The first was published early in 1970 as a *History of Africa from Earliest Times to 1800*. Although this decision solved one set of problems, it introduced new ones concerning redundancy and continuity. This introduction is an example of the former since I have already stated the reasons for writing the text, what audience it is aimed toward, and what goals I hope to achieve. Those statements are equally applicable to this volume. There are still few general studies of the continent available for teachers of basic courses in African history. Interest in the subject continues to grow on all levels including secondary education. It was partially to relieve my frustrations as a teacher because of the lack of good supporting material that I undertook the long task of writing this history.

In a single volume, continuity of theme and time is relatively automatic. In any multivolume history the author must compromise coverage and continuity in return for other advantages offered. Therefore, in this volume I have not attempted to reintroduce the reader to materials already covered in greater detail in the first book. Thus it may appear that I give little attention to such matters as the origins and development of the Bantu, the Sudanic state, or African religious systems. To have attempted a paraphrase of subjects already delineated in the earlier book would only have increased the size of an already large text and made its organization more difficult and complex.

Any historian imposes an order and unity upon the events he surveys which may not in fact have been true. Nevertheless, some organizational scheme must be used when one is attempting to survey the history of a continent over a period of almost two centuries. The pattern of geographic division utilized in the first book has again been followed with some modifications. Because of the increasing complexity of African societies and polities, it was necessary to introduce chronological subdivisions to each of the major segments. In most cases this has caused few problems since much of sub-Saharan Africa fits into a logical chronological framework without an author forcing one upon the subject matter. Thus the pre-1870 period, the scramble, organization of European control, and the period of devolution of power to African leaders are, in point of time, common to the bulk of African territories. The most glaring exceptions to this type of periodization are the two polities, Ethiopia and Liberia, which maintained their independence throughout much of the nineteenth and twentieth centuries. In surveying these areas, therefore, a different chronological pattern was utilized.

Two decisions were made early in planning this volume. One concerned the need to include events occurring south of the Limpopo River. Some histories of sub-Saharan Africa arbitrarily exclude the complex interactions of Bantu, Hottentot, Indians, and whites. This seems indefensible since southern Africa has been so important, not only because of the mélange of peoples resident there, but because of the effect which they have had upon the rest of Africa. By including southern Africa, the length of the book has been increased. Further, because of the dominance of whites in South Africa, it has been necessary to devote more space to the evolvement of their power structure than to the Bantu or Colored residents. Apartheid is one of the key potentially explosive facts of modern Africa. It seems incumbent upon a general history to elucidate the complex background of this attitude.

The second decision was to exclude any detailed history of the North African areas. Although physically a part of Africa, they are culturally, religiously, and politically more associated with the Middle East and the Mediterranean world. I wanted to avoid an expansion of the text to include the complex problems of the Ottoman Empire and its connections with European diplomacy of the nineteenth century. Obviously one could not ignore the influence of Egypt upon the Sudan, northeastern and eastern Africa, and upon the diplomacy of the scramble for Africa. Thus some attention has been given to events in Egypt in the forty-year period after 1870.

The amount of information available on almost any African area is now so great that it is impossible for one person, or for that matter a team, to be equally knowledgeable in all areas. African studies is in the fortunate state where hundreds of specialists are active in research in many fields. New books and monographs are added weekly to the already impressive list of materials available to the student, teacher, and generalist. However laudatory, this presents the author of a textbook with many problems. One cannot read all the new books and articles, much less be aware of the large body of unpublished information, known only to specialists, which might seriously modify his interpretations. Every attempt has been made in this work to minimize outright error and to guard against overspeculation. Wherever there is inadequate information, I have tried to qualify my statements in such a way as to indicate the tentative nature of the conclusion.

It is an impossible task to construct a list of acknowledgments for those persons who, either directly or indirectly, aided in the production of a general text. However, I should be remiss if I did not express my thanks to Dr. G. Wesley Johnson of Stanford University who read the complete manuscript and commented extensively and fairly upon it. My wife, Rosalie, as usual was indispensable, acting as critic, proofreader, and chief typist for the many drafts of the manuscript.

Harry A. Gailey

Los Gatos, California
September 1971

Preface to the second edition

The information given in the above preface written almost twenty years ago in the main is still true. When it was decided to update Volume II in 1981 all that was needed was to add the generalized account of what had happened in Africa in the decade since the first publication. However, I believed that this type of simplistic reworking was not sufficient for this revision. Too much had happened to simply add a few words to the survey of African states entitled Troubled Independence. Thus the decision was made to keep the materials through 1945 relatively intact with very few alterations and to issue it as the second volume in a series of three. Most of the detailed changes would then be made in a new Volume III which would cover the period 1945 through 1987. This plan allowed for more flexibility for instructors while underscoring the major differences between pre– and post–World War II Africa.

Los Gatos, California   Harry A. Gailey
January 1988

Contents

List of Maps

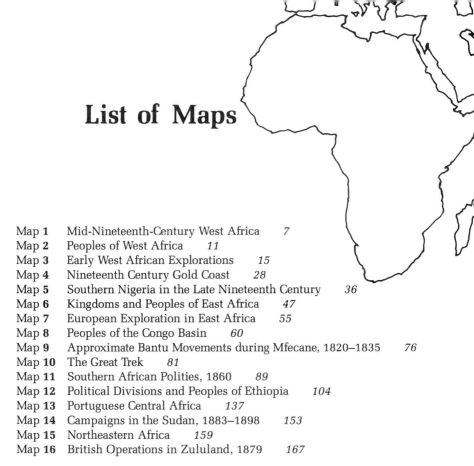

ONE
West Africa before the scramble

Islamic resurgence in the Western Sudan

The Western Sudan was in a state of flux after the Moroccan conquest in the sixteenth century. No power arose to take the place of Songhai. Rather the territory was contested by a large number of smaller polities. Trade declined partially because of the unstable political conditions and partially because European traders along the African coast diverted large amounts of goods away from the interior. The Sudan was as divided religiously as it was politically. The power of Islam was actively challenged by the states of Segu, Kaarta, Macina, and Tekrur. Nevertheless, the dream of a Dar al-Islam, a haven for Islam in the Western Sudan, persisted in the minds of Islamic teachers and holy men. They looked back at the golden age of Mali and Songhai and worked actively to foster in the minds of the people a return to the imagined purity of those days. A realization of a purified religious state was, in practice, modified by the nature of Islam in the Western Sudan. It had been strongly infiltrated by traditional religious beliefs. The carriers of the Islamic revolution in the eighteenth century were Marabouts who were teachers and holy men. However orthodox individual Marabouts might have been, they were viewed by the populace as men endowed with magical and supernatural powers. The visions of the Marabouts had particular meaning for the Fulani and the related Tucolor people. Their acceptance of the ideal of reformation created in the nineteenth century a series of Islamic states stretching from the Upper Senegal to Hausaland.

Early in the reign of Askia Muhammad, some Fulani pastoralists rebelled against their Songhai overlords. Driven out of the empire, they moved southwestward and settled in Central Guinea. Gaining adherents from non-Fulani groups, particularly the Mandinka, some of them moved northward in the mid-sixteenth century, skirted the Wolof states, and overthrew the rulers of Tekrur. Here in the Upper Senegal regions they estab-

1

lished their own non-Islamic dynasty, the Denianke, which remained in control of the new state of Futa Toro until the 1770s.

The Fulani who remained behind in the Futa Jallon settled down and took on many attributes of townsmen. Among those elements absorbed by these Fulani in the next century was Islam. In the first quarter of the eighteenth century Fulani holy men, "revivers of Islam," created a new type of state in the Futa Jallon. An imam who claimed to rule the state in the name of God was the religious, political, and military leader of the state. The imam was selected from religious teachers who were members of a few important families, and he ruled for only a specific period of time. The state was divided into nine provinces and these into further subdistricts. Each unit was administered by officials directly responsible to the imam. Located in the hilly country of Guinea, this theocratic state continued to prosper and its system remained relatively intact until the French invasions of the latter nineteenth century. During this long period, Futa Jallon acted as a training ground for religious teachers and as a practical example for Islamic reformers everywhere in the Western Sudan.

Further to the north in Futa Toro, the Denianke dynasty was challenged in the 1770s by their Tucolor subjects. The Tucolor people, basically Fulani with slight admixtures of Wolof and Serer, had long been converts to Islam. Thus the reforming movements in North Africa and the Western Sudan in the eighteenth century found early adherents among the Tucolors. Suleiman Ba was the leader of the reformers in Futa Toro and in 1776 his followers succeeded in overthrowing the Denianke rulers. The imamate of Futa Toro was subsequently created to further the goals of a revived theocracy. After the death of Suleiman, the rulers of Futa Toro were elected. Under Muslim leadership, trade which had languished was revived with other areas of the Sudan and with the French on the coasts.

Other Muslim states were created farther to the east in the same period. One such state was Bondu, located between the two Futas. Another area was Macina where the Muslim Fulani in the eighteenth century created an alliance with their still pagan rulers. In the latter eighteenth century the Islamic Fulani in Macina were almost completely free from control by the pagan rulers. The Islamic revolution was brought to the borders of the Hausa states by the creation of the town of Say. This was the work of a Marabout, Alfa Muhammad Diobo, who wished to create a center for a purified Islam. All this intellectual, religious, and political ferment was the necessary preliminary to the largest and most successful of Islamic revolutions—the Fulani jihad in northern Nigeria.

The Fulani jihad in Hausaland

The Fulani had long been resident in the Hausa city-states. Many who had forsaken the wandering pastoral life had risen to positions of prominence as teachers, traders, and public officials. The majority of these town Fulani had been converted to Islam long ago. They were not insulated from the current wave of reformism in the Western Sudan. The preaching of Muslim reformers and the practical example of the implementation of the Shari'a or Muslim law in Futa Jallon and Futa Toro gave hope of change in the same direction in the various Hausa states. Although religious motives were primary in the overthrow of the Hausa rulers, there were also many other grievances which the Fulani and many Hausa had against their government. Excessive taxation, raids on cattle herds, and unfair courts were some of the reasons why Usuman dan Fodio, the moving force behind Fulani protest, could appeal to the masses who could not become excited over the religious issue.

Usuman dan Fodio, a Fulani of the Torodbe clan, was born in Gobir in 1754. As a young man he had received an excellent Islamic education in western and northern Africa. He became a convert to the reform movement then stirring in Western Sudan. Usuman was a teacher in Gobir, and later preached his message of social and religious reform throughout Hausaland. He became famous for his learning and piety, and was selected by the ruler or sarkin of Gobir as a tutor for the royal children. He thus was in a position to convince a number of nobles of the need to reorder the state on the basis of justice and a purified religion. In 1802 the king died and Usuman's pupil, Yunfa, became sarkin Gobir. However, the new ruler, instead of putting into effect reforms suggested by Usuman, launched a campaign against him and his followers.

The sarkin Gobir's increased efforts against Muslims brought on the civil war. By 1802 Usuman had drawn a large number of followers to his base at Degel. In 1804 he was attacked by Gobir armies and forced to flee from Degel. He then proclaimed a jihad against the proven infidels. Almost immediately his army defeated a large force sent by the sarkin. With this success his fame grew among both Hausa and Fulani.

Usuman did not take part in the battles; rather he acted as the spiritual and political head of the faithful. He distributed flags to certain leaders to indicate his faith in them and charged them with supplanting the old order in various parts of Hausaland. Usuman's armies were convinced of the divine justice of their cause and quickly overran most of the north. Kebbi fell in 1805, Zaria in 1806, Katsina and Kano in 1807, and Daura and Gobir in 1808. The wars continued—particularly against Nupe, Ilorin, and Oyo in the south. However, after 1810, the largest and richest portion of Hausaland was controlled by Usuman's forces. Eastward the chief of Bauchi, although not a Fulani, received a flag and subdued the people of the plateau area. In Adamoua, the Fulani pastoralists gave their support to one of Usuman's lieutenants, Modibba Adama, and they carried the jihad into the northern Cameroun.

Eventually only Bornu, after a seven-year war, was able to resist the Fulani armies. Once one of the greatest powers in the Sudan, Bornu, by the early nineteenth century, possessed only a shadow of its former influence. In 1805 adherents of Usuman led a revolt and carved out a number of small emirates in western Bornu. Then revolt struck the southern areas and the emirate of Gombe was created. Finally in 1808 the Fulani drove the mai from his capital of Birni N'Gazargamo. Bornu was eventually saved by the appearance of irregular forces led by Al Kanemi. This army, which was composed of cattle herders from the old province of Kanem and reinforcements from the royal forces, was powerful enough to retake the capital in 1810. The final campaign was waged by the Fulani in the following year. After initial victories, the Fulani were defeated by Al Kanemi's forces and the royal army and were driven back toward the west. For all practical purposes the boundaries thus established remained throughout the nineteenth century.

The young Dunama, mai of Bornu, who had come to the throne in 1810, was retained although Al Kanemi held most of the power in the state. Dunama was deposed in 1814 and later killed; however, Al Kanemi did not seize the throne since he preferred to control affairs secretly. He consolidated what remained of Bornu, restored authority over Kanem, reformed the administrative structure, and vainly sought to recapture the territories lost to the Fulani. At his death in 1835 his son, Umar, replaced him as the power behind the throne.

In 1846 the subject state of Zinder revolted in association with the sharif of Wadai. Mai Ibrahim attempted to use this rebellion to throw off Umar's control of the state, but his army was defeated. Umar crowned his victory with the execution of Mai Ibrahim, thus extinguishing one of the longest-ruling dynasties in African history.

Umar ruled Bornu until 1880. The later years of his reign were relatively peaceful, and he retired to a life of contemplation, allowing the state to be governed by palace favorites. During this period, Kanem and a number of western tributary states broke away from centralized control and the reduced kingdom suffered from raids by Wadai. After Umar's death the corrupt bureaucracy proved incapable of efficient rule. In 1891 the slaver Rabeh, fleeing with his followers from the Bahr el Ghazal region of the Sudan, invaded the kingdom and within five years brought the whole state under his domination. Rabeh's power was finally broken by the French army in a major campaign in 1900.

Usuman dan Fodio had been the revolutionary, idealistic religious leader who had inspired first the Fulani and then a portion of the dominant Hausa to revolt against their traditional rulers. It was his son, Muhammad Bello, who consolidated the conquests and created the political structure of the Fulani empire. Even before his death Usuman, as Commander of the Faithful, had left the administration to Bello and his brother Abdullahi. The provincial rulers paid allegiance to either Abdullahi at Gwandu or Bello at Sokoto. At Usuman's death in 1817 there was a brief period of unrest until Bello assumed the title of sultan. Abdullahi remained an emir with, however, political control over one half of the empire. In both sections the empire was divided into areas which were each ruled by an emir. In normal administrative matters the emirs were supreme in their territory; however, they were required to defer to the political judgment of Sokoto and Gwandu. In religious matters the Commander of the Faithful at Sokoto was supreme. Each emir was required to obey the orders of his superior and to pay tribute to him. The viziers of Gwandu and Sokoto visited the emirates regularly to settle disputes and to review the administrative practices. The Fulani retained to a very large extent the administrative machinery found in the Hausa states revising it only to make it more amenable to centralized control and a purified Islamic state. Usuman and Bello did not discriminate against the numerically more powerful Hausa. In most cases the emirs were Fulani but the other offices within the emirates were open to men of piety and talent whether Hausa or Fulani.

The sultan was forced to garrison some of the emirates—such as Katsina, Kebbi, and Zamfara—more heavily than others, because in the period before 1830 a significant portion of the population of these cities had not accepted the new system. Forty times, Sultan Bello in his twenty-year reign led the Fulani forces against dissidents within the empire and against unbelievers in the south. By the time of his death resistance against Fulani rule had been broken in all areas except the south. The Fulani emir of Nupe had forced back into two small towns the adherents of the traditional rulers. Eventually the entire area became subject to the emir who ruled the area from Bida. In the extreme south the Fulani, during the height of the jihad, were halted at Ilorin, a predominantly Yoruba town. It wasn't until 1829 that a Fulani commander was given a flag in recognition of his conquest. Despite the weakness of the Yoruba after the breakdown of the kingdom of Oyo, the Fulani were not able to occupy much Yoruba territory permanently. The forest line and the tsetse fly acted as allies of the Yoruba and limited the effectiveness of the Fulani cavalry.

The unification of the competing city-states resulted in an economic resurgence in the north. Kano became the most important trading city of the Western Sudan. The major export product was cloth which was produced in the villages and major cities. It was then dyed and some of it made into clothing. Such cloth from the north found its way into markets throughout the Western Sudan and also into the forest states. Other important manufactures were finished leather goods, metal products, and dyes. Horses and cattle also provided the north with considerable income as did the slave trade. Many slaves were taken to Kano for transport to the oases of the Sahara, North Africa, and to the Eastern Sudan. A far larger number collected as spoils of war against pagans from the southern border areas were sent southward and eventually found their way to the European slavers at Badagry, Lagos, Bonny, and Calabar.

Many European observers in the nineteenth century reported that the centralized control of the sultan began to wane after the death of Bello in 1837. Recent research has indicated that this assessment is only partially true. As late as 1860 the sultan had the power to depose the emir of Zaria and select a new man for the position. All emirs, even those most distant such as Adamoua, needed the sanction of the sultan to rule. Where there were rival claimants to the throne each would, if necessary, travel to Sokoto to secure the sultan's underwriting of his legitimacy. The united empire without doubt underwent a number of changes in the years after Bello's death. The fervor of the jihad died away and the emirs became increasingly materialistic. There were attempts by individual emirs to rid themselves of the practical links that bound them to the sultan and there was open jealousy between emirs. However, when the British forces under Lugard in the last years of the century occupied the north, they found a well-ordered, stable Islamic empire. Far from being decayed, it functioned so well that the British modified only a portion of its administration and were content to allow the sultan and emirs to continue their rule relatively unchanged into the twentieth century.

The Tucolor empire and other reform movements

The successful Fulani jihad in Hausaland spurred on religious reformers elsewhere in the Western Sudan. In the early nineteenth century Sheikh Ahmadu bin Hammadi Boubou who had studied with Usuman at Sokoto returned to Macina and opened a Koranic school there. This became the centrum of a reform movement designed to create an Islamic state in Macina. His activities worried the rulers of Macina and their overlords, the Bambara of Segu. In defense of the faith, Ahmadu proclaimed a jihad in 1818 which overthrew the old government of Macina. Ahmadu's forces took the city of Djenne and even held the city of Timbuktu for a short period. The reconstructed Islamic state followed an organizational pattern similar to that established by Usuman and Bello in Hausaland. There were five emirates with each ruler responsible to Ahmadu at his new capital city of Hamdullahi. The government based upon the Shari'a was puritanical and efficient, but the revised laws and their implementation were more fair to the people than the laws of the previous regime. Although Timbuktu was soon lost, the greater portion of the new state remained faithful to Ahmadu's successors until it was incorporated briefly into the empire of Al Hajj Umar after 1862.

Al Hajj Umar was a Tucolor born and educated in Futa Toro. Like so many of his learned contemporaries, he traveled a great deal in order to study with renowned teachers. In 1820, when about thirty years of age, he undertook a five-year pilgrimage to Mecca and Medina. On his return to North Africa he came under the influence of the Tijaniyya brotherhood. This movement created by Ahmad al Tijani stressed the special place reserved by Allah for the faithful ones. Despite their sins they were destined for salvation. Thus a member of the Tijaniyya believed himself to be superior to all Muslims who did not subscribe to the teachings of al Tijani.

Al Hajj Umar was appointed caliph of this movement in the Western Sudan. However, his wanderings were not yet completed. He resided in Sokoto in the golden years of Sultan Bello's rule and there absorbed the details of political and military organization. While in Hausaland he gained considerable wealth and presumably a number of faithful followers. The respect shown to him is indicated by his marriage to one of Bello's daughters.

In 1838 Umar left Sokoto and established a religious center in the Futa Jallon. His teachings and the attitudes of his followers frightened the orthodox imams and he was expelled. Umar then established a religious

Mid-Nineteenth-Century West Africa

L. Chad

BORNU

ADAMWA

FULANI EMPIRE

• Kano

• Zaria

NUPE

Benue R.

• Sokoto

Niger R.

IBO

Calabar

Bonny

Fernando Po (Sp.)

YORUBA

Brass

DAHOMEY

Lagos (Br.)
Cotonou (Fr.)
Whydah (Fr.)

Príncipe (Port.)

São Thomé (Port.)

Niger R.

• Gao

FULA

MOSSI

Volta R.

ASHANTI

Accra (Br.)

Cape Coast (Br.)

FANTI

GULF OF GUINEA

TUCOLOR EMPIRE

• Timbuktu

MASSINA

KAARTA

BAMBARA

• Segu

MANDE

SAMORY

Grand
Bassam (Fr.)

FULA

• Kankan

SUSU

Bissandugu

TEMNE

MENDE

Monrovia

Senegal R.

MANDE

WOLOF

Gambia R.

ATLANTIC OCEAN

Conakry

Freetown (Br.)

Bissau (Port.)

St. Louis

Dakar

Goree

Bathurst (Br.)

Miles

0   100   200   300

French Controlled

British Controlled

7

and military base at Dinguiray near the source of the Niger River. There
he continued to attract followers and prepare for war. Many of his Tucolor
and Fulani recruits were armed with modern weapons acquired from European traders along the coast. In 1852 some of his soldiers clashed with the
forces of a local Bambara chief. Proclaiming a jihad, Umar's armies in 1854
swept northward conquering Bambauk and humbling the Bambara state of
Kaarta. Turning his attention eastward Umar sought to gain a hold in the
middle Senegal area. However, the French under Governor Louis Faidherbe
blunted this drive in the two-year period after 1857. Thwarted there, Umar
then attacked Segu, the most powerful Bambara state. Segu capitulated in
1861.

Umar's Tijaniyya forces then confronted the Islamic state of Macina
that was ruled by Ahmadu III, a grandson of the founder. Despite much
provocation, Ahmadu III appealed to Umar in a manner similar to that of
Al Kanemi of Bornu when under attack by the forces of Usuman dan Fodio.
He wished to know how it was possible for one Muslim leader to make war
against another under the excuse of a jihad when this was expressly
reserved for conversion of pagans. Umar's reply was that Ahmadu III had
given help to the pagan rulers of Segu and thus could be considered an ally
of those who struggled against the faithful. Umar's armies subsequently
defeated those of Ahmadu in 1862 and Macina was incorporated into the
empire. With the taking of Timbuktu in 1863 his personal empire reached
its zenith.

The Tucolor had conquered a vast territory, but they had not gained
the allegiance of the people. The Bambara remained obstinately pagan. In
Macina the new rulers were hated because of Umar's breach of Islamic law
in attacking them. Further a policy of forced conversion to the concepts of
Tijaniyya was attempted. The unrest in Macina resulted in a revolt against
Umar's authority in 1863 and he was killed trying to repress the uprising.
With the loss of its charismatic leader, the Tucolor empire began to fall
apart. In the extreme west the French were actively undermining Tucolor
authority. In the north the empire had to thwart periodic Tuareg attacks.
Throughout the empire the conquered rebelled against the rule of Umar's
son, Ahmadu; but by the early 1870s he had regained nominal control over
most of his father's empire. However, the constant fighting had disrupted
trade and left some areas such as Macina little more than desert. Ahmadu
and Tucolor rule were so hated by subject peoples that large segments of
the population welcomed the French in the 1880s and 1890s, not as con-
querors, but as deliverers.

Although not specifically a part of Islamic state building, the Mandingo
empire of Samory Touré must be mentioned briefly. It was created at the
same time that Ahmadu's Tucolor empire was crumbling. Samory controlled
only a small chiefdom in the Kankan region of Guinea in the early 1860s.
In fifteen years, through his administrative and military skills, he had transformed this tiny, weak state into the most powerful interior state west of
Hausaland. He first incorporated the small neighboring Mande states within
his kingdom and in 1873 conquered Kankan. From this date he was continually at war until his power was broken by the French twenty-five years

later. At its greatest extent in the early 1880s, Samory's well-administered domain extended from the Futa Jallon in the east to the area of the Upper Volta in the west. Samory, not Ahmadu, provided the French with their most implacable opponent in their drive to occupy the interior of West Africa.

In the Senegambia area there was also a spilling over of reforming Islam. The juxtaposition of Wolof, Mandingo, Jola, Serer, and Fulani in the area as well as the presence of the French and British along the coast prevented the creation of a single Islamic polity. However, the fifty-year period of struggle between the protagonists of Islam, the Marabouts, and the traditional leaders, the Soninke, had important ramifications for the future of the area.

The first religious reformers appeared in the Gambia area in the early 1850s. These teachers had been involved in similar movements in Algeria or other parts of the Sudan. They found the majority of the population of the Wolof kingdoms of Jolof, Cayor, Sine, Saloum, and chieftaincies along the Gambia relatively untouched by Islam. Those chiefs who had accepted Islam were at best occasional conformists, and religious observances among them were highly colored by animistic practices. Those who listened to the teachers and followed the war chiefs in the 1850s and 1860s were a minority of the population, but an organized and at first inspired minority. However, along the Gambia River the only way to convert the Soninke was by conquest. As the internecine wars continued the religious motivation of some of the leaders dimmed and many of the small wars were caused by political and economic desires of individual leaders.

The only leader to emerge with attributes similar to the most successful religious revolutionaries, Usuman dan Fodio and Al Hajj Umar, was Maba. During a brief career in the early 1860s he sought to create a large Islamic state in southern Senegal. His objective was thwarted not only by the Soninke but by the French and British. After Maba's death in 1867, the leaders of the Marabout movement such as Fodi Kabba, Fodi Silla, and Musa Mollah were content with expanding their own small kingdoms and engaging in the slave trade. The religious motive by the 1880s had become secondary. Continuing warfare along the Gambia River destroyed many of the traditional ruling houses and left a vacuum of power that was easily filled by the British and French in the 1890s. Despite the inability of the early Muslim reformers to create a single purified state, they were successful in this period of warfare in converting the mass of the riverine population to Islam. In the Wolof states the successors of Maba in Sine and Saloum continued his work of conversion. Lat Dior, another of Maba's disciples, came to power in Cayor as did Alboury N'Diaye in Jolof. Thus by the time of the French occupation much of the population of these areas had been converted to Islam.

European attitudes toward West Africa

European interest in Africa from the first hesitant coastal voyages of the Portuguese in the fifteenth century had been primarily economic. The original impetus for the Portuguese crown to underwrite these explorations was the hope of by-passing the Mediterranean and thus undercutting the Italian states that controlled trade in Eastern luxury goods. Profits from gold, ivory, pepper, feathers, and gum from Africa justified the investment and danger to the pioneer explorers. The Portuguese, from their trading stations and forts in West and East Africa, were the first beneficiaries of the demand for slaves without which the plantations of the New World could not have functioned. The slave trade, a trickle in the sixteenth century, reached flood tide in the eighteenth and displaced thousands of Africans every year. French, Danes, Brandenbergers, Courlanders, Dutch, and British all were eager to tap these riches. At the opening of the eighteenth century the French, Dutch, and Portuguese, although active in the slave trade, had confined the bulk of their activities to restricted areas in West Africa. British merchants dominated the trans-Atlantic carrying trade.

Coastal African societies came to depend largely upon the export of slaves. This interaction between native polities and European legitimate slave merchants belongs to the period before 1800. It is sufficient to note that states such as those of the Ibibio and Ijo east of the Niger had completely reoriented their political and social systems because of the slave trade. In areas such as the Senegambia, Gold Coast, and Angola, where Europeans were firmly established in towns or forts, the lives of neighboring African people came to be centered on the slave trade. Inland states, which could not be conquered by Europeans, tended to develop into large autocratic militaristic polities. The creation of the Ashanti Union, Dahomey, Oyo, and Kasanje depended upon issues other than the slave trade, yet the profit motive of increased trade with Europeans was an important factor in their development.

The reversal of British attitudes toward slavery in the early nineteenth century had ramifications which, in time, affected most of Africa. On the most obvious level it restricted British merchants from engaging in the trade after 1807. All British governments in the nineteenth century were committed to halting the traffic in slaves. Due in large measure to British pressure, other European states eventually outlawed it thus placing most European slavers beyond the law. The logic of commitment led British governments to support a series of activities designed to enforce the paper decrees of abolition. These included the maintenance of a permanent West African squadron to seize suspected slave ships, establishment of permanent stations along the coast, and treaties with native rulers that elicited promises to cease selling slaves. Inevitably Britain was drawn more deeply into the internal affairs of African states to secure compliance with these agreements.

The abolition of the slave trade was but one offshoot of a more generalized development within British society. The Evangelical movement, a reinterpretation of Protestant Christianity, was the dominant theme of British life in the nineteenth century. Biblical Christianity became the driving force for political, economic, and social change. One area almost totally neglected by the Established Church in the eighteenth century was mis-

Peoples of West Africa

10°
0°
KANURI
Benue R.
TIV
IGALA
IBIBO
DOUALA
I B O
OYO
HAUSA
BENI
F U L A N I
NUPE
YORUBA
IJEBU
EGBA
FON
Niger R.
FULANI
MAHI
BARIBA
ADJA
Mono R.
EWE
SONGHAI
GURMA
DAGOMBA
Volta R.
GA
MOSSI
MAMPRUSSI
FANTI
DIOULA
ASHANTI
BAMBARA
GUR
Komoe R.
BAOLE
MALINKE
AGNIS
Niger R.
MALINKE
GREBO
Sassandra R.
KRU
BAMBARA
TOMA
BASA
FULA
Cavalla R.
KPELLE
Loffa R.
Senegal R.
MALINKE
MENDE
SHERBRO
MALINKE
LOKO
SERER
FULA
TEMNE
Gambia R.
SUSU
TUCOLOR
MANDINGO
Rokel R.
SERAHULI
BAGA
WOLOF
JOLA
PAPEL

ATLANTIC OCEAN

GULF OF GUINEA

0°

10°

10°

0°

0   100   200   300
Miles

11

sionary activity. Evangelicals, however, took seriously the call to preach the word to "heathen" peoples. To facilitate this, proselytizing Baptists, Wesleyans, Independents, and Anglicans established missionary societies. Within a few years these agencies had missionaries placed in territories from Africa to the Pacific Islands. This phenomenon coincided with and reinforced official activities to end the slave trade. By the end of the first five decades of the century British-sponsored missionaries were at work throughout West Africa. They expected and received active support for their efforts from their government. Thus, despite official statements to the contrary, the missionaries drew the government into deeper intervention in the internal affairs of African polities.

Although the abolition of the slave trade did not immediately end the traffic in human beings, it did result in cutting back British trade with Africa. Large trading firms in Liverpool and London lost very little from the reversal of policy. The British empire was large enough and its manufacturers and bankers so dominant that it was a simple matter to reorient the direction of their trading activities. However, smaller trading houses were damaged and began to seek out new African products to substitute for slaves. In some areas this search was short. East of the Niger Delta, oil palm products became the major trade items even before the African middlemen had been forced to abandon completely the sale of slaves. Elsewhere it took longer to develop alternate exports. Exports of peanuts, cocoa, and rubber from West Africa did not assume major proportions until the latter years of the nineteenth century. With the increasing effectiveness of measures to limit the slave trade, Africa became an economic backwater for Europe. As first Britain and later other European states embraced free trade they began to reduce government expenditure by closing down unprofitable stations. Government officials at those permanent bases that were retained for noneconomic reasons were under orders not to expand the territory under their jurisdiction.

Another set of factors closely joined to evangelical and economic motives also worked to undermine the official position against expansion. Curiosity about the unknown parts of the world had been growing in the eighteenth century and had resulted in government sponsorship of many exploratory ventures. Perhaps the most fruitful of these had been the three Pacific Ocean voyages of Captain Cook. Africa, whose periphery was so well known, became the focal point for private and government-sponsored explorations in the early nineteenth century. The African Association, formed in 1788, led the way by underwriting efforts to unlock the secrets of the interior of West Africa. Their most successful venture, Mungo Park's journey from the Gambia to the Niger, was but a prelude to a series of explorations which by 1850 had solved most of the geographic mysteries of West Africa. The British government sponsored many of the expeditions for the dual purpose of checking the slave trade and discovering, if possible, new sources of wealth that could be exploited by British merchants.

The generalized picture of European activities in West Africa is a strange picture of increasing involvement limited by the official attitudes that stressed noninvolvement. Explorers, missionaries, and officials work-ing for the destruction of the slave trade committed European states, par-ticularly Britain, to greater intervention in the affairs of African rulers. At the same time the economic facts dictated an official policy that would minimize expenditures. The resultant tension between these divergent fac-tors produced inconsistent government activities that confused Europeans concerned with Africa as much as they did the Africans. Although it is not totally possible to separate the many European activities, it will be con-venient to survey each area in some detail.

European exploration in West Africa

In 1788 the African Association was founded, due largely to the efforts of Sir Joseph Banks who had accompanied Captain Cook on his first voyage to the Pacific. Although the association had economic motives and later developed humanitarian overtones, its primary purpose was the scientific collection of data concerning the unexplored world. The first major ques-tion that its members sought to answer was the riddle of the great river mentioned in Arabic texts of the Western Sudan. Although Europeans had been active along the coasts for 350 years, no European had observed such a river. There were many theories about this mysterious stream. Some geographers believed as did Herodotus that it was the same as the Nile. Somewhere beyond the limits of European knowledge, the river, flowing eastward, changed its course to become the Nile. Another theory stated that the two rivers were separate. The one in the Western Sudan flowed eastward and lost itself in a great lake where the bulk of its waters simply evaporated. Yet others thought that its direction of flow was not eastward but westward. It branched into three rivers—the Senegal, Gambia, and Rio Grande (Jeba)—whose mouths were already familiar to Europeans. All of these elaborately developed theories rested on no firm foundation. No one knew whether there was such a stream, let alone its source, direction, and outlet. It was to solve these problems that the African Association dis-patched its first explorations.

By 1793 the association had sponsored three expeditions into the Western Sudan. All had failed although Major Houghton who used the Gambia River as a point of departure had, before his death, communicated enough to the association to convince them that there was a river and it flowed eastward. A young Scots doctor, Mungo Park, undertook to com-plete Houghton's work. Arriving at Pisania on the Gambia River in the summer of 1795, he studied the language and talked to as many Africans as possible before departing for the interior. After enduring hardships and sickness that would have killed most men, he reached the Niger near Segu almost a year later. The broad river did exist and it flowed eastward. Exhausted and without supplies, he was forced to turn back to the coast. The results of Park's first expedition were modest, but they fired the imagi-nations of many powerful Englishmen. The association boldly announced that the way was open for commercial penetration of the hinterland.

By 1805 the Colonial Office had been convinced of the worth of further detailed explorations of the Niger. It financed a large utterly inexperienced expedition led by Park whose purpose was to uncover the remaining secrets of the Niger. Thirty-eight Europeans, including Park's brother-in-law, accompanied the explorer on the second expedition. They carried with them the equipment necessary to construct boats that would presumably carry them down the Niger to its outlet. Arriving during the rainy season, the expedition soon discovered the perils of travel in West Africa. By the time they reached the Niger near Bamako, in August 1805, only ten Europeans were alive and most of these were in no condition to continue. Ultimately Park, four Europeans, and four Africans set off from Sansanding to float down the river on a raft. Later Park and his surviving companions were lost in the rapids near Bussa after a fight with the inhabitants of that town. Park's Mandingo servant, Isaaco, fortunately managed to carry Park's manuscript back to the coast where it was subsequently delivered to the British government.

The Napoleonic Wars brought a halt to further explorations and it was not until 1820 that Dr. Walter Oudney was invited by the British government to undertake a new expedition. Associated with him in the venture were Major Dixon Denham and Lieutenant Hugh Clapperton of the Royal Navy. The group left Tripoli in early 1822, crossed the Sahara via the Fezzan and Tibesti, and arrived at Kuka in Bornu. Denham moved southeast from there exploring Bornu and the regions of the Shari River. Oudney and Clapperton proceeded westward. Oudney died at Murmur in January 1824, but Clapperton reached the great trading city of Kano and eventually Sokoto. He was kindly received there by Sultan Bello, spiritual and temporal head of the all-powerful Fulani empire. However, Bello would not allow him to explore southward toward the Niger only 150 miles away. He then retraced his steps to meet Denham at Kuka and together they recrossed the desert to Tripoli. Arriving in England in June 1825, he was almost immediately commissioned by the colonial secretary, Lord Bathurst, to lead a further expedition to the Fulani-Hausa states following a new route northward from the coast of Guinea. One reason for the Colonial Office's haste was the naïve belief, fostered by Sultan Bello's request for a treaty, that he would be willing to abolish the slave trade in his empire.

Clapperton's second expedition included four other Europeans. One of these was Clapperton's twenty-one year old Cornish servant, Richard Lander. The small group landed at Badagry near the end of 1825. Very soon after leaving the coast two of the Europeans died and another decided to explore Dahomey, thus leaving Clapperton and Lander to proceed northward alone. Their journey took them through Bussa to Zaria and Kano and thence to Sokoto. Clapperton was dismayed to discover that Bello had no intention of abolishing a lucrative and traditional source of income on the basis of the arguments of a wandering European. Clapperton became ill in December 1826, and died the following March. Despite evidence that the rulers of Hausaland in the midst of their troubles with Bornu were becoming suspicious of him, Lander decided to travel southeast toward

Early West African Explorations

15

what he believed to be a town on the Niger called Funda. From there he hoped to make his way to the mouth of the river. However, he was halted by soldiers of the emir of Zaria before he reached his objective and was compelled to return to the coast by the same way he and Clapperton had come. In April 1828 Lander arrived in Britain with all the notes of the expedition.

After delivering Clapperton's papers to the Colonial Office, Lander wrote two accounts of his adventures. No longer just a servant, but one of the few living experts on West Africa, he was able to convince the Colonial Office to underwrite a further attempt to trace the Niger from Bussa to the sea. The government subsidy was far from munificent. It consisted of £100 each for Richard and his brother John, and a guarantee of an additional £100 for the maintenance of Richard's wife in his absence. The two brothers landed at Badagry in March 1830, and from there they followed the previous route taken by Clapperton to Bussa. Richard was remembered by the ruler of the town and they were warmly welcomed. Procuring two canoes and the men to row them downstream, they left Bussa and had few problems with the riverine Africans until they reached the vicinity of Asaba. Despite difficulties with the Ibo, they eventually reached Brass in November and persuaded a British captain to transport them to Fernando Po. From there they sailed via Brazil to Britain and did not arrive home with the news of their discovery until July 1831.

Other explorers had also been active in the period immediately after the Napoleonic Wars. The Frenchman Gaspard Mollien in 1818 had investigated the Futa Jallon and discovered the sources of the Sengal, Gambia, and Rio Grande rivers. Four years later Major Alexander Laing had identified the source of the Niger. In the two years after 1827, René Caillie traveled from the Senegambia via the mysterious Timbuktu to Morocco. Caillie exposed the low level to which the once great trading city of the Western Sudan had fallen.

In the decade and a half after Waterloo, the hinterland of western Africa had been exposed to Europe by the exploits of a few intrepid, lucky explorers. Each of them had upon their return to Europe put down their adventures in writing and had found an eager market for their books about the unknown continent. The British government, which had sponsored many of the expeditions, was particularly receptive to the information about peoples, their activities, and particularly the economic possibilities of the new territories. It is possible, however, to overstate what the early explorers had done. Much of West Africa remained a mystery to Europeans. The later activities of the Landers, Macgregor Laird, Dr. Baikie, and Heinrich Barth would provide more information to solve the puzzle of the hinterland. Nevertheless, large segments of the interior remained a mystery until after the scramble for Africa had been completed seventy years after the Niger River ceased to be a mystery.

Enough of the territory had been explored by the 1830s to indicate several things. The various expeditions had exploded the myth of the great wealth of the interior cities such as Timbuktu and Kano. This tended to confirm the dominant attitude of European governments that trade in most of the areas was not worth the trouble and expense of any territorial expansion. Some businessmen, however, saw in a few of the areas opportunities to expand preexisting trading activities. The most important of these areas were believed to be those adjacent to the Niger River northward to the Fulani states.

Trade and exploration along the Niger

European activities along the Niger coast in the nineteenth century were a complex amalgam of old and new forces. The slave trade continued to play an important role until the British occupied the area in the latter decades of the century. Coastal African rulers and middlemen, particularly in the Ijo and Ibibio states, at the same time were dealing with legitimate trade products. In some areas, such as Bonny, the oil palm trade had become more important by mid-century than slaving. However, the economic and political structures created for the exploitation of the slave trade remained intact; only the trading materials changed. Most European traders respected the coastal merchants' claim to the sources of supply and did not seriously attempt to bypass them and trade directly with the interior. New merchant entrepreneurs such as Macgregor Laird did not. Intrigued with the potential of the hinterland as reported by the explorers, they became active in further exploratory ventures designed to establish trading centers in the interior. Although not necessarily connected to the latter movement, the growing missionary interest tended to reinforce attempts to open up the hinterland. Missionaries and business interests concerned with activities that were hostile to the traditional closed system of the African middlemen expected and grudgingly received the support of the British government.

The first attempt to take advantage of the newly discovered Niger route for trade proved a disaster. In 1832 a Liverpool merchant, Macgregor Laird, dispatched two iron oceangoing steamships to the Niger with forty-eight Europeans including Richard Lander on board. The purpose was to reconnoiter the river and establish a trading station. Although the party traveled past the Benue confluence, it was forced to return to the coast because of the heavy death rate. Thirty-nine Europeans including Lander died of malaria. This expedition dampened enthusiasm until 1841 when the Church Missionary Society sent another large group to the Niger to establish a permanent station upriver. Representatives of European merchants trading with African coastal cities vainly protested this attempt to bypass them. The society, supported by the government, believed that such a station would enable missionaries to reach many thousands of interior Africans. The station was to be converted into a model farm. Thus European technology would reinforce Christianity. Hopefully in the future the station would be but one of many and would stimulate direct trade with Europe. This costly experiment also failed since over one-third of the Europeans involved lost their lives. The disaster convinced the directors of the Church Missionary Society that, because of the appalling European death rate, the major hope of Christianizing the interior lay in sending more African missionaries such as Samuel Ajayi Crowther who had been one of the missionaries on the 1841 venture. The Church Missionary Society also changed the focus of their attention from the Niger to the Yoruba states to the west.

Meanwhile the Church of Scotland in 1846 had sent Hope Wadell and a contingent of Jamaican Christians to work at Calabar. They established a mission near Duke Town and later one in Creek Town. These missionaries, in the following decade, worked to subvert some inhumane practices of the Ibibio society such as the killing of twins and human sacrifice. In this struggle they enlisted the reluctant support of European traders of Calabar. Their success can be measured by the fact that in 1858 upon the death of the ruler of Creek Town there were no official sacrifices of slaves.

Beginning in the 1830s large numbers of freed Yoruba slaves began to return from Freetown to their homeland. Many of these people had become Christians and formed colonies of Westernized Africans at Badagry and Abeokuta. There they established trade and cultural links with Freetown and the Gold Coast. Soon Methodist, Baptist, and Church Missionary Society missionaries followed them. In 1842 Thomas Freeman, a part African Methodist minister, established a mission station at Badagry. In the same year Henry Townsend of the Church Missionary Society visited Abeokuta prior to opening missionary work there. In the following year Townsend and Crowther set out to bring Christianity to Abeokuta. The disturbed affairs of the Egba states and a war with Dahomey prevented this and they had to be content with working at Badagry until 1846. Even after that date it was extremely trying and dangerous for the missionaries at Abeokuta. By the 1850s there were many missionaries from England representing most of the mission societies at work throughout southern Yorubaland.

In 1850 the British government commissioned an Englishman, James Richardson, and two Germans, Adolf Overweg and Heinrich Barth, to explore Hausaland and the Western Sudan. This expedition was a belated continuation of the efforts of Oudney, Denham, and Clapperton of over two decades before. Richardson and Overweg died, but the indomitable Heinrich Barth spent five years crossing and recrossing the Sudan from Timbuktu to Bornu. His book recounting these adventures in extraordinary detail became the standard work on the Western Sudan almost immediately. In response to a letter from Barth in 1852 concerning the Benue River, the British government in conjunction with Macgregor Laird sponsored a new expedition designed to collaborate with Barth. This venture commanded by Dr. Baikie, a naval surgeon, discovered little of geographic note and never contacted Barth. Nevertheless, it was one of the most important of all the explorations of West Africa because Baikie insisted upon the daily use of quinine. As a result none of the Europeans died. With such protection, the way was clear to open the Niger for further European economic and missionary activity.

One of the members of Dr. Baikie's expedition was the Reverend Samuel Crowther who with other African missionaries established the Niger River mission of the Church Missionary Society at Onitsha. Later smaller stations were begun at Lokoja and Gbebe. Despite early problems, the Niger River mission prospered and in 1864 Crowther was nominated as the Bishop of Western Equatorial Africa. By this time the missionary ventures of all the societies were flourishing throughout southern Nigeria. At the close of the first half of the nineteenth century, missionaries were at work in almost all of the major towns and cities from the Cross River to Badagry. Wherever they were they exercised an influence far beyond their numbers. Because of their success at conversions, the missionaries undermined the traditional closely knit African political, socioeconomic systems. They brought sorely needed medical knowledge to the people under their charge. Most important for the future, they opened schools and thus developed an ever-growing number of Western-educated Africans. Missionary influence on education continued to be dominant in all Nigerian areas even after British annexation later in the century.

West African naval patrols and the slave trade

British Evangelicals who succeeded in pressuring Parliament to end the slave trade naïvely believed that the trade would soon end and with this slavery itself would wither away. It became quickly apparent that neither of these goals would be accomplished easily. In order to enforce the ban on British subjects engaging in the slave trade, the crown assumed jurisdiction over the colony of Freetown and sent two old ships to patrol the West African coast. An admiralty court was established at Freetown to deal with captured ships whose captains were charged with engaging in the trade. Eventually courts of mixed commission were also created as Britain entered into treaties with other European powers who had also outlawed the trade. In 1810 four ships were assigned to the slave patrol. Although old and slow, their activities caused a series of protests from other European states that Britain was interfering with their trade.

Immediately after Waterloo, British statesmen brought diplomatic pressure to bear on all European powers then active in the trade. The result was that Portugal in 1815 and Spain in 1817 agreed to limit the activity of their slave ships to south of the equator. France outlawed the trade in 1818 and Brazil, which was one of the great markets, agreed in 1826 not to import any more slaves. The United States had declared the slave trade illegal in 1808. Thus in the ten years following the close of the Napoleonic Wars, almost all of the nations concerned with slave trading had either outlawed the practice or agreed to limit its scope.

There were a number of interrelated factors that made these treaties and agreements almost worthless. The first was the increasing demand for slaves in the New World. The sugar industry in Cuba was expanding and needed more men to work the plantations. In Brazil, where vast new territories were being opened, the economy depended upon tobacco, cotton, and coffee culture—all of which demanded a cheap labor force. In the

United States, the invention of the cotton gin completely changed all but the most liberal attitudes toward slavery. New lands in Alabama, Mississippi, Louisiana, and later in Texas were given over to the production of cotton. Thus the demand for slaves increased greatly after the trade abolition. Government officials charged with upholding the laws openly condoned the importation of slaves. African rulers had no intention of abandoning the profitable enterprise of gathering and selling slaves. Most African middlemen were eager to sell as long as there was someone to purchase the commodity. Much later in the 1880s, the emir of Kontagora expressed the feelings of so many African rulers when he said: "Can you stop a cat from mousing? I shall die with a slave in my mouth." The price of slaves on the west coast remained generally stable, actually declining in many areas, in the 1830s and 1840s when the West African patrol became more effective. At the same time, the price of slaves increased in the markets in Cuba and the United States. By 1850 the price of a good field slave in the New World had more than quadrupled since the opening of the century. With such profits to be gained, slave traders of all nationalities were willing to take chances to secure their share.

The British West African Squadron, even had there not been such a demand for slaves, would have had a near impossible task. There were over 4,000 miles of deeply indented coastline to patrol. The rivers of West Africa tend to lose themselves in a number of mouths or swampy mangrove delta land. These provided many excellent hiding places for the slavers. By the 1820s Britain was maintaining an average of twenty ships on the patrol, and all available statistics indicate that many more slaves were being shipped than before the abolition. It was not until the mid-1820s that the ships of the Royal Navy were fast enough to apprehend some of the better-equipped slave ships. In some cases the slavers were as well armed as warships; one of the larger slave ships mounted twenty guns. There were many instances of slave captains fighting after being overtaken. During the chase the slaves might be thrown overboard because until 1839 they were the only evidence that could convict a captain of slaving.

The problem had hardly begun when a slave ship was captured. A prize crew was put on board and the ship and its cargo sailed to a port where there was a mixed commission. In West Africa this port was normally Freetown. The voyage could be thousands of miles long. The sufferings of the slaves on board did not stop with its capture since these ships were normally packed with slaves. Upon landing, the senior naval officer filed his papers and in due time the case would be heard by the commission. Unless everything had been done exactly right and there was no question of the nationality and the purpose to which the ship was put, the commission would find for the ship owner. Until 1839, when the British law was amended, slaves had to be found on the captured ship. Equipment or other circumstantial evidence as to the ship's purpose was not considered. Captains of British warships could be held personally responsible for losses to the owners of ships brought into port when the navy could not prove their charges. Ships of the United States that were apprehended by the American squadron were sent to United States ports. Most American captains and owners who were found guilty were given relatively small fines.

One obvious answer to the problems of patrolling waters where slavers of different nationalities operated was reciprocal search agreements. Britain obtained treaties allowing this from Portugal and Spain in 1817, from the Netherlands in 1818, and from Sweden in 1824. In 1831 France agreed to allow British naval vessels to search French ships in the restricted area from 10° south to 32° north latitude extending from 0° to 30° west longitude. However, an attempt in 1841 to extend the area was refused by France. The official position of the United States, stated prior to the War of 1812, that no naval vessel of a foreign power had the right to stop an American trading vessel on the high seas, remained until the Civil War. This position gave American slavers a relatively free hand in West Africa. Furthermore, it led to the use of the American flag by slave captains of all nationalities. The United States sent four warships to West Africa in 1820 to maintain its own patrol. These were withdrawn within three years. The Webster-Ashburton Treaty of 1842 provided for joint cruising by British and United States warships. In 1843 two ships under the command of Lieutenant Matthew Perry were assigned to this duty. In the 1840s the United States never had more than seven ships on station compared with Britain's twenty or more. The United States ships were based on Cape Verde, 1,000 miles from the slaving areas. It is, therefore, little wonder that the joint cruising concept did not work. The United States squadron in the ten years following its reestablishment took only nine slave ships.

Despite the difficulties, the antislave patrols began to make real progress in the 1850s. This was partly because of the more active role of the British government and the missionaries on the mainland. Another reason was that the equipment treaties with most nations allowed slave ships to be taken even if there were no slaves on board. France began to maintain its own naval patrol off the Senegambia after 1845. Britain increased the numbers of its ships. Many of these were new, well-armed, fast steam vessels. In the early 1850s, the United States squadron of five ships was under the command of Lieutenant Andrew Foote who cooperated more fully with his British counterparts than any other previous American commander. However, the turn of the tide against the slave trade did not come until the American Civil War. All the major countries except the United States had by then abolished slavery in their territories. This became an accomplished fact in the United States in 1865. Brazil alone of western hemisphere areas recognized the legal status of slavery until 1888. Denied markets where great profits could be made, the slaving entrepreneurs were forced to turn to other areas for profitable investment. The practical abolition of the trans-Atlantic slave trade, far from being the simple process envisioned by Evangelicals, took almost sixty years. It had cost the British government millions of pounds and thousands of lives. Despite the difficulties encountered, the British squadron, in the forty years after 1825, had captured over 1,250 slave ships and released over 130,000 slaves alive. However, the slave patrol and the diplomatic maneuvering of the British government were only two facets of the total problem. Another phase of the antislave trade movement concerned the maintenance of bases on the African coast, the resettlement of captured slaves, and the attempt on the part of abolitionists to return freed slaves to African colonies. In this context the two areas of Freetown and Liberia became extremely important.

Freetown

The small settlements of what later became Freetown were located in the hills abutting upon the mouth of the Rokel River and had been promoted by Evangelicals in 1787. They visualized a haven for freed slaves in Africa. These settlers, already committed to Christianity and Western ideas, not only found a good future in Africa, but acted as carriers of civilization. As detailed elsewhere, the original plans of the Evangelicals foundered because of the hostility of local Africans, the inexperience of the original colonists, and the unhealthy climate. In 1791 the Sierra Leone Company was formed to continue the work of colonization. New settlers were brought from Nova Scotia, England, and Jamaica, and by the beginning of the nineteenth century, despite all difficulties, there were over 1,500 settlers in the Freetown area. The cost of administering the private colony, however, was prohibitive, and the directors of the company were delighted to turn their responsibilities over to the crown in 1808.

After 1808 the history of the settlement was tied closely to the drive to end the slave trade. Freetown became the major British naval base in West Africa. The British squadron was stationed there and the majority of the captured slave ships were taken to Freetown. The great increase in the population of the colony was due almost entirely to freed slaves. By 1822 the population of the area was estimated at 22,000, and by mid-century over 70,000 captives had been liberated at Freetown. Throughout most of the century the government was autocratic with the governor and his staff appointed by the Colonial Office. Until mid-century the governors were almost always military men.

The most active governor in the early history of the colony was Sir Charles MacCarthy who was appointed in 1814. He was deeply committed to eradicating the slave trade and to accomplish this he enlarged the territory responsible to the crown. MacCarthy wanted to annex islands that were known slaving territory and to extend the government's influence over the native peoples immediately adjacent to the colony. The Colonial Office refused to sanction most of MacCarthy's schemes for the expansion of British influence. Even so, the expenses of administering Freetown increased fourfold during MacCarthy's administration.

In 1821 MacCarthy became the governor in charge of all British West African territories. Thus the governor's time was increasingly devoted to the affairs on the Gold Coast and in the Gambia. The major area of concern at this time was the Gold Coast and the danger of an Ashanti invasion. MacCarthy was killed there in 1824 while attempting to carry out an activist policy against the Ashanti. His death had wide ramifications for British policy, not only in the Gold Coast but throughout West Africa. Thereafter the governors at Sierra Leone were under direct instructions not to expand British territory or to enter into alliances with chiefs who might call upon the British for help in time of trouble. This policy was enforced through the 1880s. A parliamentary commission in 1865 investigated the feasibility of abandoning all British possessions on the west coast. It reluctantly recommended holding those areas that Britain already controlled because the government had assumed certain moral responsibilities to the people of these colonies, particularly those at Freetown. The British presence had to remain, but with the distinct understanding that no new territories were to be added. This policy was scrupulously followed and resulted in the French occupation in the 1880s of the coastal area northwest of Sierra Leone and the Isles de Los.

During the half century following the assumption of control by the crown, a homogeneous population owing more to the culture of Western Europe than to Africa developed in the colony. The original settlers from Britain, Nova Scotia, and Jamaica and their immediate descendants at first held aloof from the freed slaves who were brought in increasing numbers to the colony. Government and missionary groups attempted to provide these liberated slaves with land and a small amount of relief funds. Since the liberated slaves had come from all parts of West Africa, they tended to drift toward their countrymen who congregated together in small villages around Freetown or in specific areas of the city. Within a generation the gap between the early Christian settlers and the new arrivals had narrowed, because the latter had begun to adopt the dominant language, religion, and mores of the colony.

The early settlers of Freetown did not regard themselves as Africans. Most held the native people of the interior in contempt for their backward "pagan" ways. The ethos of Freetown was a blend of evangelical Christianity and the materialism of nineteenth-century Britain. Christian missions continued to play an important role in the colony. A "Christian Institution" of learning was established in 1827 and this became Fourah Bay College in 1845. From this institution came a long list of men who would distinguish themselves as ministers, doctors, lawyers, and tradesmen, not only in Freetown, but throughout West Africa. The merchants based in Freetown traded with the interior of Africa and Europe and many made large fortunes. Others became artisans or entered the lower echelon of government service. They built substantial homes and copied the dress and manners of the British middle class. The newly arrived freed slave, if he chose, could adopt Christianity, work hard, and perhaps be accepted by the dominant families of Freetown as almost an equal. By 1865 this process of assimilation had gone on so long that there was little practical distinction between descendants of the 1790 settlers and those of freed slaves of the 1820s and 1830s. This mixed, Westernized creole population, protected from the Mende and Temne tribesmen of the interior, thrived in a manner that could be envied by the freed slaves in Liberia who were sponsored by American Evangelicals.

Liberia

Many concerned public officials and Evangelicals in the United States had viewed the Freetown experiment with great interest. Resettlement in Africa appeared to offer a solution to the poor conditions under which many freed slaves were forced to live, particularly in the southern United States. The first attempt at colonization was by a Negro Quaker, Paul Cuffee, who led thirty-eight settlers to Freetown in 1816. Governor Mac-Carthy did not welcome adding the care and possible maintenance of large numbers of Americanized Negroes to his many other problems; therefore, he suggested to Cuffee, who relayed the information back to the United States, that the Cape Mesurado area southeast of Freetown would be an excellent locale for any further similar experiments.

In late 1816 the American Colonization Society was formed. Its major function was to sponsor colonies of free Negroes in West Africa. In addition to the many ministers and abolitionists attracted to the new society, it also had the support of influential men in government such as Henry Clay, Bushrod Washington, and Daniel Webster. There was considerable support for the resettlement scheme by many slave owners who wanted to get rid of the free Negroes in the South. The United States government reluctantly agreed to provide transportation for the colonists but disclaimed any direct responsibility for the undertaking. The first settlement attempt sponsored by the society was by a group of eighty who landed on Sherbro Island in 1820. Within a few months, disease had all but destroyed the experiment and the survivors were taken to Freetown. Another group of thirty-three tried to establish themselves on Sherbo Island in 1821 but also failed. In December 1821, Dr. Eli Ayres and a small number of settlers arrived at Cape Mesurado. Upon landing they negotiated the purchase of the area from a local Bassa chief for approximately $300 in trade goods. It is reported that the most effective argument Ayres had for the cession was a pistol aimed at the head of the unfortunate chief. The land thus obtained later became the site of the city of Monrovia.

The society had meanwhile formed state branches, some of which later would plant their own small colonies in West Africa. For the settlement at Mesurado the society issued a constitution that conferred upon its resident agent administrative, legislative, and judicial powers. The laws of the new colony were to be those of the United States. In 1822 Yehudi Ashmun arrived in Mesurado to assume the post of agent, and until his death in 1828 he was the most important influence within the colony. The new town was named Monrovia and Ashmun supervised its fortification against the raids of neighboring African peoples. From the beginning the Kru, Bassa, and Grebo had not wanted the settlement and their antipathy soon took the form of raids against the colonists. In 1823 there was a minor war when the Africans attempted to drive the settlers from Monrovia.

Another problem closely related to the hostility evinced toward the settlers that Ashmun tried to solve was the continuation of slave trading almost within sight of the settlement. In July 1824, he reported that over 800 slaves had been sold from the vicinity of Monrovia in a three-month period. The slavers, most of whom were Spanish, refused to recognize the jurisdiction of the society over the territory. Ashmun and the settlers, in conjunction with the United States Navy, eventually raided a number of slave centers, burned the barracoons, and released the slaves. However, the society did not possess the power to stop the activities of the slavers along the entire coast. They continued to operate even after Liberia had become an independent state.

Tension, similar to that which had disrupted the Freetown colony in its earlier years, quickly developed between the settlers and the agents of the society. Most of the settlers were unprepared for the hard life in Africa. Disease, threats from native Africans, and the hard work necessary to clear the ground and plant crops were the actual reasons for the colonists' dissatisfaction. The agent represented rules that governed the colony and many of the colonists' complaints were focused upon this symbol of authority. The situation became so bad that a special agent of the society was sent in 1824 to investigate settler charges against Ashmun. Despite this the society did little to mollify the settlers until the late 1830s when the agent's title was changed to that of governor and the settlers received a portion of legislative and executive authority by having a resident council to represent their views.

In 1834 the Maryland branch of the society established a small colony near Cape Palmas. Later the New York and Pennsylvania branches began one on the St. Johns River. In 1838 the Greenville colony was begun by the Louisiana and Mississippi societies. Each of these small establishments was governed separately from Monrovia until 1838 when the society merged all except the Maryland venture into one colony. This new unified entity called the Commonwealth of Liberia was administered by a governor and a council, but the society still retained veto power over their decisions. The Maryland settlement was not absorbed by Liberia until 1857.

The first governor, Thomas Buchanan, was white, but in 1841 J. J. Roberts, a Negro settler, was appointed governor. Roberts thus began a long career of service to Liberia. After independence he was elected president five times, the last time in 1872. The first governors attempted to raise revenue for the state by levying customs duties on imports and exports. This led immediately to protests to the society from missionaries and, most important, the British government. In 1843 Britain asked the United States to clarify its relationship with Liberia. Was it a colony or protectorate of the United States? The answer, although not definitive, indicated that Liberia had never been considered a possession of the United States. This imbroglio led directly to the severing of connections between the American Colonization Society and Liberia in 1846. In the following year, a constitutional convention met in Monrovia in June to consider adopting a declaration of independence and constitution. On July 26, 1847, Liberia proclaimed its independence.

The Liberian Constitution established a system of government patterned directly upon that of the United States. There was to be a president, vice-president, congress, and supreme court. The laws of Liberia were basically the laws of the United States. It also adopted United States currency, weights and measures, and, in theory, its educational system. Despite the close historical links with the United States and the establishment of parallel institutions, the governments of Presidents Taylor, Fillmore, Pierce, and Buchanan tried to ignore the new state. Britain and France recognized Liberia immediately, but the United States did not recognize it until 1862. Herein lies the major difference between Liberia and the similarly created British colony of Freetown. The Liberians were all but cut adrift in the nineteenth century whereas the creole population at Freetown received the support of British protection and British investment.

The survival of Liberia as an independent state, particularly in the period of the later scramble for Africa, is one of the minor miracles of the nineteenth century. In 1860 there were fewer than 10,000 settlers in Liberia. They did not think of themselves as Africans; they were Christian, had some education, spoke English, and attempted to live according to current standards in the United States. Posts in government service were restricted to these Americo-Liberians. No concrete attempts to associate Africans in the government were made until well into the twentieth century. Although there was at the beginning a two-party system, the Whig party came to dominate public life. There were wars with the adjacent African peoples. The Grebo War of 1857, which resulted in the incorporation of the Maryland colony, was particularly savage. By the close of the nineteenth century the Americo-Liberians controlled the narrow coastal strip, but they had no practical authority over the large hinterland area which they claimed.

Liberia had to depend upon agriculture for its existence. It had few exports of value; therefore, it had little enough money to operate the government let alone to undertake major developments. Foreign investments and loans were almost impossible to get. After the default on a British loan of 1871, Britain proposed a joint Anglo-American protectorate but was thwarted by United States and French opposition. During the last two decades of the nineteenth century when Africa was being divided up, Liberia was saved by the jealousy of the competitive powers. The United States, although not wishing to assume the responsibility for the area, did not want to see its independence liquidated. In 1906 a British development company, in return for a loan, gained brief control of the customs office and frontier forces. This led to the establishment of a consortium composed of Britain, France, and the United States which, until World War I, collected the customs duties.

Despite its long history as an independent state, Liberia is practically a twentieth-century phenomenon. Large-scale investment in rubber plantations during the 1920s rescued the finances of the state, and the discovery of iron in the 1950s made Liberia financially independent. The effective policy of integration of members of the twenty tribes of the hinterland into the state is only a generation old. The bulk of the important positions in government are still held by Americo-Liberians. The one great advantage Liberia possessed over the new African states created in the late 1950s was a long history of governing itself within the context of a constitution which allowed it to extend freedom and government participation to Africans without revolution or even major government reorganization.

The Gold Coast

Much of the history of the Gold Coast for the century following the accession of Osei Kojo as Asantahene in 1764 seems to be a series of repetitious actions. The rule of the Ashanti was supreme over kindred Akan clans in an area of approximately 100 miles north and south and 150 miles east and west with its center in Kumasi. Far beyond this nucleus the Ashanti controlled vassal states through a system of treaties and the fear of Ashanti armies. These dependent states were so different that they could not be assimilated into the Ashanti Union. Thus the Ashanti were continuously involved in punitive expeditions and small wars against chiefs who wished to sever their connections with the Asantahene. One objective of Ashanti was to dominate the coastal Fante, Wassaw, Akim, and Ewe people. Although none of these polities was powerful enough to stand alone against the Ashanti, they did ally themselves with the Europeans who dominated the export trade from their many coastal forts. The combinations of Europeans and native allies denied the Ashanti practical control of the coast. However, these combinations were short-lived and were not powerful enough to keep the Ashanti from trying repeatedly to dominate the coast.

European activities along the coast were divided between Danish, Dutch, and British merchants. Each group attempted throughout the early nineteenth century to secure the major part of the trade for themselves. This competition made it impossible to present to the Ashanti a common economic or political policy except in times of extreme crisis. There were no clearly demarcated spheres of trading influence. The Danes attempted to play the Fante and Ashanti off against the British, and British merchants intrigued against the Dutch. The only long range common trade policy concerned the restriction of trading firearms to the Ashanti. In order to obtain guns, the Ashanti turned their trade more toward merchants operating from the Ivory and Slave coasts. This became increasingly true after the British abolition of the slave trade.

It is a mistake to assume that the three European governments were greatly concerned with the Gold Coast. Merchants of each country kept alive the old claims to the coast and were responsible for the upkeep of the trading forts. The British areas after 1783 were administered by the Company of Merchants Trading in Africa. They received a small annual

GURUNSI

WALA

Black Volta R.

DAGOMBA

White Volta R.

MAMPRUSSI

●Tamale

NANUBA

Oti R.

Approximate limits
of Akan speakers

BRONG

BANDA

Mono R.

Comoe R.

ASHANTI

●Kumasi

●Bekwai

Volta R.

AHAFO

Tano R.

Ofin R.

Pra R.

AKIM

EWE

GA

Ft. William

SEFWI

ASSINES

TWI

EFUTU

Prampram

Christianbourg

Accra

Barracoe

Winneba

AHANTA

FANTI

Cape Coast

Elmina

St. Sebastian

St. Anthony

Acquodah

G U L F   O F   G U I N E A

Key to Possession of Forts:

□ English

■ Dutch

0   10   20   30

Nineteenth Century Gold Coast

28

subsidy from parliament for the upkeep of the forts. The company could not afford to maintain the military force necessary to counter Ashanti power or to act effectively against the slave trade. A complex combination of events in the first two decades of the nineteenth century eventually convinced the British government to assume direct control of the company's forts.

The period from 1800 to 1820 was probably the apex of the power of the Ashanti Union. The Ashanti claimed to be the overlords of the Fante middlemen living within the trading sphere of the European forts. In 1806 they defeated the Fante and European forces, captured the Dutch fort of Kormantin, and elicited from the chief representative of the British company the promise to pay the Ashanti rent for the continued occupation of the forts. By extension the Europeans had agreed that the Fante were vassals of the Ashanti. In the next ten years, the Ashanti armies continued to humble the divided Fante, Wassaw, and Akim peoples. In 1817 the British sent a mission to Kumasi and entered into an agreement whereby the Asantahene promised to protect the British forts. In return the British promised Ashanti traders along the coast equal treatment with the Fante.

The disturbed conditions in the hinterland, combined with evangelical pressure to end the slave trade, resulted in the reversion of the eight trading forts to the British crown. In 1821 Sir Charles MacCarthy assumed the responsibility of governing all British West African possessions. He began a more aggressive policy to rid the coast of the constant threat of an Ashanti invasion. MacCarthy obtained assurances of help from the Fante and Ga and rejected any idea of compromise with the Ashanti.

The result of this ill-conceived policy was war between Britain and the Ashanti. MacCarthy had underestimated his enemy and paid for this mistake with his life in 1824. After MacCarthy's death, Britain sent reinforcements to the coast to prevent the Ashanti from profiting from their previous victories. The British government then announced that it would stop all payments to the Ashanti for use of the forts. Despite victories over the Ashanti armies in 1826, the war dragged on. The following year the Colonial Office, in another reversal of policy, withdrew all British troops and officials from the Gold Coast, leaving their traders to extricate themselves from the results of the disastrous expansionist policy.

The British government, while still claiming the territory on which the forts were located, turned over actual administration of Cape Coast and Accra to three of the largest companies trading in the Gold Coast. Their representatives formed the London Committee, which made the general policy for the British Gold Coast. In the Gold Coast, resident executive authority was exercised by a Council of Seven. The president of the council, appointed by London, was the chief executive officer. Parliament paid the committee a small annual subsidy to help meet the expenses of maintaining the forts. In 1830 George Maclean, a young army officer, was appointed president of the council. He, more than any other person, was responsible for retaining the Gold Coast for Britain.

In 1830 the war still continued, trade with the interior was disrupted, and the Dutch and Danes were spreading their influence into areas that had been British spheres. Worst of all, the Fante and other allies had lost faith when British troops had been withdrawn. Maclean, who had served there during the disturbances of the mid-1820s, was no stranger to the territory. He was dynamic, shrewd, and relatively unhampered by unwanted, potentially harmful orders from London. He had only a small militia force and his intelligence with which to counter his enemies. In a short time he had restored the trust of the Fante in Britain by mediating quarrels between competing chiefs. He convinced the Dutch and Danes to abandon their differential policies that were ultimately harmful to all European traders. Finally he negotiated an end to the long war with the Ashanti. In return for recognition of their right to trade directly with the coast, the Ashanti relinquished their claims to be paid rent for the British forts. This was a trader's peace. Both the Ashanti and British merchants wanted to reopen the normal channels of trade. Therefore, there was no attempt to define the relationship of the coastal people with the British and the Ashanti.

Following this agreement with the Ashanti, Maclean interfered more in the affairs of adjacent people. He worked to stop such practices as human sacrifice, handed down rules that he considered binding on the Fante, and, if necessary, sent out punitive expeditions. He thus created an unofficial protectorate over the coast behind the British forts extending approximately forty miles into the interior. Exports during Maclean's rule increased fivefold. By 1840 they had risen to £325,000 per year and imports had increased threefold in the same period to £425,000 per year. Maclean's masterly tour de force was not applauded by all. Missionaries who arrived in the Gold Coast in this decade were very critical of Maclean. They believed he had not interfered enough to stop "heathen" practices, to end domestic slavery, and to spread Christianity. Other more legal-minded critics pointed, on the contrary, to the degree to which he had assumed control over the hinterland. To them the establishment of a de facto protectorate was illegal. Maclean had been given authority only over the affairs at Cape Coast and near Accra and should not have meddled in native affairs.

In 1841, in response to his critics, the Colonial Office sent a committed antislavery advocate, Dr. R. R. Madden, to investigate the charges. His report, despite the fact that he had spent little time in the Gold Coast, was so negative that in the following year a select committee of parliament was appointed to investigate the full range of British problems on the west coast. The report of the committee exonerated Maclean of wrongdoing and praised him for what he had accomplished with so little funds. The report stated the need for more money and for a more consistent policy for all British areas in West Africa. It suggested that this could be facilitated by a return to the system of one governor-general for all of British West Africa. In 1843 this system was approved and the Gold Coast reverted to direct administration by the crown through a lieutenant-governor. Maclean was retained as chief justice with special reference to native peoples. However, from this date until his death in 1847, he had little influence over major policy making in the Gold Coast.

The Foreign Jurisdictions Act of 1843 enabled the administration to legalize the de facto arrangements he had made with the hinterland chiefs. This was done by means of treaties, called "Bonds," with individual rulers. The chiefs promised to protect European property and lives, abolish certain practices repugnant to Europeans, and allow British judges to assist them in major cases such as murder and robbery. These "Bonds" did not convey to the British specific rights of government. However, in the Gold Coast, as elsewhere in West Africa, the administration of justice was difficult to separate from executive and legislative authority.

The resumption of authority by the crown did not succeed in establishing a consistent policy. Administration by the Colonial Office, through appointed officials who knew nothing of the peculiar problems of the area and who at best stayed for only a few years, could hardly have achieved what Maclean, acting without interference, could not do. Nor were the administrators given the money necessary to do much more than maintain the government establishment. The forts fell into even greater disrepair. In 1852 an attempt was made to improve finances by having chiefs collect a poll tax from their subjects. This plan never functioned well and was eventually abandoned. Dutch and Danish competition limited the funds that could be raised by increasing customs duties. In 1850 the Danes, after having struggled unsuccessfully to find enough profit from legitimate trade in troubled times, ceded their forts to the British. However, the Dutch continued to refuse to cooperate in establishing standardized policies.

Failure to clarify the relationship between the Europeans, the coastal people, and the Ashanti resulted in a series of minor incidents in the 1850s. The situation reached crisis proportions when Governor Pine refused to release to the Ashanti certain persons accused of various crimes. In 1863 Ashanti armies crossed into the area ostensibly under British protection. Pine was convinced that peace and prosperity would come to the coast only when the menace of the Ashanti was removed; therefore, he recommended launching a major counterattack against the invaders. The British government refused to authorize the expenditure. The coastal people again lost faith in the British ability to protect them, and trade, which had steadily declined in the 1850s, came almost to a complete halt.

These were the conditions which inspired the Colonial Office to send Colonel H. St. George Ord in 1864 and a select committee of parliament in 1865 to study the feasibility of a complete British withdrawal from West Africa. Both reports applauded this as a long-range objective but agreed that it was impossible to achieve immediately. The main proposals implemented were the restriction of the areas of British jurisdiction in West Africa, and once again the unification of all British West African territories under a governor-general at Freetown. In the Gold Coast, British authority was to be confined to the forts at Accra, Dixcove, Anomabu, and Christianborg, and to a five-mile radius around Cape Coast.

Educated Fante were encouraged to work for a meaningful association between the many competitive polities that would give them the ability to defend themselves against the Ashanti. In 1867 the British, in order to have their possessions on the Gold Coast grouped in one area, made a treaty with the Dutch. By this arrangement all British forts west of Cape Coast were to be exchanged for all Dutch forts east of Elmina. Although logical to colonial officials in London, this treaty set into motion events that destroyed the retrenchment policy of 1865. African chiefs and their subjects had not been consulted about the transfer. Many Africans did not want Dutch protection. The Denkara actually prevented the Dutch from occupying Kommenda. The inhabitants of Elmina were definitely anti-British and their attitude led to conflict with other nearby coastal polities. To complicate matters, the Ashanti reinvaded the coastal areas in 1868.

With such prevalent conditions and faced with a steadily declining trade, the Dutch in 1869 began negotiations for reversion of all their forts to the British. These complicated discussions were not completed until 1872 when the British, much to the dismay of some high officials, controlled all the Europeans forts on the coast. Complications arose immediately after the transfer. The people of Elmina were pro-Ashanti and encouraged the intervention of the Asantahene to prevent the British from occupying the fort. The Dutch had claimed that the rent that they paid to the Ashanti for their forts was simply another form of "dash" which enabled them to trade in peace. The Asantahene, however, claimed that all the forts were his. The Dutch had not consulted him about any transfer and he wanted them. The British attempted negotiations with the Ashanti and one of their envoys erroneously reported that Asantahene Kofi Kari-kari had renounced his claim to the disputed area. At this juncture the educated Fante proudly announced the completion of their attempts to create a meaningful federation. At Mankessim they had formed a confederation of thirty-three member states with a federal assembly and a king-president. Having been encouraged to do this, they were surprised and chagrined when the British government viewed this as a pro-Ashanti conspiracy and briefly arrested the leaders of the confederation movement.

In January 1873 the main Ashanti army invaded the coast once again with the express purpose of occupying the territory formerly ruled by the Dutch. Rains, an outbreak of dysentery, and smallpox halted the Ashanti and gave the British time to reassess their position and reluctantly accept the advice Governor Pine had given a decade before. Ashanti power in the coastal areas had to be eliminated. In October Major General Garnet Wolseley assumed the position of administrator and commander in chief of the Gold Coast. Over 2,500 British regular soldiers and large numbers of native auxiliaries gave General Wolseley enough strength to invade Ashantiland in early January 1874. Two major battles were fought in late January and early February. The Ashanti military organization and individual bravery proved no match for British firepower, and on February 5 Wolseley's forces entered Kumasi. Since the purpose of the expedition was not to occupy Ashantiland, Wolseley retired after burning the city. Representatives of the Asantahene soon after sued for peace. The terms dictated by the British demanded that the Ashanti pay an indemnity of 50,000 ounces of gold, renounce their claims over the coastal areas, promise to keep trade routes to the north open, and cease human sacrifice.

In July 1874 the conservative government of Disraeli proclaimed the direct takeover of the previously protected areas on the Gold Coast. Administration of the enlarged colony was separated from the authority of the governor-general at Freetown and placed under its own governor. These actions effectively killed any hope that the Fante might have had for a resurrection of their confederation schemes. Britain, despite its hesitant vacillating policies, had decided to increase its territory in the Gold Coast. Nevertheless, the Colonial Office was unwilling to sanction any further expansion at the expense of the Ashanti. The 1874 war thus did not settle in a final way the question of hegemony over the interior. The proud, warlike Ashanti still retained their land, organization, and military forces. Supremacy of the hinterland was not finally settled until 1900.

Oyo and the Yoruba states

The structures of government in Oyo were under stress in the eighteenth century. The system had been developed to rule directly over a much smaller area than that of the Oyo empire. Expansion of the empire and trading sphere brought a schism between the great councillors of state, the Oyo mesi, and the palace administration that the alafin used to carry out the government of the state. The alafin was theoretically a divine king, but in practice his power was considerably less than that of the kings of Dahomey, the Asantahene, or the Hausa rulers. If he abused his powers, he could be removed from office by the Oyo mesi and forced to commit suicide. By the mid-eighteenth century all the conditions were present for radical alteration of the way that Oyo was governed. This occurred when Prime Minister (Basorun) Gaha seized authority and became the real power in Oyo for over twenty years.

Before the mid-eighteenth century, the alafin directly controlled most of the western Yoruba towns and was represented there by officials charged with supervising tribute payments and securing the safety of trade caravans. The kingdoms of Borgu, Nupe, and the Egba states to the south were also tributaries of Oyo. Dahomey had finally agreed in 1747 to pay an annual tribute to Oyo and the alafin gave his protection to the trading cities of Porto Novo and Badagry. The power struggle in Oyo between Basorun Gaha and the alafins weakened the power of the central government. Finally in 1774 Alafin Abiodum killed Gaha and ended the power of the basorun's subordinates in the central government, but he was not able to purge the entire empire of Gaha's supporters.

The empire had been held together not only because of efficient administration, but also partly because the tributary monarchs feared retribution by the armies of Oyo. The armies' efficiency was also damaged by the long contest for central power on Oyo. The tempo of the slave trade had increased in the latter eighteenth century, and Oyo found that the few secure places for obtaining increased numbers of slaves were the Yoruba areas themselves and the adjoining non-Yoruba tributaries to the south and east of Oyo proper. The greater volume of trade in these areas increased the tensions between the central government and these territories. Beginning in the 1780s, the authority of the alafin was successfully challenged by a number of client rulers. In 1783 Borgu and in 1791 Nupe defeated the armies of Oyo and declared their independence. Dahomey ceased paying its tribute on a regular basis, and in 1818 King Gezo declared Dahomey's complete independence from Oyo. Armies dispatched by the alafin against territory dependent on the oni of Ife in 1796 refused to act and subsequently the alafin committed suicide. Afonja, the commander of the armies of Oyo, defected from Oyo and joined the Fulani armies in establishing a separatist rule over Ilorin.

These events coincided with an increase in the demand for slaves by Europeans along the coast due to increasing activity of the British Navy eastward from the Niger delta. Oyo's supply of slaves from the north had been cut off by the revolts of Nupe and Borgu and the actions of Afonja at Ilorin. The disturbances in Oyo, which had begun largely for reasons unconnected with the slave trade, degenerated into a long series of wars between competitive Yoruba rulers for the main purpose of gathering slaves. These Yoruba civil wars lasted until 1893 and resulted first in the fragmentation of the Oyo empire and later made it virtually impossible for the Yoruba to resist European incursion.

There are a few important developments in the early stages of these complex wars that must be mentioned. In 1827 a combination of Ife, Ijebu, and Oyo forces took and destroyed the powerful eastern city of Owu. Refugees from Owu returned to Egbaland and precipitated a decade of warfare that destroyed many villages and provided the victors with large numbers of slaves from the homeless. In 1829 some Ijebu, Ife, Egba, and Oyo refugees settled in the vicinity of the small town of Ibadan. Subsequent quarrels between factions at Ibadan resulted in migration southward of a sizeable portion of the Ibadan settlers. These established themselves at Abeokuta where they created a federal system of government that the Egba tended to dominate. In Ibadan itself there were a series of disputes throughout the 1830s that ended with the Oyo faction supreme. Ibadan soon became the most important of all the Yoruba towns, generally allied, but not subservient to Oyo.

During this period the Fulani at Ilorin were attempting to subjugate as much of Yorubaland as possible. If the Yoruba had not been so deeply divided, the Fulani would have posed no real threat. However, the internecine wars enabled Ilorin to conquer the previously powerful city-states of Ikoyi and Gbogun. The Fulani cavalry was halted in the hilly, wooded area of Ijesa, but there was no such protection for Oyo and the alafin fell under the domination of the Fulani rulers of Ilorin. In an attempt to throw off his control, Oyo allied itself with Borgu and Nikki. Oyo received no assistance from the rulers of other Yoruba states and in 1837 Muslim armies took and sacked Old Oyo so thoroughly that little remains today of the center of the once powerful Oyo empire. Ile Ife, the spiritual center for the Yoruba, was also abandoned temporarily during this phase of the wars.

Refugees from Old Oyo and nearby villages moved southward under their new alafin and settled in the small town of Ago Oja which henceforth became the capital of the Oyo kingdom. Soon after the founding of New Oyo, the Yoruba of Ibadan delivered a resounding defeat to the Fulani at Oshogbo in 1840. Although the Fulani threat remained active throughout the nineteenth century, they never afterward were able to mount a major offensive. However, the troubles of Yorubaland were not over. Wars between various city-states continued widening the gulf between Yoruba so that in some cases Muslims from the north were used in the fighting. In the mid-1840s the king of Dahomey, still deeply involved in the slave trade, began to encroach upon Yoruba territory. The greatest Dahomean threat came in 1851. King Gezo, taking advantage of Ibadan's preoccupation in a war with Ilesha, sent a strong army against Abeokuta. The Egba needed missionary assistance and ammunition supplied by the British Consul John Beecroft in order to repel the Dahomean invaders.

Southern Nigeria and Dahomey to 1865

In southern Nigeria the twenty-five year period after 1845 witnessed a curious liaison between three, at times, antagonistic elements—the traders, the missionaries, and the British government. As previously noted, the missionaries were very active among the Ijo and Ibibio east of the delta. The Atlantic slave trade was still present, but by mid-century had been greatly restricted by the British Navy. Even more important, the rulers of the leading coastal towns had found that oil palm products brought profits without the dangers attendant on the seaborne slave trade. Bonny soon became the most important city for this trade, while New Calabar and Brass also turned more in the direction of legitimate trade. African middlemen still controlled the bulk of the new trade. Although there were over 200 individual European traders along the coast, Liverpool traders predominated. They were content to allow the Africans to gather the oil so long as they could have the largest share in the trade. In the early 1850s, Europeans in most of the trading cities established courts of equity in order to discipline their members and to keep African rulers from retaliating against Europeans en masse for the activities of a few.

There were, however, Europeans who were not content with dealing with middlemen. Macgregor Laird and his associates were quick to take advantage of the interior discoveries of explorers. In 1857 he contracted with the British government to maintain a steamship on the Niger. The use of quinine made possible permanent trade stations such as Aboh, Onitsha, and Lokoja in the interior. Dr. Baikie established himself at Lokoja after his expedition in 1854 and pioneered new trading routes to Nupe and the north. These growing activities in the interior were resented by the Liverpool merchants along the coast as well as the African rulers. Between 1860 and 1870 Laird's ships were escorted on the river by naval vessels. The tension between the new European merchants and the traditional form of trading activity continued throughout the nineteenth century

Map Labels

Niger R.

5°

0 50 100 150

●Kontagora

Bussa●

10°   10°

Jebba

OYO●   ●Bida

●Ilorin

Benue R.

Oshogbo●   Lokoja●

●Ilesha

●Ife

●Ibadan   ●Owo   ●Idah

●Abomey   ●Abeokuta

●Ijebu-Ode

Whydah●   ●Benin

Porto   Lagos   ●Onitsha   ●Afikpo
Novo

●Arochukwu

5°   Aba
                                                    ●   Abak Calabar
                                                              ●
G U L F   ●Opobo

        O F   Brass● Bonny●
                G U I N E A

▨ Metropolitan Oyo 18th Century

▥ Lagos Colony & Protectorate 1890

▤ Niger Coast Protectorate 1887

▨ Administrative Limits of Royal Niger Co.

Southern Nigeria in the Late Nineteenth Century

until the great African trading houses were broken by the British invasions during the scramble. In the 1850s and 1860s these conflicts were open invitations for British officials to begin their intervention in African affairs.

In 1849 John Beecroft was named British consul for the Bights of Benin and Biafra. He had been active in west coast affairs since he left his ship at Fernando Po as a young sailor in 1827. In the intervening years he had explored the hinterland regions of the delta, become a successful trader, served the British government in a number of missions, and in 1843 had been named governor of Fernando Po by the Spanish. Beecroft favored more direct involvement of Britain in the affairs of African states to secure trade, advance missionary activity, and end the slave trade. In his six-year tenure as consul, he made the British presence felt in a variety of ways. Because of complaints of European traders and factionalism, he used British power in 1851 to depose and exile William Pepple, the ruler of Bonny, the most powerful delta trading state. Although Pepple was returned a decade later, the internal affairs of Bonny were never the same afterward. Beecroft also was very active in attempting to influence policy at Calabar.

It was at Lagos that his intervention had the most immediate effect. Continuing wars in the Yoruba states and the expansion of slave raiding activities by the king of Dahomey had made Lagos and Badagry major slave trading ports. British missionaries at these places and at Abeokuta continually bombarded the British government with pleas to end the internecine conflict, halt the slave traffic, and open the interior for legitimate trade. To them Kosoko, the ruler of Lagos, represented all that was wrong with the system because he was a confirmed slaver. However, his position was not secure because there were powerful factions within Lagos who resented the methods by which Kosoko had come to power. Beecroft interjected himself in this complex internal situation. He obtained a promise from Akitoye, Kosoko's uncle, that he would suppress the slave trade if he were selected oba. In 1851 Beecroft attempted to force Kosoko out by invasion, but failed. However, elements of the British West African squadron drove Kosoko from Lagos and Akitoye was later confirmed as the ruler. In 1853 after Akitoye's death, Docemo, his choice as a successor, was confirmed as oba. A full British consul was appointed for Lagos in the same year.

Kosoko, from his base at Epe, continued to harass interior traders. The Yoruba wars were an ever present deterrent to the establishment of legitimate trade, and Dahomey was a constant threat to the missionaries at Abeokuta. Thus in 1861, the British, in order to obtain a more permanent base in Yorubaland, gained the cession of Lagos from Docemo in return for an annual pension of £1,030. Soon afterward the governor at Lagos annexed the slaving town of Badagry and destroyed the town of Epe. The interior wars usually involving Ibadan continued in the 1860s unchecked by the growth of British influence on the coast. During one of these wars in 1867, the ruler of Abeokuta, angered at continuing interference from Lagos, expelled all European missionaries. For over a decade thereafter missionary activity among the Yoruba was almost nonexistent. In the same period, British trading firms became well established at Lagos and legitimate trade with the Yoruba in oil palm products and cotton increased. The reality of this trade with the Yoruba was at variance with the report of the 1865 select committee, which recommended a nonexpansive political policy. The combination of trading and missionary activities dictated a forward policy. When the British government decided to support such a policy in the 1880s, they found little opposition from the Yoruba states weakened by seventy years of civil war.

Westward from Badagry lay the coastal areas dominated by the powerful Fon kingdom of Dahomey. This well-organized, militaristic state had been checked in its expansion in the eighteenth century only by the Ashanti in the west and Oyo in the east. The ports of Whydah, Jaquin, Little Popo, and Porto Novo were most important for Dahomey's major export, slaves. European traders at these ports were never allowed to gain the power and influence that they exercised on the Gold Coast. Nevertheless, they played an important role in the complex competition for power between the kings of Dahomey, local rulers, and the alafin of Oyo. The kings of Dahomey managed to defeat the trading nobility at Whydah and Jaquin and to humble the European traders by the latter eighteenth century. By becoming a tributary of Oyo, they protected their eastern borders from invasions from this great Yoruba power. The focus of European slave trading activity in the latter eighteenth century moved from the Dahomean coast to Badagry and Lagos, and to the states east of the Niger delta.

The Dahomean state in the nineteenth century depended upon the slave trade, and its kings were, at first, helpless to reverse the trend of the trade away from Dahomey. The French, who were the dominant European traders in the area, also struck at the prosperity of Dahomey when in 1794 the republic banned the slave trade. However, in the early nineteenth century, a series of events gave the Dahomeans a chance to regain their supremacy in the trade of the Slave Coast. The French returned, to be sure, in lesser numbers after 1802. More important was the breakup of the mighty Oyo empire and the subsequent civil wars in Yorubaland. King Gezo of Dahomey felt secure enough to stop paying the annual tribute to the alafin of Oyo. The activities of the British West African patrol along the eastern Nigerian coast made Dahomey once again an inviting area for trade. Lagos, Badagry, and Porto Novo, because of the Yoruba wars, became almost independent entities. It, therefore, was only natural for King Gezo to try to absorb western Yorubaland into his sphere of influence.

When King Gezo actually began to attempt incorporation of Yoruba territory into his kingdom in the 1840s, he was opposed not only by individual Egba and Yoruba rulers, but also by Britain. Abeokuta was one of the major collection points for slaves in troubled Yorubaland, and Gezo attempted in 1845, 1848, and 1851 to absorb the Egba states into his kingdom. Reference has already been made to the contributions of Consul Beecroft and the missionaries to the defense of Abeokuta which foiled Gezo's plans. The establishment of British hegemony over Lagos and later

Badagry made it impossible for the Dahomean kings to incorporate these rich ports into their sphere of influence. Thus, due largely to the British, Dahomean efforts were only an additional cause for disorder in Yorubaland.

The Dahomean slave ports prospered during the first half of the nineteenth century because of restrictions on the trade elsewhere along the coast. British efforts to get Gezo and his successor, Gelele, to abandon the trade proved fruitless. A British mission in 1850 was flatly told that the king had no intention of giving up trading in slaves. In 1852 Gezo did sign a treaty but made no attempt to enforce it. All that could be done was to impose a rigid blockade on the Dahomean ports. The British government at one time considered military operations against Gezo but rejected it. Dahomey was one of the stronger powers in West Africa and could not be as easily defeated as the divided polities of coastal Nigeria. The active antislavery policy of Britain warned the Dahomean rulers that they had to maintain their military forces. Since they had not developed legitimate trade to any degree, the export of slaves was necessary to buy the guns that would assure their supremacy.

The history of the Slave Coast in the latter nineteenth century is bound up with the conflicting colonial ambitions of Britain and France. Britain had already staked out a sizeable sphere of influence from Badagry to Calabar. The French, after the abandonment of their fort at Whydah, were quiescent until the 1870s. However, when the scramble began, Dahomey became one of the major areas of French interest. Opposing this new imperialism, the autocratic rulers of Dahomey would be crushed in two bloody wars in the 1890s.

French activities to 1870

France, the second European power with considerable territorial and trading interest in West Africa, suffered from more handicaps than did Britain. The British government, despite changes of government, was stable throughout the nineteenth century. The French had been deeply divided ideologically and politically by the revolutions of the latter eighteenth century. These wide differences between conservative and liberal forces were reflected in the nineteenth century by the revolutions of 1830 and 1848. No less profound was the coup of Napolecn III in 1852 and the War of the Commune in 1871 following the Franco-Prussian War. Thus a succession of different governments based upon divergent theories of rule could hardly be expected to follow consistent imperial policies. French activity in Africa until the period of the Third Republic was very limited by comparison to its rival Britain. Two other factors should be remembered in discussing French imperialism. The first is the inferior nature of the French manufacturing and banking sectors in comparison to Britain. Thus mercantile and manufacturing pressure on French governments for overseas expansion was not great until the last quarter of the century. Another factor was that France had lost the bulk of her overseas territories in the wars with Britain in the eighteenth century. In Africa this meant that they had no substantial spheres until after the Napoleonic Wars. Even afterwards they were relatively restricted to the posts in the Senegambia which Britain had returned to them in 1817.

The major French enclave was St. Louis du Senegal which had been established in 1659. In addition the French controlled the island of Goree off Cape Verde and had a station at Albreda on the Gambia River. The major trade product in the early part of the century was gum gathered at Portendic and shipped from St. Louis. In the 1820s the French experimented with establishing a plantation economy based on cotton in Senegal. This venture was largely unsuccessful. Later peanuts were introduced, but this crop proved to be more suited to the land of the African kingdoms of Sine, Saloum, and Cayor. Peanut exports did not become significant until the 1850s. It is not surprising that the governments of Charles X and Louis Philippe were not eager to obtain any more territory of such dubious value.

Nevertheless, St. Louis had grown by 1851 into a small city of over 15,000 of whom almost 300 were Europeans. The myth of further riches to be gained by trade with the Niger territories had not been dispelled by the investigations of Mollien, Caillie, and British explorers. This expectation of wealth remained and became one of the reasons for Governor Louis Faidherbe's more active policy of the 1850s. In 1852 all the areas south of St. Louis were taken from the governor and placed under the authority of the naval commander on the west coast. At that period naval officers were extremely skeptical of the value of West Africa and resented the manipulations of French merchants to involve them more directly in African affairs. They acted as another brake on activist policies.

Some French merchants proved that they could compete with the British on the Ivory and Slave coasts. They brought pressure on the government to assure them protection from hostile Africans. Chief among these merchants was Victor Regis from Marseilles. He had been involved in the gum trade in Senegal until he quit in 1840 because of what he felt was government favoritism shown to his competitors. Subsequently he became involved in the palm oil trade further south. Due largely to his endeavors, the French became established on the Gabon coast and at Assinie and Grand Bassam on the Ivory Coast in 1843. Regis' company was also active at Lagos and Whydah. In 1850, when he withdrew from the Slave Coast, the navy stayed on to protect some of the smaller merchants involved in the scanty trade.

In 1841 Regis' agents secured a near monopoly of oil palm exports from Whydah in return for small payments to local officials and the king of Dahomey. His trading influence extended westward to Grand Popo. In 1851 he devised a scheme to export laborers from Africa for work in the West Indies. This was foiled by British opposition to what appeared to them as slavery in another form. Regis' position at Lagos was undercut by its transfer to the British crown in 1861 when almost immediately traiff rates on alcohol and tobacco drove him to seek an alternative port that would still allow his agents entrance to the trade of Yorubaland. His agents obtained a treaty of protection from the local ruler of Porto Novo and this was eventually approved by Napolean III's government in 1863. Regis' agent became the French consular agent for the area. However, the sandbar across the harbor there meant that another better port was needed. This led to the temporary occupation of Cotonou, which was directly ruled by King Gelele of Dahomey. The French government was in no position to undertake any real military action if Gelele moved against the European traders there. Because of the threat of possible war, the navy ordered the evacuation of Cotonou and Porto Novo in 1864. Although Regis had not been successful in his attempt to bypass Lagos, he had given the French a claim to Porto Novo. In 1868 Gelele ceded a small amount of territory at Cotonou to the French, and this together with Porto Novo gave the French bases from which much later they expanded northward into Dahomey proper.

Another place of growing French involvement during the 1860s was the Mellacourie and Scarcies River area northwest of Freetown. Creole merchants from Freetown and some French traders had been involved there for years since it was one of the outlets for trade from the Futa Jallon. In 1865 a civil war broke out between competing chiefs and protection for all European merchants became imperative. Almost all merchants trading in the Mellacourie signed a petition requesting British protection. The British government, operating on the philosophy of no expansion, was extremely reluctant to get involved. The French vice-consul at Freetown in conjunction with Governor Pinet-Laparde of Senegal decided to guarantee the security of the merchants. By using troops and naval vessels, a de facto French protectorate was established by 1868. Although British traders were in a majority in the Mellacourie, they lodged no great protests over the actions of the French authorities.

The French position in Senegal at mid-century was very weak. To the north, Moorish subgroups controlled the gum-producing areas and they charged French merchants what amounted to tribute to trade for gum. The Wolof states located between the Senegal and Gambia rivers were not controlled in any way by the governor at St. Louis whose military strength was such that he could not protect merchants even along the lower Senegal River. The rise of the Tucolor empire under Al Hajj Umar presented a definite threat to the French enclaves as well as to the Wolof. This was the situation when in 1854 a thirty-six year old engineering officer arrived in St. Louis to assume the position of governor. During his two periods as governor, Captain (later General) Louis Faidherbe's activist policies firmly established the French as the dominant force in the Senegambia.

His first area of difficulty was with the Moors. Faidherbe absorbed the Walo in 1855 and soon afterward defeated the powerful Trarza group. Thereafter the Moors could expect to be paid a standard three percent duty for gum exported through their areas. In 1857 an agreement with Britain exchanged the French post of Albreda on the Gambia for the relinquishment of British claims to the gum trade at Portendic. The French had established a fort at Podor in 1854 and one further east at Medina near

the border of Tucolor territory. Faidherbe attempted to protect French
merchants in the Wolof states and to further their dominance of the growing peanut trade. In the late 1850s he aroused the enmity of Portugal
by establishing French claims to the Casamance north of Bissau. Faidherbe
was provided with more troops and supplies from France than had any of
his predecessors. He increased his potential military strength further by
recruiting and training a Senegalese battalion in 1857. In 1857 Goree was
returned to Faidherbe's jurisdiction, and a new town, Dakar, was established on the adjacent Cape Verde peninsula.

In 1855 Al Hajj Umar had proclaimed a holy war against the infidels
in Senegambia. This did not pose any immediate threat to the French since
it was directed primarily against Africans, and Umar was busy with his
wars along the Niger. However, some of Umar's followers attacked French
posts, and in 1857 a large segment of his army attempted to take Medina.
After a siege of three months, the Tucolor were driven off. Faidherbe was
concerned with the demarcation of French and Tucolor spheres of influence on the upper Senegal River and opening of trade routes to the Niger
River. The first of these objectives was achieved by an agreement in 1859.
During Faidherbe's second administration (1863–1865), he commissioned
Lieutenant Abdon Eugene Mage to retrace Mungo Park's route to the Niger
and to secure, if possible, a treaty with Umar that would encourage trade
between St. Louis and the deep hinterland. Mage signed a very general
agreement with Umar's son, Ahmadu, in 1866. Faidherbe's successor, Pinet-
Laprade, did nothing to follow this up and there were no further French
activities in that direction for over a decade.

The major sphere of French activity in the decade after 1857 was in
the Wolof and Serer states. In 1859 Faidherbe, acting on many complaints
from merchants, moved with approximately 350 well-trained troops against
the alleged troublemakers in the kingdoms of Cayor, Sine, and Saloum. On
March 18, the French defeated the army of Sine and soon afterward
marched to Saloum. He dictated treaties to the two monarchs that gave the
French a near monopoly of trade subject only to a three percent export
duty. Each monarch granted extraterritorial rights to French citizens. Continuing threats from Sine and Saloum dictated another punitive expedition
in 1861. The French established forts at Joal in Sine and Kaolack in Saloum
in addition to the one previously constructed at Rufisque. In 1861 a quarrel
erupted with the ruler of Cayor over French rights to build a telegraph line
across his territory. The ruler, Macadou, was deposed and a puppet was
installed. A strong Wolof leader, Lat Dior, disputed the throne of Cayor
and it was not until January 1864 that the French were able to restore even
their tentative position in Cayor.

In the mid-1860s the southern Senegambia was wracked by the
religious upheavals called the Soninke-Marabout Wars. The rise of the
religious reformer Maba threatened for a time not only "pagan" chiefs, but
also the French presence. The kingdom of Rip, which he created, was constructed to recreate a powerful single government over the Wolof that had
not existed since the breakdown of the power of the kingdom of Jolof in

the eighteenth century. The growing crisis in Europe following the Austro-Prussian War meant that Governor Pinet-Laparde could not hope for replacement troops and certainly no reinforcements. Maba defeated the French a number of times and, if he had waited, he might have been successful in driving the French from the Wolof areas and thus assuring himself of the eventual domination and conversion of those states. However, he attacked Sine in 1867 and was killed in a battle against that king's forces. His death removed the greatest threat to French supremacy over the Wolof states.

The conquests of Faidherbe and Pinet-Laparde in Senegal gave France the largest European colony in West Africa. They had transformed what had been little more than a colony of two islands into extensive productive mainland possessions. In those territories where French merchants had once paid to trade, the governor at St. Louis in the 1860s claimed the right to control trade and, to varying degrees, the political life of those client states. France was thus in a very favorable position to expand control over the interior in the decades of the scramble.

Competition between Britain and France was not severe in the period 1860 through 1870. Contrary to usually stated reasons for economic conflict between the two states, it was free-trade Britain which was responsible for closed markets at this time. British territories were supposed to be self-sufficient; therefore, duties had to be imposed in order to provide the necessary funds. No such stricture was placed on French areas. The British placed high duties on alcohol and tobacco, the trade goods most used by the French. Thus, in effect, French traders were always at a disadvantage in British areas. In the mid-1860s the growing number of disagreements between British and French merchants all along the coast began to alarm both governments. Schemes for exchanges of territory and, by extension, spheres of influence were welcomed by both governments. Each wanted a grouping of areas. Most of Britain's interests were concentrated from Freetown to Lagos while the French were in the Senegambia. Thus plans for exchange involved trading Bathurst for French areas on the Ivory Coast. In 1866 and 1868 plans for such an exchange were foiled by a British parliamentary opposition that believed the compensation for British territory was not enough. Bathurst merchants and citizens also protested against being transferred to France. Despite this setback, plans for the exchange of the Gambia were revived after 1871 and this remained a possibility until World War I.

TWO

East and Central Africa
before the scramble

The peoples of East Africa and the Arab traders

East Africa in the nineteenth century was inhabited by a bewildering number of differing Bantu, Nilotic, Nilo-Hamitic, and
Semitic people. Populated by a series of invaders from the north
and west over more than a thousand years, there was little
political unity. Only in the interlacustrine areas had there developed complex large-scale polities which could compare with
states in West Africa. Between the great lakes and the coast
the typical polity was small and generally clan oriented. Most of
the Bantu groups were agriculturists although wherever they
could they did keep and prize their cattle. Pastoralists such as
the Masai and Nandi with their more aggressive societies controlled a substantial portion of territory between the agricultural Bantu clans. However, they were never able to create a
state which functioned on the same high level as the interlacustrine kingdoms. Along the coast were the Zenj states dominated at the beginning of the century by local trading Arab
oligarchies. The population of these coastal towns was mixed,
the dominant language was Swahili, and the tempo of life considerably different from that of the interior villages and towns.

The most stable, affluent, and powerful of the East African
kingdoms was Buganda. Energetic rulers early in the century
had successfully declared their independence from Bunyoro.
Under Suna and later Mutesa—the greatest of the kabakas of
the century—its army and navy had brought Koki, Karagwe, and
western Busoga under Buganda control. The neighboring rulers
of Toro and Ankole were also directly affected by Buganda's
power. Buganda, blessed with excellent soil, its cattle herds
prospering, and with an already efficient government structure
improved by Mutesa, was invulnerable from outside attacks
until the arrival of the Europeans.

The kingdom of Bunyoro had by mid-century recovered
from the internal dissensions which had brought about the

separation of Buganda and Toro. Its rulers, Karmurasi and later Kabarega, strengthened the bureaucracy loyal to them and developed a powerful military force. They dominated trade and politics in the area between Lakes Kyoga and Albert. Arab traders, usually from the Sudan, traded freely with Bunyoro but only at the discretion of the ruler. It appears that a conflict between Buganda and the resurgent Bunyoro to determine dominance in the interlacustrine territory would have been inevitable had it not been for the arrival of Europeans. The entire energies of Bunyoro were taken up, throughout the two decades following 1870, with attempting to repulse the Europeans and Egyptians. And Kabarega did successfully fight off the attempts of Baker and Gordon to make Bunyoro an appendage of Egypt. However, in the late 1880s he attempted to supplant the kabaka's influence in Ankole and Toro and thus brought a coalition of Buganda and the British against him. Bunyoro was finally conquered in 1898.

East of the great lakes in what is modern Kenya there existed a multiplicity of Bantu and Nilo-Hamitic groups, many of them still unsettled. The Luo and Kikuyu were the most important of the agricultural Bantu of this area but neither group was well organized in a central state form. The Kikuyu of central Kenya were probably the largest Bantu group in eastern Africa. However, their clan system of government obscured their size and greatly reduced their potential power. The Kikuyu, hungry for land, were still in the process of moving into the Kiambu district in the latter nineteenth century. Harassed by the Masai, they had not fully brought this southern segment within the context of the Kikuyu land system by the time that the Europeans arrived. First Kikuyu contacts with Europeans were in this yet unstable region. Smallpox and rinderpest epidemics in the 1890s combined to depopulate large areas of the fertile highland, leading Europeans to believe that the territory was uninhabited. Herein lay the seeds of much future discord.

The proud Masai pastoralists were also still in the process of migration during the nineteenth century. By 1800 they were firmly established on the grasslands from an area west of Lake Rudolf south to Kilimanjaro. Few in number, the Masai's peculiar military-political system enabled them to fight effectively against strangers. However, they could not combine into larger, more powerful political units. Nevertheless, advance elements of the Masai reached deep into modern Tanzania until halted by the Bantu Gogo in the 1830s. At mid-century the Masai were driven out of the territory immediately to the west of Lake Rudolf by the southward migrating Turkana. Even with this loss the Masai clans controlled the bulk of the high hill country of central Kenya. Toward the end of the nineteenth century, partially weakened by smallpox and internecine struggles, one large segment of the Masai moved permanently into northern Tanzania.

Adjacent to the Kikuyu were located another pastoral people, the Nandi. Although not as aggressive as the Masai, they did raid their neighbors' lands and successfully defended their own grazing lands against everyone, even the Masai. It was the Nandi later in the century who caused the British government and the railroad builders the most trouble. But after

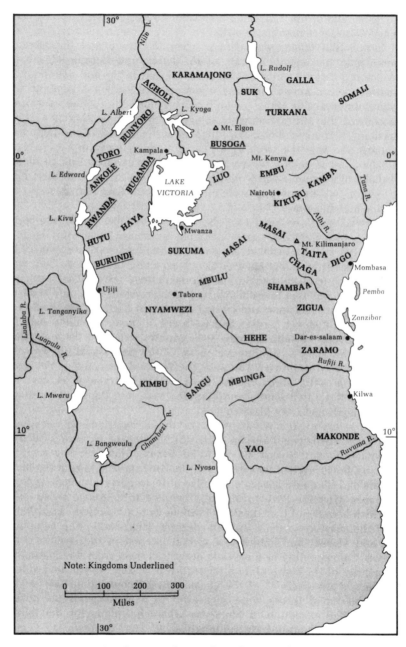

Kingdoms and Peoples of East Africa

many futile attempts by government forces, they were finally, in the early 1900s, induced to accept British rule.

The peoples of the Tanzanian area were no less complex in their numbers and differences than those of Kenya. There were no major states there until late in the nineteenth century when the Hehe and the Sambaa, responding to the outside threats of the Arabs and Europeans, created larger, more powerful entities. The Hehe located in the hill country near present-day Iringa were united by the work of two leaders, Myugumba and his son, Mkwawa. The Hehe not only helped block the further southward expansion of the Masai, but were later the chief opposition to German expansion. The powerful Sambaa kingdom was centered in the Usumbara Mountains and was the work of an early nineteenth-century ruler, Kimweri. The Sambaa ruler's control over his subjects was as firm as that of the kabaka of Buganda. The Sambaa, however, partially due to their location, did not play an important role in the history of East Africa during the latter nineteenth century.

Centered on Kaze (modern Tabora) were the many differing Bantu groups to which Europeans gave the common name, Nyamwezi. In actuality the Nyamwezi consisted of over one hundred separate clans each varying in size from a few hundred people to many thousands. They were basically an agricultural people, but the mark they left on the history of eastern Africa was due to their skills as porters. Arabs first, and then the Europeans, depended upon and trusted Nyamwezi carriers. Many of them were also long distance traders and were not adverse to selling their fellows into slavery. Partially because their country straddled the main slave route from the coast to the interior, many of the slaves sold on the coast were Nyamwezi. In southern Tanzania, the Yao and remnants of the Nguni in conjunction with Arabs carried on a profitable trade in slaves. The activities of these two Bantu groups spilled over into the territory of the Shire Highlands and Lake Malawi.

The movement and development of these hinterland peoples were hidden from European observers until the coming of explorers such as Livingstone, Baker, Speke, Burton, and Stanley later in the century. Europeans, however, had long known of the Zenj states. Ships in the lucrative India and China trade regularly called at these ports, although no European power after the Portuguese had attempted to dominate these cities. The British because of their position in India were particularly knowledgeable of the coastline and its Swahili-speaking inhabitants. The sultans of Oman and Muscat had long had a special interest in the eastern coast. However, the instability of their state prevented them from dominating the trading cities of the coast. Only after 1810 was Sultan Seyyid Said able to turn much of the energies of the Omani toward controlling East Africa. By 1820 his naval forces were successful in overawing all the coastal towns with the exception of Mombasa where his plans for domination were opposed by the ruling Mazrui family.

Sultan Said's conquest of Mombasa was postponed by the interference of Captain William Owen of the British Navy who in 1824 posted a small detachment at Mombasa and offered British protection to the Mazrui rulers. Owen did this without prior consultation with his government because he believed it the only way to significantly check the eastern sea-borne slave trade. Said, not wishing to go counter to the most powerful naval power in the Indian Ocean, did not want to risk a confrontation at Mombasa. Finally in 1826 London repudiated Owen's policy and ordered all British personnel withdrawn from Mombasa. The British government did not want additional responsibilities in East Africa, and the Indian government preferred to see Said dominant on the coast. After the British withdrawal, Said's forces occupied Mombasa briefly in 1827 and 1828 and then permanently in 1837. Almost immediately the sultan entered into economic and political negotiations with the United States and Britain. The United States sent a consul to Zanzibar in 1837 and the British did so in 1841. This reflected Zanzibar's growing importance as a way stop in the Far Eastern trade. In 1840 Said transferred his residence to Zanzibar and began a policy which encouraged the planting of clove trees on the island and oil palms elsewhere along the coast. By these decisions he created a plantation economy which demanded an ever-increasing supply of slaves.

There were already extant trade routes which had brought interior products to the markets of the Zenj states for a thousand years. However, the urgings of Said and the increased demand for slaves caused adventuresome merchants to open new trade routes as they pushed farther into the hinterland. In 1842 the first Arab coastal caravan reached Lake Tanganyika and a few years later Arab merchants were trading regularly with Buganda. In 1852 an Arab caravan crossed the continent from Bagamoyo to Benguela. Tabora became a major interior entrepôt for caravans in the 1840s and a substantial number of Arabs established permanent residence there. One trader of mixed Arab and African descent from Tabora was Hamed bin Muhammad, better known as Tippu Tib. He became, for Europeans, the epitome of the wealthy, successful Arab trader. In the 1870s he had established himself southwest of Lake Tanganyika near the Lualaba River. There he built a vast commercial empire extending far westward into the Congo basin.

Despite the increasing importance of slaves during Said's reign, the main product which drew the Arabs into the interior was ivory. Slaves were either purchased or taken by force to provide the porters necessary to carry the equipment of the caravan and the heavy elephant tusks. After the completion of a trading venture, the slaves would then be sold.

An Arab caravan of the nineteenth century was a major undertaking which cost its backers a considerable investment. Depending upon the time and the route planned, caravans would stay in the field from one to two years before returning to Tabora or to the coast. On these long excursions Arab entrepreneurs preferred peaceful trading relations with the Africans. In most places they had little difficulty in obtaining ivory or slaves by offering a variety of goods for the desired products. In some places however, particularly when operating against Bantu people with a weak military organization, they utilized force in raiding for slaves. Trade with

Buganda and other similarly powerful states was on a more regularized basis. Tippu Tib and other major traders could not have operated successfully far into the interior with as few men as they had if powerful African states had not been well disposed toward them.

Arab merchants, by the time European explorers and missionaries began to arrive in great numbers, had established a complex system which tapped the interior trade from Gondokoro in the north to the Shire Valley in the south, and from the Congo River eastward to the coast. An integral part of the system was the involvement of Africans directly in the process of collecting slaves. In the south the Yao and Nguni were soon renowned for their slave raiding and in the north the Nyamwezi, Baganda, and Karagwe were deeply committed to the trade. One should note that these Arab princes of commerce owed no definite allegiance to any state or man. Some, like Tippu Tib, established their own interior states. The sultan of Zanzibar ostensibly was their overlord, but his power to punish stopped a few miles inland from the coast. His control over the activities of his subjects who could be absent for anywhere from one to five years was mostly economic. Until the Europeans by their interference diverted much of the trade, the best place to sell ivory and slaves was in the coastal towns. This gave the sultan a certain control over the traders—enhanced by the degree of his own investment in these interior ventures. But if the sultan could not effectively control all the activities of his Arab subjects, he was even less powerful in directing the political destinies of the African people. Until the 1880s he was relatively unconcerned with political power, being content to tap the riches of the interior. Despite this obvious fact, the British government throughout the early nineteenth century persisted in acting as if the sultan's edict would be enforced in the hinterland.

British antislavery activity

Britain early concerned itself with East Africa merely as an adjunct to its dominant position on the Indian Ocean. The British East India Company's government was deeply involved in the affairs of the Persian Gulf which in turn made events in Oman and Muscat important to them. After 1807 the new factor of the abolition of the slave trade was added to British policy toward territories abutting upon the Indian Ocean. It is important to note that while the British government recognized that it had certain interests in East Africa, it did not assign a very high priority to them. If the British could achieve their goals without undue expenditure of funds or risk of a major conflict, they would pursue them. If heavy expenses or the possibility of unnecessary open hostility with another European power intruded, Britain could retreat from her preestablished position. This latter development was particularly noticeable during the period of the scramble for Africa when Britain was confronted with German imperial ambitions in East Africa.

Early in the nineteenth century some British officials believed that the slave trade could be curbed by entering into formal agreements with rulers of territories which supplied slaves. In pursuance of such a goal Captain Fairfax Moresby, in 1822, acting for the governor of Mauritius negotiated a treaty with Sultan Said. By the terms of the Moresby Treaty the sultan promised to end the trade in slaves between his subjects and that of any Christian power. It did not interfere with the trade within the sultan's own possessions or with any Muslim state. Said also granted the British Navy the right to stop and search vessels suspected of being in violation of the treaty.

The next step in attempting to curb the slave trade was taken by a British naval officer who decided to act on his own initiative against the trade. Captain William Owen, while employed in charting the coastline of eastern Africa in 1822 and 1823, came to the conclusion that the sultan's agents were not complying with the terms of the Moresby Treaty. While in India in 1823 he tried to convince the governor of Bombay to intervene more directly in the sultan's affairs. Receiving no help from this quarter, Owen concluded that in the process of completing his survey he would strike at the malefactors whenever he could. On his return to eastern Africa he stopped at Oman and informed Said that on his return to Mombasa he would give protection to its Mazrui rulers if they requested it. Said, not wishing to offend a British naval officer, gave orders that all assistance should be given to Owen when he arrived on the African coast. Privately he later complained to the government of Bombay and other British representatives about Owen's contemplated action.

In February 1824, Owen was asked by the Mazrui rulers of Mombasa to offer them protection from possible conquest by Oman. Owen concurred and signed a treaty of protection on February 9 whereby the Arab leaders of Mombasa promised to give up the slave trade. Owen agreed to help Mombasa reinstitute its control over Pemba. He was not successful in this venture having to be content with the reopening of trade between the two areas. Owen soon sailed away to attempt to gain support for his undertaking from the governor of Mauritius. He left Lieutenant John Reitz, Midshipman George Phillips, a marine corporal, and three sailors behind to collect the customs and keep order in Mombasa. Reitz died in less than three months and Midshipman Phillips was left to deal with the Arab leaders, Indian merchants, and the slave trade. In August 1824, Phillips was replaced by Lieutenant James Emery.

Meanwhile Owen was having little success in convincing higher authority to support his protectorate. However, neither the government of Bombay nor Sir Lowry Cole, governor of Mauritius, ordered the abandonment of Mombasa. Rather, before taking a definite stand, they waited for instructions from London. Without active support from Britain and with the growing hostility of the Mazrui who were disappointed at the meager assistance they had received, Emery was forced to withdraw from Mombasa in July 1826 before orders to do so reached him from London. Thus ended the first, near comic, British protectorate in East Africa.

Once the British presence was safely removed, Said attacked Mombasa and his agents ruled there until the end of 1829 when the Mazrui once again asserted their independence. Said sent one more expedition against the town without success before turning to diplomacy to gain his ends. In 1836 on the death of Sultan Salim of Mombasa, Said allied himself with a strong faction within the town and forced the new sultan, Rashid, to accept the overlordship of Oman. A few months later with Omani troops garrisoning the town, Said had Rashid and many of his leading supporters murdered. Thus Said was able to end the local oligarchy and administer the town directly from Zanzibar. Said's control over Mombasa and the other coastal towns increased immeasurably when he moved the seat of government from Oman to Zanzibar in 1840.

The increase in the number of slaves taken in the interior in the 1830s and early 1840s showed clearly that the Moresby Treaty was not working. The primary task of Consul Hamerton, the first British permanent representative to Zanzibar, was to rectify this situation. Said depended upon continual British support to ward off encroachments by other powers, particularly the French, on his territories. Thus Hamerton exercised great influence over the sultan from the beginning. Hamerton on direct orders from Lord Palmerston suggested as early as 1841 a new, more comprehensive agreement which would replace the Moresby Treaty. Said resisted, knowing how unpopular any restrictions upon the coastal trade would be with many of his most powerful subjects. He agreed to the new treaty only after it became obvious that Britain would make such an agreement the price of continuing to support the sultan's position in the Indian Ocean. In 1845 the Hamerton Treaty was signed which proscribed the seaborne trade by the sultan's subjects except between Lamu and Kilwa. It gave the British the right to search Zanzibari ships suspected of carrying slaves.

Negotiations for the Hamerton Treaty were carried out against a background of renewed French activity in the Indian Ocean. French planters on Bourbon Island needed to obtain more "free workers" from eastern Africa for their sugar plantations and thus French agents were active along the Zenj coast. A French naval patrol was posted to the Indian Ocean area in 1845 and the British squadron gave up its right to search French ships suspected of carrying slaves. The French attempt to gain dominance on Madagascar and their occupation of the island of Nossi Be frightened Said and certainly contributed to his willingness to accept the Hamerton proposals.

The French openly supported the claims of Said's elder son, Hilal, to succeed his father. Said had made it clear that he wished his empire divided between two other sons, Thwain and Majid. The opportunity for the French to intervene to their advantage in this question was briefly ended by the death of Hilal in 1851. However, when Said died in 1856 leaving Thwain to rule in Oman and Majid in Zanzibar, the French once again attempted to gain influence by supporting one faction against another. They first supported Thwain, but soon shifted to uphold the claims to Zanzibar of a young brother, Barghash. In 1859 a French naval force visited Zanzibar and its commander and the French consul, presumably hoping for a coup, openly declared for Barghash. In response the British sent three warships to Zanzibar and General Rigby, the British consul, was able to convince the French representatives that they were creating a situation which would have serious diplomatic ramifications. After this brief sortie at rebellion, Barghash caused no more trouble and succeeded his brother as ruler of Zanzibar in 1870. French interest in the coast waned, and in 1862 they signed a declaration with Britain recognizing the independence of the sultan of Zanzibar.

In 1866 Dr. John Kirk, who had accompanied Livingstone on his explorations of the Shire Highlands, became consul. Partially because of Majid's need for British support and partially because of Kirk's skill as a physician, the new consul gained an influence over the sultan which none of his predecessors had enjoyed. This influence was continued after Barghash became sultan and it seemed at times that Kirk was more concerned about the political well-being of the sultan's empire than was Barghash. Despite this feeling of responsibility, Kirk was as convinced as his superiors that Barghash should be forced, if necessary, to sign a more definitive treaty concerning the slave trade as had been suggested by an 1871 parliamentary Commission of Inquiry.

In 1873 Sir Bartle Frere came to Zanzibar as a special commissioner to negotiate a comprehensive agreement. He wanted the sultan to forbid the export of slaves from any part of his kingdom and to close down all the slave markets. Barghash believed such an agreement would be economically disastrous and resisted until the presence of elements of the British Navy in the harbor and Kirk's threats to blockade the sultan's territory convinced him to capitulate. On Kirk's advice, Barghash later forbade marching slaves from one town to another along the coast. In order to make the new agreement more effective a new Zanzibari military force was created under the command of Lieutenant Lloyd Matthews of the British Navy and British ships quelled any signs of revolt from disaffected merchants in the coastal towns.

The agreement of 1873, although ending the bulk of the coastal and seaborne trade, did not stop the traffic in East Africa. Arab traders in the interior were merely forced to seek new and more difficult routes. Slaves from the Sudan became more important since one of the best markets for slaves in the early 1870s was Khartoum. The 1873 agreement showed how dependent the sultan was upon British support. His empire was a commercial one with little political control being exercised over interior African people. Barghash's tenuous control could be maintained as long as Britain was uninterested in expansion and would champion the sultan's cause against other European powers. In the 1880s the diplomatic scene changed radically and Britain slowly but definitely moved away from protecting the sultan, thus making possible the division of his empire.

European explorations

European curiosity concerning the mysteries of the East African hinterland did not become active until the mid-1850s. Until then West Africa had absorbed the attention of most geographers, adventurers, and missionaries.

True, there were continual speculations concerning the Nile source, but no one seemed willing to investigate the interior. The first European explorers of the hinterland of East Africa were German missionaries in the employ of the Church Missionary Society. Dr. Ludwig Krapf in 1844 had been given permission by the sultan to establish a mission on the mainland. Two years later he was joined by Reverend Johann Rebmann who opened a station fifteen miles west of Mombasa. Rebmann became interested in the people of the Taita hills and particularly the Chaga. In the course of one of his visits to them he sighted the snow-topped Mt. Kilimanjaro. Dr. Krapf, on a journey to the interior, was the first European to glimpse Mt. Kenya. When these reports reached Britain they were disbelieved. One noted geographer pointed out how impossible it was for snow to exist on the equator. A map drawn by another German missionary, J. J. Erhardt, who had obviously talked to Arab traders, introduced to Europe the possibility of a great inland sea which he called the Unyamesi.

These reports, particularly that of Erhardt, led Sir Roderick Murchison of the Royal Geographic Society to sponsor an expedition in 1856 to investigate these rumors. The two explorers chosen for this task had been officers in the Indian Army, and although possessing completely different personalities, they had already cooperated on one exploration in Africa. Richard Burton was a scholar, linguist, and adventurer, deeply attached to Eastern forms of life and to the exotic. Only thirty-six years old in 1856, he was already famous for his audacious visit to Mecca and later to Harar when in both cases he had disguised himself as a Muslim. John Hanning Speke had served ten years in the Indian Army and was regarded as a steady man and an excellent hunter. He previously, in 1854, had planned to investigate the source of the Nile. However, he had met Burton in Aden where he was persuaded to participate in the Harar and Somali venture on which he had been seriously wounded.

The two men, still good friends, left the East African coast on June 16, 1857, after forming their caravan. Following the southern slave route they reached Tabora in November. Both the explorers suffered constantly from a variety of illnesses. Despite such handicaps they reached Lake Tanganyika in February 1858, and returned to Tabora in June. Until this point the journey, although hard and reasonably productive, had not divided the two men. At Tabora they decided to trace the source of a rumor that there was a greater lake to the north. Since Burton was ill Speke proceeded alone and on August 3, 1858, at Mwanza he first glimpsed the huge lake which was later named Victoria. He was ill and low on supplies and, therefore, did not explore the shoreline of the lake. Nevertheless, he concluded that this vast expanse of water was the source of the Nile.

After hearing Speke's report, Burton dismissed the idea that the lake, named by them Victoria, could be the point of origin of the Nile. Speke had not investigated the lake and therefore there was nothing to substantiate his theory. This disagreement became the basis of hostility between the two men which developed into a hatred that lasted until Speke's unfortunate accidental death in September 1864. Speke who preceded Burton to

Gondokoro
Juba
L. Rudolf
Albert Nile
Faloro
L. Albert
L. Kyoga
△ Mt. Elgon
Jinja
Mt. Kenya △
0°   0°
L. Edward
Tana R.
LAKE
VICTORIA
L. Kivu
Mwanza
Athi R.
△ Mt. Kilimanjaro
Mombasa
Luolaba R.
Ujiji
Tabora
Pemba
Zanzibar
Mpwapa
Bagamoyo
Luapula R.
L. Tanganyika
Rufiji R. Zungomere
Kilwa
L. Mweru
10°   10°
L. Bangweulu
Chambezi R.
Ruvuma R.
L. Nyasa

⎯⎯⎯⎯⎯⎯   Burton & Speke 1856-58
✦✦✦✦✦✦✦✦✦✦✦   Speke 1858
⎯ ⎯ ⎯ ⎯   Speke & Grant 1860-63
▪▪▪▪▪▪▪▪▪▪▪   Stanley 1871
⎯✦⎯✦⎯✦⎯   Baker 1863-64
⎯·⎯··⎯··⎯   Thomson 1883

0   100   200   300
Miles

|30°

European Exploration in East Africa

55

Britain after their journey certainly did nothing to moderate Burton's dislike of him. He had promised not to discuss their findings until Burton had joined him. Despite this he gave interviews, delivered addresses, and was active in arranging government support for a new expedition. Thus when Burton arrived in London he found himself all but ignored. He never forgave Speke for breaking his promise and for years continued to agitate against Speke's conclusions concerning Lake Victoria.

Speke chose Captain James Grant as his companion on the new expedition. Grant was self-effacing and not likely to challenge Speke's authority or conclusions. They put together their party in Zanzibar and Bagamoyo in mid-1860, then followed the established southern route to Tabora and thence to Karagwe in November 1861. The journey was replete with the problems which were typical of explorers in East Africa. Supplies were lost and stolen, porters deserted, and both men were ill during much of the year which it took to reach Karagwe. Since Grant was ill in late 1861, Speke set out by himself to visit the court of Kabaka Mutesa of Buganda. His small party was welcomed by Mutesa and Speke had a number of long conferences with the ruler in the five months he spent in Buganda. Speke was the first European to visit this interlacustrine kingdom. His later description of Buganda, although in part unflattering, was important in introducing Europeans to this advanced but strange African state. After Grant joined Speke they proceeded northward to Bunyoro. On July 21, 1862, after having left Grant behind again, Speke encountered the Victoria Nile and one week later sighted Ripon Falls. The expedition then explored more of Bunyoro and, running low on supplies, moved northward according to plan to Faloro and thence to Gondokoro in the Sudan.

At Gondokoro Grant and Speke discovered that Samuel Baker and his wife were waiting for them. The Bakers had decided to spend their honeymoon exploring the Upper Nile. Speke and Grant because of lack of supplies had not been able to investigate rumors of another lake lying southwest of Victoria. They suggested to the Bakers that they should follow up this rumor. To facilitate their journey Speke gave Baker his own map of Bunyoro. In March 1863, the Bakers moved south toward Bunyoro. One year later, despite the usual difficulties with terrain, transportation, and illness, they arrived at the new lake which they named Albert. Traveling along the eastern shore they discovered a river flowing in from Victoria and followed this to the falls which they named Murchison Falls. They later confirmed that Lake Albert also contributed to the Nile. These discoveries which went far in vindicating Speke's theories could not be announced until after the Baker's finally reached Suez in October 1865. By that time Speke was dead and another expedition had been sponsored by the Royal Geographic Society to settle finally the questions of the lakes, mountains, and rivers of East Africa. This expedition was begun in 1866 by the most famous of the explorers of his time, David Livingstone.

Although Livingstone was only fifty-two years old when he began his third expedition, he had spent almost a quarter of a century traveling throughout Africa and popularizing the problems of Africa. He had come first to Kuruman station in Bechuanaland as a missionary for the London Missionary Society. Convinced of the need to search out routes for further missionary stations, Livingstone first explored the route to Lake Ngami and thence to the Makololo country of the upper Zambesi River. On these early journeys he was introduced to the interior slave trade and became obsessed with the need to develop legitimate trade with the interior people while at the same time opening routes for further missionary activity. It was in search of alternate routes into the interior that he undertook his solitary journey across the continent from Luanda to Quelimane. On this long (1853–1856), hazardous journey he discovered Victoria Falls and was the first European for centuries to venture into most of the lands bordering the Zambesi. Livingstone's book, *Missionary Travels and Researches,* describing these adventures was extremely popular and Livingstone became a celebrity. His activities inspired the organization of the Universities Mission to Central Africa.

In 1858 Livingstone was back in Africa as consul to Mozambique, a position which gave him free scope for explorations. The British government sponsored him on a detailed examination of the lower Zambesi and Shire rivers and Lake Malawi. From 1858 to 1864 in a series of explorations, aided by a substantial party of Europeans, he plotted out the significant features of the Malawi area. By their work in the field and then in subsequent books they laid the groundwork for the later missionary endeavors in Malawi.

Livingstone held aloof from the passions of the debate generated by Burton and Speke on the probable source of the Nile. Nevertheless, he did not believe that Lake Victoria was the source of the river. He appears to have thought that the river rose in an area west of that lake. On his third journey to Africa, Livingstone decided to operate from two bases, Zanzibar and Ujiji on Lake Tanganyika. His old friend, Dr. Kirk, the British consul in Zanzibar, was to be responsible for keeping Livingstone's interior base supplied. This link later broke down and left Livingstone grievously short of supplies. He found it difficult to recruit porters. The Arab slavers were suspicious of him and his letters from the interior in many cases were never delivered to Kirk. Nevertheless, Livingstone continued his investigations, discovering Lake Bangweulu in 1868, and the Lualaba River on a further journey.

If Livingstone's memory is that of a devoted Christian, Stanley's is that of bula matari, the breaker of rocks. Measured by the impact he had on both Africans and Europeans, he was the greatest of the explorers. An English orphan (born John Rowlands) who had made his way to the United States, Stanley had by 1871 clawed his way at age thirty to preeminence as a reporter for *The New York Herald.* He was commissioned in that year, as a part of a series assignment, to investigate whether the world famous Dr. Livingstone was lost and, if so, to find him. Despite the lack of cooperation of British officials at Zanzibar and his lack of experience in Africa, he put together a caravan on the coast and drove it by way of the southern slave route to Ujiji, making the journey in the record time of 104 days.

Here he found Livingstone who had just returned from his investigations of the Lualaba River to discover that supplies promised by Kirk had completely disappeared. The two men further explored Lake Tanganyika, but Livingstone refused to return to the coast with Stanley. Stanley left his newly discovered friend at Tabora with all the supplies he could spare in March 1872. However, Livingstone died near Lake Bangweulu in April 1873 before more aid could reach him.

Livingstone's contributions to European understanding of Africa were very great. In a long career of exploration he had been the first European in modern times to visit the Kalolo, see Victoria Falls, Lake Malawi, Lake Bangweulu, and the Lualaba River. He had popularized Africa by his books and speeches. More than all this, he had symbolized for his countrymen the selfless humanitarian who cared for Africans and sincerely wanted to improve their conditions.

On Stanley's return to Britain he wrote a best seller, *How I Found Livingstone*, which in connection with his brusque manner did nothing to endear him to the British upper classes. Nevertheless, he managed to convince *The New York Herald* and the *London Daily Telegraph* to finance him on further explorations of East Africa. Stanley left Britain for Zanzibar in August 1874, with three objectives in mind. He intended to circumnavigate Lake Victoria to determine, finally, its connection with the Nile. He then planned to do the same for Lake Tanganyika, and finally he hoped to check on Livingstone's theories that the Lualaba River was the true source of the Nile. Stanley's expedition which left the coast in November 1875, was the best equipped of any which had previously penetrated the hinterland. He had over 350 men to carry eight tons of supplies and the dismantled forty foot steel boat which was so important for his plans.

From the south shore of Lake Victoria in March 1875, Stanley and eleven others sailed along the east shore and in three weeks sighted Ripon Falls, then proceeded to Buganda in early April. Stanley was very impressed by the kingdom and by Mutesa. While he was at the kabaka's court, General Gordon's deputy, Linant de Bellefonds, arrived and agreed to take back a dispatch for the *Daily Telegraph* urging that missionaries be sent to Buganda. In early May, Stanley had proved Speke's theory that Victoria was a single, large lake and that it had only one major outlet at Ripon Falls. Later in 1875 after joining Mutesa in a battle with some natives on two islands in Lake Victoria, Stanley was provided by Mutesa with a guard for further explorations toward Lake Albert. The guard fled at the first opportunity and Stanley proceeded without them to Karagwe.

After returning to Ujiji and resting for some months, Stanley launched his boat on Lake Tanganyika in June 1876, to carry out the second of his objectives. In less than two months he had circumnavigated the lake and determined that there was no outlet which could be taken for the Nile. This discovery, combined with his investigations on Lake Victoria, finally confirmed Speke's and Baker's conclusions on the source of the Nile.

The third phase of Stanley's journey was begun in August 1876, when he set out with only about half of his original force to investigate the

Lualaba River. With the help of agents of the Arab slaver, Tippu Tib, he reached the river and launched his boat for the long voyage down river. After a series of adventures which included attacks from Africans, shipwreck, and loss of supplies, he reached the mouth of the Congo, 999 days after he had left Zanzibar. The African survivors of the journey were sent by boat back to Zanzibar and Stanley proceeded to Europe to write his book, *Through the Dark Continent*. He eventually accepted the offer to become Leopold II's chief agent on the Congo.

Other explorers at the time of Stanley's epic second journey were busy filling in the blank spaces of eastern Africa. Colonel Chaille-Long, one of General Gordon's assistants, traced the Nile from its source to Karuma Falls. He also discovered Lake Kyoga. Another of Gordon's lieutenants, Romola Gessi, circumnavigated Lake Albert and followed its course northward. With these discoveries European geographers could plot with great accuracy the major features of eastern Africa. Every explorer after Burton and Speke added new information, not only on the geography, but also on the people. Interior journeys which had been considered by Europeans to be the height of adventure and novelty in 1870 had become commonplace by 1890. The isolation of the hinterland peoples of eastern Africa from the European world had ended and in a short period of time they would become pawns of the Europeans in the scramble for Africa.

The Congo basin

Much of the history of Central Africa is concerned with the establishment of different Luba polities and various kingdoms and empires derivative of the Luba. Although the events relative to the creation of these states is crucial to the Congo basin, little is known of the complex migrations of Luba people or the genesis of individual chiefdoms. Some general background to nineteenth century Central Africa can, nevertheless, be abstracted. By the sixteenth century there had evolved in the Katanga area a major Luba kingdom. In time other smaller Luba states such as Kaniak and Kikonja also developed in the Katanga. All these states had a similar political structure. Power in each was exercised by a chief who was a descendant of one lineage. There was a relatively tight bureaucracy responsive to the will of the chief. However, the Luba kingdoms never evolved into large permanent empires since the chiefs were content only to gather tribute from subject people. The pattern of migration which had brought the Luba to the Congo originally continued, presumably because of population growth and political differences within the established states. The Bemba, Bisa, Lozi, Katanga Lunda, and Kazembe Lunda all developed from basic Luba stock.

The Katanga Lunda empire was established by the early seventeenth century. In contrast to the smaller Luba polities the early Lunda kings established a policy of politically incorporating neighboring people within the Lunda sphere. The ruler of this Sudanic-type state, the mwato yamvo, exercised tight control over his subjects. Chiefs of conquered people were

Peoples of the Congo Basin

allowed to retain their authority subject to good behavior and direct affiliation with the Lunda system of rule. Many of the smaller Luba polities of the Katanga were incorporated into the Lunda empire. In the 1740s one of the Lunda generals with a raiding force crossed into the Luapula Valley and conquered the Bantu people there. The new kingdom which developed from this conquest took the name Kazembe from its first ruler, Kazembe II, who established a strong centralized state. The Lualaba River became the frontier between these two Lunda empires although the Kazembe rulers continued to consider the mwato yamvo as their titular overlord well into the nineteenth century.

The Bemba were a Luba people who in the latter seventeenth century moved eastward across the Lualaba River. For over a century divisions within the original group and various complex migrations resulted in the settlement of the area between the Luapula and Luangwa rivers. The main group of Bemba after 1760 settled down in the territory between Lake Bangweulu and Lake Tanganyika. Another segment which became known as the Bisa established themselves east of Lake Bangweulu and south of the Chambesi River.

Another Luba migration was that of the Luyi, or as they were later called, the Lozi. They migrated southward to the upper Zambesi Valley in the late seventeenth century. In the following century they absorbed many of the other smaller Bantu groups into a federal type state. This peaceful, well-organized polity was by 1800 composed of over twenty distinct groups. The Luyi king, called the litunga, received ritual as well as political loyalty from his subchiefs who were drawn from leading Luyi families. The kingdom was divided into northern and southern segments. The north was directly under the control of the litunga while the south was ruled by a queen of the royal family and was sometimes almost completely free from northern rule.

There had been continuous trading contact for many centuries between all the hinterland kingdoms and the coastal towns of Angola and East Africa. These had increased after the arrival of the Portuguese in the late fifteenth and early sixteenth century. This trade had been one of the reasons for the creation of large, more aggressive Bantu polities in the Congo. Some of the early Luba-Lunda people had received guns in trade and this had given them the necessary power advantage over their neighbors allowing them to expand their influence. In the early nineteenth century due to a variety of factors, the trade between the interior and both coasts increased tremendously with ensuing revolutionary effects upon the Bantu states. The more centralized governments of the interior kingdoms allowed for more expeditious trade within a polity. In the immediate interior both in the east and west, certain African people reoriented their societies primarily toward trade. In the west the Imbangala of the Kasanje became the middlemen between the mwato yamvo's kingdom and the up-country trading agents of the Portuguese at Luanda. In the east the Bisa and the Yao were the first to act as intermediaries in trade with the east coast. Later the Nyamwezi became the dominant African long-distance traders. Africans were the primary agents in the upsurge of trading activities although the Portuguese and Swahili merchants still remained important for interior trade.

Portuguese demand on the Atlantic coast for African products remained relatively constant throughout much of the century. The great expansion in the volume of the slave trade occurred in the stable mercantile empire of the sultans of Zanzibar which demanded more slaves to work the clove and oil palm plantations. French planters on a number of sugar growing islands in the Indian Ocean were in great need of workers and they were willing to flaunt the regulations against the slave trade to obtain labor. The demand in Europe for ivory increased greatly in the nineteenth century. It is not surprising that African merchants and chiefs took advantage of such favorable conditions. The Nyamwezi are the best example of an African people who radically altered their society to meet the new economic demands. The Nyamwezi in the early nineteenth century were a collection of decentralized polities located in a most favorable position to dominate the east-west routes from Katanga to the east coast as well as the north-south interior trade toward Lake Victoria. In time Nyamwezi traders and porters became a fixture in most of the East and Central African territories. Under strong pressure from Swahili merchants in the early 1870s a Nyamwezi chief, Mirambo, using guns and Nguni mercenaries, created a powerful centralized state. This enabled the Nyamwezi to remain in control of the rich eastern trade in ivory, slaves, and copper from the Katanga. After Mirambo's death in 1884 the united kingdom fell apart and the Nyamwezi became easy prey to the Germans in the 1890s.

The increase in the demand for slaves in the mercantile empire of the sultan of Zanzibar spurred on the Swahili traders of the east coast to pioneer new trading routes into the interior. There traders, erroneously referred to as "Arabs," had by the 1870s already penetrated into the eastern Congo. Their outpost, Nyangwe, became a major trading entrepôt. The man who best exemplifies this new adventuresome attitude was Hamid bin Muhammad, better known as Tippu Tib. During the 1860s in a series of far-ranging ventures he pioneered trade routes into the Bemba sphere and became a Tetela chief in the Lomani area. In 1875 Tippu Tib established the center for his ivory and slave trade at Kasongo in the eastern Congo. From there by the strength of his administrative ability and a large force of well-armed retainers, he ruled a huge area of the Lomani and Lualaba valleys. In this empire he assessed taxes, built roads, regulated the hunting of elephants, and controlled all trade. In less than ten years he had extended his trading sphere as far down the Congo River as Stanley Falls. It was Tippu Tib who provided Stanley with the general knowledge and the physical support which enabled him to succeed in his exploration of the Congo River. Tippu Tib continued to be the most important political and economic force on the upper Congo River throughout the 1880s despite the inroads made by Stanley and other agents of the Congo Independent State. After he left the Congo permanently in 1890, no other "Arab" trader could gain supreme authority and very soon Tippu's territory was absorbed by the Congo Independent State.

Elsewhere in Central Africa the upsurge in trade also affected the state structures. The Bemba in the late eighteenth century had already developed an active trade with the people to the north for salt and with the Bisa for meat and fish. They also traded ivory to the Nyamwezi and Swahili. Traditionally the Bemba were ruled by a series of chiefs from one royal clan. Before the nineteenth century the paramount chief called the chitimukulu had performed mainly ceremonial and religious functions. In the first half of the nineteenth century the chitimukulus became paramount in political, military, and trading matters as well. Trade became a royal monopoly and the chief utilized the militaristic Bemba to secure more ivory and slaves. Much of the centralization was the work of Chitimukulu Chileshe who expropriated the throne at mid-century. From 1866 to 1887 the ruler was Chitapankwa who further extended the Bemba sphere of influence and the state became richer than ever. Bemba power continued even after the declaration of a British protectorate over their area in 1893. Quarrels over succession to the throne eventually weakened the Bemba and the British South Africa Company was finally successful after 1898 in making practical the paper claims to Bemba territory enunciated five years earlier.

An even more powerful polity than Lubemba was the Kazembe kingdom of the Luapula Valley. The Portuguese explorers, Monteiro and Gamitto, reported in the 1830s that the mwato kazembe had over 5,000 warriors, many well armed with guns. He also was a merchant prince controlling a major link in the trade which in the nineteenth century extended from the Atlantic to the Indian Ocean. Livingstone reporting his visit to this Lunda kingdom in 1868 indicated that the Kazembe's potential power had not waned. However, quarrels over succession weakened the Kazembes. This enabled a Nyamwezi merchant, Msiri, to build up a competitive state which stripped the Kazembe of much of their control over the Katanga trade. Msiri with a number of well armed Nyamwezi, later called Yeke, settled in Kazembe territory in 1856. Utilizing the Yeke and an extremely harsh rule, Msiri gathered slaves and ivory throughout the southern Congo basin. Many of the smaller Luba chieftancies to the north paid tribute to him.

The Lunda empire of the mwato yamvo was also deeply affected by the increase in trading profits. The king alienated large numbers of his people by his arbitrary use of power. He would designate whole villages to be sold into slavery. The dissatisfaction of his people combined with the ever-present centrifugal forces within a Sudanic type state caused a series of struggles for power at the center. This enabled the Chokwe, a seminomadic people from the south, to encroach upon the kingdom. Taking advantage of the disturbances and using guns obtained in trade, the Chokwe by the mid-1880s had taken over most of the territory formerly ruled by the mwato yamvo. Wars between the Chokwe and the Lunda continued for years and sufficiently weakened both sides so that they resisted very little the takeover of their territories by agents of the Congo Independent State.

Elsewhere in the Congo basin the agricultural Bantu who had not evolved larger, more elaborate state structures became the prey of African and Swahili slave raiders. European explorers and missionaries in the latter nineteenth century were witnesses to the side effects of the trading revolution which had done so much to transform the politics of Central Africa. Their reports of slave raiding and the huge ivory and slave caravans were important factors in creating the necessary climate of opinion in Europe which supported the new imperialism. Ultimately this European imperialism destroyed the great kingdoms whose existence was based largely upon the long-range trade.

THREE
Southern Africa to 1872

British-Boer relations in Cape Colony to 1836

In June 1795, almost 150 years of rule by the Dutch East Indies Company was brought to an end by a British invasion fleet. The reasons for this occupation are closely tied to the upheavals in Europe begun by the French revolution. In 1794 the armies of revolutionary France invaded Holland, captured the Dutch fleet, and forced the aristocratic government to flee to Britain. The Prince of Orange entered into an agreement which allowed the British to occupy strategic Cape Colony before the French and the new Dutch revolutionary regime could do so. After minor resistance the Dutch commander at the Cape surrendered to General Craig and the British became responsible for the government of a territory with undefined boundaries, economic difficulties, independent frontiersmen, displaced Hottentots, and threats from the Bantu.

The European settlers, descendants of Dutch and Huguenot settlers of the seventeenth century, numbered approximately 20,000. The majority were concentrated in Cape Town and in the western Cape region. The settled burghers at Cape Town followed a variety of trades and professions, were in contact with the latest trends in Europe, and maintained schools and churches. The farmers of the western Cape were further removed from direct European influence but they, too, were generally prosperous and had developed various specialized agricultural pursuits. Both the Cape Town residents and those farmers located near such towns as Stellenbosch or Tulbagh were amenable to control by the central government. The Dutch East Indies Company had granted these interior areas a modicum of local government by the establishment of drotsdys. These were administered by an official, usually a local farmer, aided by a council of local government called the heemraaden. There was only one court for the entire colony located at Cape Town. Despite some tensions between these local authorities and the central government, the British took over a relatively well organized political system and found it necessary to make few changes.

A small group of Boers living far to the east of Cape Town near the settlements of Swellendam, Uitenhage, and Graaf Reinet, however, soon showed the British that their aims were far from those of the British governors. The basis of livelihood of these frontier areas was cattle farming. More than their settled kinsmen, these veld Boers exhibited characteristics which made it impossible for them to accept British rule in the nineteenth century. They disliked any authority, believed in their God-given superiority over all black men, were normally uneducated and fiercely Calvinistic, and wandered freely over the countryside to stake their claims to huge cattle ranges.

The frontier Boers in the eighteenth century had reduced their competitors, the cattle-keeping Hottentots, to a servile state of landless men. In the 1770s they encountered their first real African opposition from the southward moving Xosa clans of the Nguni Bantu. This began a series of conflicts over cattle and land which periodically exploded into general warfare. These so-called Kaffir wars will be treated in more detail later. It is only necessary to note here that the frontier Boers who resented authority and disobeyed government edicts expected first the company and later the British to help them exterminate the Xosa. When such aid was not forthcoming they were not immune to rebellion against central authority. In 1795 when the British first landed, the Boers at Swellendam and Graaf Reinet were in the midst of such a rebellion. The rebels reluctantly accepted the new government in hopes that the British would adopt an aggressive policy against the Xosa. Cattle raiding continued across the ill-defined borders and the Boer unrest in 1799 exploded in another rebellion by some of the disgruntled farmers at Graaf Reinet. British dragoons, infantry, and some Hottentot soldiers soon ended the experiment of a separate Boer government. No sooner had this been settled than a quarrel between two Xosa chiefs spilled over the frontier and began the third Kaffir war. The new liberal landdrost Maynier attempted to deal justly with all factions, forbade private military forays into Xosa land, was concerned with the condition of the Hottentots, and believed in the rule of law. The frontier war ended in 1802, but the Boers were again on the verge of rebellion against Maynier and he was recalled.

Maynier's problems on the eastern frontier can be viewed as prophetic of later British-Boer relations. Whenever a government official attempted to view problems objectively, particularly those connected with Hottentots or Bantu, he could expect no help from the frontier farmers. Government to the frontiersman should exist only to further his interests. A rule which was almost invariably true was that in a quarrel the native people were always in the wrong. Any government which did not subscribe to this could expect continuing problems from the Boers.

The first British occupation was ended by the terms of the Treaty of Amiens in 1802. The British governors had viewed their mission in almost completely military terms and had not attempted any major changes in the system of local and central government. Except where conflict was inevitable such as at Graaf Reinet, the British had left undamaged Boer presumptions of their superiority over blacks. The representatives of the reconstituted Dutch government (the Batavian Republic), Commissioner de Mist and General Janssens, who assumed responsibility for administration in February 1803, found themselves caught in an impossible dilemma. Imbued with ideas of liberty, equality, and fraternity, they wished to institute sweeping changes in government to regulate better the association between Boer, Bantu, and Hottentot. Little could be done to effect permanent change since war between Britain and France broke out once again in May 1803. Janssens, who was in charge at the Cape after 1804, could not afford to alienate the Boer population in the face of a potential second British invasion. In 1805 the British, acting once again to protect their trade routes, dispatched a large invasion fleet to the Cape. Early the next year after only a token resistance Janssens surrendered to the overwhelming British strength.

Although this second occupation was to prove permanent, British governors at the Cape did not know this until 1814. Therefore, the British governors in this interim period, Lord Caledon and Sir John Craddock, wanted to make as few changes as possible. However, it was necessary to intervene more directly into the lives of the Boer population. The abolition of the slave trade in 1807 applied to Cape Colony at a time when the economy was expanding because of the Napoleonic Wars. Thus a premium was placed upon the once despised Hottentot population. Many of the landless Hottentots had already been used by the farmers of the eastern Cape. After 1807 the Boers urged the government to pass legislation which would force the Hottentots to settle down in one place and work for them. Two Hottentot ordinances of 1809 and 1812 created the necessary rules to force the Hottentots to become workers and servants of the Boers. However, they also provided rules concerning contracts, terms, and conditions of employment of Hottentot workers. Although these regulations were largely ignored in practice, they did give theoretical protection to the Hottentots.

The London Missionary Society which had been active in Cape Colony after 1799 emerged as the champion of the Hottentots. The society had established a number of stations throughout the colony to minister to their needs. As the government policy and the farmers' attitudes began to press in upon the mission-station Hottentots, the missionaries appealed first to the governors and eventually to evangelical opinions in Britain. They represented the life of the Hottentot to be that of a slave who could expect no protection from the laws or officials of the colony. Particular charges made by the Bethelsdorp missionaries, combined with the obvious necessity of providing a court for the interior, led to the establishment of the circuit court in 1812. The second circuit court investigated the missionary allegations against fifty Boer farmers charged with everything from extreme cruelty to murder. The Roman-Dutch law of evidence and the wandering nature of Hottentots made the task of proving the charges almost impossible. Nevertheless, seven Boers were convicted of the lesser charge of mistreatment. More important, the precedent was established by the "Black Circuit" of accepting the testimony of natives against their white masters. Although the Cape government had been reluctant to alienate Boer opinion, the Boers had thus been introduced to the more liberal attitudes of the British.

At this time the eastern frontier was in turmoil with constant cattle raiding by both Boers and Xosa. In 1811 the fourth Kaffir war began and resulted in the Xosa being driven from the Zuurveld. After the war the British, instead of supporting the farmers' demands for continued commando and military action against the Bantu, ordered the Boers to retire behind a series of forts constructed west of the Fish River. The most important of these was Grahamstown which soon became an important white town. Although such a system, designed to keep contact between the races to a minimum, could not work, it could and did irritate the Boers. The Land Ordinance of 1812 revoked much of the old Dutch land law and tried to restrict individual landholding to 1,200 acres on which a high annual quit rent was required. This attempt also eventually proved unsuccessful, but it was another link in the chain of Boer grievances against a meddlesome British government.

By 1814 when the British government negotiated the permanent transfer of Cape Colony from Holland, there was already a deep estrangement between the British government and the Boer farmers. An example of this conflict which would assume an importance to many Boers far beyond its actual significance was the Slachter's Nek incident. A Boer, Frederick Bezuidenhout, was accused by a Hottentot servant of mistreatment. Pleading illness, Bezuidenhout did not appear in the circuit court to answer the charges. Subsequently a contingent of Hottentot police were sent to arrest him. Refusing to be arrested by blacks, he fired on them and was killed. Frederick's brother Johannes, a neighbor Hendrick Prinsloo, and other Boer farmers vowed vengeance for the killing. Prinsloo wrote to Gaika, one of the Xosa chiefs, proposing an alliance against the British. The message was intercepted by British authorities who then arrested Prinsloo. A few of the dissident farmers tried to rescue him. They could gain little support from most of the settlers and were easily beaten by the British. Those captured at Slachter's Nek were tried under the traditional Roman-Dutch law before Boer judges, found guilty, and sentenced to death. Their execution in 1815 was marred by the collapse of the gallows and the hanging had to be repeated. Very soon those who had been executed came to be viewed as martyrs, killed only because they stood for the traditional freedoms of the veld Boer against the autocratic British system.

Lord Charles Somerset became governor of Cape Colony in 1814. This descendant of Plantagenet kings represented the ambivalence of the British government. A Tory, he was extremely suspicious of radicals, humanitarians, and missionaries, yet his sense of order, propriety, and his autocratic nature guaranteed his estrangement from the frontier Boers. In 1818 a quarrel between clan leaders of the Xosa soon involved the British. Ndlambe and Makana, both unyielding enemies of the white settlers, challenged the more malleable Gaika for control of the western Xosa. Gaika was severely defeated and appealed to the British government for aid. In December white troops crossed the Fish River, burned huts, and captured over 20,000 cattle. Makana retaliated in April by invading the colony and with 10,000 warriors laid siege to Grahamstown. The war ended three months later after European reinforcements had arrived and Makana had surrendered. Gaika, for whose protection Lord Charles had used imperial forces, was forced to cede almost 3,000 square miles of Xosa territory to the British. The area between the Fish and Keiskama rivers was declared neutral territory. This action, far from ending the border crisis, was calculated to increase tensions since one of the major problems of the Xosa had been the necessity for them to find more land.

In 1813 the officer primarily responsible for the Xosa defeat in the Kaffir war, Colonel Graham, proposed that the government should underwrite the emigration of British settlers to the eastern Cape frontier. Significant numbers of sturdy British peasants would presumably dilute the Boer control of this region and they would provide a buffer against Xosa invasions. Lord Charles approved of the plan even before he left Britain. After the fifth Kaffir war of 1818 had begun, parliament voted £50,000 to subsidize sending out British settlers. As was usual for colonization schemes of the nineteenth century, this one was badly planned and poorly managed. Few of the settlers who arrived in 1819–1820 had any farming experience, and the area was suited to raising cattle, not to sedentary agriculture. Droughts, locusts, floods, and Xosa raiders in the first five years drove most of the settlers off their farms and into the towns. The major objectives of the plan outlined by Colonel Graham, therefore, were never achieved. However, the bulk of the 5,000 settlers did not return to Britain but remained in Cape Colony. Their demands that they be treated as British citizens struck at the very root of the autocratic unreformed government of Cape Colony. These British settlers demanded the primacy of the English language in legal transactions, English common law, a free press, and a curb upon the actions of the governor.

A series of personal confrontations with Lord Charles and sensation-provoking law cases brought by the government highlighted the Albany settlers' demands. Lord Charles quarreled with and secured the dismissal of his lieutenant-governor, Sir Rufane Donkin, and his colonial secretary, Colonel Bird. Each of these men upon their return to Britain joined the chorus of those already demanding Somerset's recall. Charges by two citizens against the collector of customs led to two long trials of the principals for libel. A printer, George Greig, whose paper was banned and his press seized, also became involved in litigation with the Cape government. Charges of maladministration of the relief funds for the Albany settlers also added to Lord Charles' discomfiture. The sum of all these allegations added to the depressed economic state of Cape Colony in the early 1820s and led the colonial secretary to send a commission of inquiry to investigate the whole range of government activity.

The man who came to personify to Lord Charles all the unprincipled radical activity was the newly appointed superintendent of the London Missionary Society in Cape Colony, John Philip. Although Somerset's assessment of Philip was untrue, the superintendent did become his most implacable opponent. In 1819 Philip believed that most of the trouble between the government and the mission stations was caused by the missionaries. Within two years he had completely reversed himself and was convinced that the missions could only begin to function as centers for Christianity when the Hottentots were treated as human beings. He criticized the government for being in league with the farmers to provide them with a steady, cheap Hottentot labor supply. To Philip, the Hottentot ordinances, far from protecting natives, guaranteed them a status as near slaves. Somerset used all his influence to have Philip removed. However, after 1826 Philip managed to convince the powerful parliamentary evangelical faction that Hottentot emancipation was only another facet of their struggle against slavery. Lord Charles was recalled to London to answer the many charges against him and eventually resigned in 1828.

The period after the arrival in Cape Colony of acting Governor Bourke in 1825 witnessed a series of near revolutionary changes which went far toward anglicizing the society. The Dutch language could no longer be used in the civil service, courts, or schools. The churches which were state established were also forced to adopt English for their services. The courts were reconstructed in the British mold with appointive judges, the jury system, and the common law. Roman-Dutch law was retained for civil cases, but business and criminal law followed the British model. Local government was completely changed. The office of landdrost gave way to magistrates appointed by the central government and responsible to it. The traditional commando leaders, the veld cornets, were stripped of their military and civil powers. Most of these changes recommended by the commission of inquiry were necessary for the modernization of the colony. However, they went far to convince the predominantly Dutch-speaking population that the British government aimed at the eventual destruction of all that was good and familiar in the old system.

The action of General Bourke which had the greatest impact and most lasting effect was Hottentot emancipation. Philip in the early 1820s had concluded that the only way that men of color in Cape Colony could be protected was to have the British government specifically grant them equality with whites. Toward this end Philip after 1821 devoted most of his energies. In 1826 he returned to Britain, met with Thomas Buxton and other parliamentary Evangelicals, and enlisted their support for his cause. He also wrote a two volume work on his experiences with the Cape government while championing the cause of the Hottentots. This served to enlist more influential support for his cause. In 1828 parliament passed a resolution which declared men of color equal to their European counterparts. Before the Colonial Office could put this resolution into effect word was received that General Bourke had already acted to achieve the same goal by issuing the Fiftieth Ordinance.

The ordinance allowed Hottentots, Griquas, and even Bushmen theoretical equal rights with white settlers. They no longer had to carry passes, could not be arrested for vagrancy at the whim of the police, and had easier access to the courts to complain of civil or criminal maltreatment. British and Boer alike protested that the ordinance had let loose on the colony a horde of indolent potential criminals and had robbed the farmers of the needed labor services of the Hottentots. Although most Hottentots continued to work for their employers, large numbers took advantage of their newfound freedom to wander from place to place living off relatives and stealing. Despite attempts by later governors, Lowry Cole and Benjamin D'Urban acting on the complaints of farmers to restrict the Hottentots, the Fiftieth Ordinance remained in force until the early 1840s. Its spirit was carried forth by a series of legislative acts which retained for the Hottentots, now generally called the Colored, equality in Cape Colony well into the twentieth century.

The Boer farmers had hardly recovered from the shock of Hottentot emancipation when the British parliament in 1833 abolished slavery. Although almost 40,000 of the ex-slaves were required to serve four years as apprentices, emancipation was a heavy blow to the affluent Boer farmers, particularly those of the western Cape. The money provided by parliament for compensation was not quite half the market value of the slaves. This sum was not paid directly to individual slave owners in Cape Colony but rather in drafts redeemable only in London. The Boer farmers thus lost even more in payments to London agents.

It has been commonplace to attribute the decision by thousands of Boers to trek away from the colony to the abolition of slavery. However, this action was seen by the Boers as only the latest of a long series of unwarranted tamperings with their attempt to live the good life. One other factor contributed heavily to the Boers leaving Cape Colony. The population of the colony had grown considerably in the decade and one-half after 1820, yet no significant land additions had been made. For cattle grazers on marginal lands who had large families, this lack of land was crucial. In response to the many-remembered grievances and the Boers' land hunger, three exploring parties or kommissie trekkes were sent north and east of Cape Colony. Their task was to investigate the new lands across the Orange River and report by the beginning of 1835 on such crucial matters as the presence of African tribes, the fertility of the land, and the availability of water.

It was at this crucial period that the sixth Kaffir war began. John Philip and other missionaries had urged upon Governor Benjamin D'Urban a policy of moderation toward the Bantu which would recognize the sovereignty of Xosa and Griqua states to the north and east of Cape Colony. Such a policy had little chance of success given the instability of the eastern frontier, continued cattle raiding, and the land hunger of the

Boers and Xosa. Along the coast northeast of the Kei River and in the deep interior the wars of Shaka and the mfecane had displaced tens of thousands of persons. The Xosa had also been affected by these events. Just before Christmas over 10,000 Xosa swept across the neutral territory and into the eastern Cape and with this invasion changed D'Urban's policy of moderation to one of force. In the first week of the war over one hundred Europeans were killed and the Xosa burned farmsteads and drove off thousands of cattle, horses, and sheep. Colonel Harry Smith who took command of the frontier found the bulk of the 7,000 European settlers concentrated in Grahamstown. However, imperial troops, Hottentot levies, and Boer commandos drove the Xosa across the Fish River and took the war to their kraals.

The sixth Kaffir war cost the farmers of the eastern Cape £300,000 and the imperial government over £150,000. To D'Urban this was a clear mandate to change previous policies which had not solved the problem of the unquiet frontier. He, therefore, declared all the land between the Keiskamma and Kei rivers to be British territory. All Xosa who stayed in this area which was named Queen Adelaide Province became British subjects. Africans friendly to Europeans such as the Fingoes (referred to by the Xosa as their dogs) were to be settled in the area. The Boers who had expected the bulk of the lands in the new area were disappointed, but they still confidently expected to be rewarded with land in the area between the Fish and Keiskamma rivers and in the Stormberg territory. However, they were totally disillusioned by the actions of the colonial secretary, Lord Glenelg. On the advice of Philip and other critics of D'Urban, Glenelg repudiated the annexation of Queen Adelaide Province. Instead D'Urban was ordered to withdraw behind the Fish River boundary. The eastern Cape was put under the control of a commissioner, Andries Stockenstrom, who was instructed to enter into treaties with various Xosa chiefs which would secure peace on the frontier.

Although some Boers led by Louis Trigardt and Janse van Rensburg had left the colony in 1835, no great numbers had departed until Glenelg's decision became known. Almost immediately Andries Potgieter and Sarel Cillers led the first large group northward away from ambivalent authority and really began the Great Trek. This wholesale movement of Europeans from Cape Colony will be discussed in more detail later. However, before a full understanding of how easy it was for the trekkers to occupy the area from the Orange to the Limpopo rivers one must survey the great changes which had taken place among the Sotho and Nguni groups in the forty years prior to the beginning of the Trek.

The rise of the Zulu and the mfecane

Before investigating the causes of the mfecane or "time of crushing," it is necessary to recapitulate briefly the general organization of the southern Bantu. Large groups of Bantu had moved across the Limpopo in the years after the sixteenth century. These people can be classified into two groups according to language and also by their place of settlement. The Nguni filled up the coastal strip east of the Drakensberg Mountains while the Sotho settled on the high plateaus of the interior west of these mountains. All the southern Bantu had similar social, political, economic, and military organizations. There were no extensive Bantu kingdoms in the south. Clans were the highest level of political organization. Originally members of a clan were denoted by kinship relations with the semi-mythical creator of the clan. However, by 1800 the larger clans had absorbed neighboring groups and there were hundreds of different clans in southern Africa. It has been estimated that in 1800 there were over 800 clans in the area of Natal alone. Clan size varied from a few hundred people to many thousands. Each clan was governed by a chief whose autocratic power was balanced by tradition, religion, and the unique limits placed upon him by other political institutions of the clan. The land itself dictated the type of economic development. In the rich valleys of Natal, sedentary agriculture was the basis of life and cattle keeping served primarily to indicate the richness of an individual and the clan. Further west and southward in marginal agricultural land, cattle and other livestock assumed a more important role. The stress placed upon different economic pursuits served along with language and customs to differentiate between the many Bantu groups. In the same locale because of constant regrouping of the clans and the practice of exogamy, there was cultural homogeneity.

The confrontation of some Xosa clans and Boer farmers along the Fish River in the 1770s was an event whose meaning transcended the series of Kaffir wars which followed. It indicated that the long period of Bantu wandering into open territory was almost at an end. No longer could the Bantu relieve population and political pressures by simply moving. Expansion into other areas after the 1770s would have to be done at the expense of other Bantu clans or white settlers. Thus all that was needed to set in motion a disastrous series of wars was the proper opportunity and the right African leaders. The opportunity presented itself in the first decade of the nineteenth century to the first of the great Bantu nation builders, Dingiswayo.

Dingiswayo (the troubled one) was a younger son of Jobe, chief of the Mtetwa clan. This clan of approximately 4,000 people was one of the largest in the Natal area. Fearing his sons, Jobe attempted to kill them all and believed he had succeeded. However, Dingiswayo was only wounded and took refuge with another clan, the amaHlubi. Tradition relates that during this short period he met and cared for a white man, probably a survivor of an expedition sent out in 1807 by Lord Caledon. After the death of his patient Dingiswayo took his horse and gun and with these established himself as the new chief of the Mtetwa. With the Mtetwa army he began to expand his authority. In his eight-year reign he established control over more than fifty adjacent clans. Dingiswayo's wars were designed to secure total submission of his enemies. Once his dominance had been accomplished he left the defeated clans in peace to be governed by their own leaders. His aim was not extermination but the creation of a larger, more viable state.

One of the smaller clans which fell under his overlordship was that of the amaZulu, the people of the heavens. They had been settled near the White Umfolozi River since the late seventeenth century. In the late 1770s the amaZulu, comprising not over 1,500 people living in a ten square mile area of rolling, grass-covered hills, were ruled by Chief Senzangakona. The chief was guilty of an indiscretion with Nandi, a woman of the neighboring eLangeni clan. Upon the announcement of her pregnancy the Zulu elders who had been shamed by their chief sent word to Nandi that she was mistaken. Her problem, they said, was caused by an intestinal beetle, *iShaka*. The child born to Nandi was given this name and lived most of his youth in the shadow of shame. About 1787 he was at his father's kraal, but he and his mother were driven out six years later and returned to the eLangeni. In 1802 because of famine, the eLangeni forced Nandi and her young son to leave and they finally found refuge in a clan directly controlled by Dingiswayo. About 1810 Shaka joined the other young men of the clan who had been called to serve in Dingiswayo's army. The embittered young man assigned to the izi Cwe regiment found his vocation since his bravery and innovations soon brought him to the attention of Dingiswayo and eventually he was given the izi Cwe to command. Shaka, during this period, evolved the military concepts which would later make his armies invincible.

The changes Shaka made are deceptively simple. The basic weapon of the southern Bantu had been the throwing spear. Shaka shortened the shaft and enlarged the blade, creating a stabbing spear. He increased the size of the shields for men in his regiment. He organized boys who were not yet warriors into a supply corps which was charged with keeping his men in food and drink. Shaka also threw away their oxen hide sandals and forced his men to toughen their feet. More important than any of these was the iron discipline and training techniques which enabled his men to cover over fifty miles in a day's march. These improvements created of the izi Cwe regiment first, and later all the Zulu armies, the most merciless and effective fighting machine in Africa.

In 1816 Shaka supported by Dingiswayo returned after Senzangakona's death to claim the chieftainship of the Zulu. He soon broke all opposition, destroying many of those who had ridiculed him when he was young. Shaka applied his military theories to the Zulu and in the early wars with his neighbors he evolved the ox-head formation. This formation which remained unchanged until the final destruction of Zulu power in 1879 was composed of four parts. The head met the enemy directly and held them fast while the horns, the left and right wings, fanned out and enveloped them. The fourth division, the body, was held in reserve and the commander could direct their attack wherever it could do the most good. After a victory, the Zulus killed all the enemy who could be found. By 1817 Shaka had incorporated some smaller clans and quadrupled the size of his kingdom. His army had grown to approximately 2,000 warriors.

Shaka was still the loyal servant of Dingiswayo when he was called in 1818 to participate in an expedition against Chief Matiwane of the emaNgwaneni clan to the north. Matiwane entrusted the bulk of his cattle to an ally, the amaHlubi clan, who were located in the foothills of the Drakensberg. Dingiswayo's campaign against Matiwane was inconclusive. After peace had been restored Matiwane demanded his cattle from the amaHlubi and was refused. At this juncture Chief Zwide of the Ndwandwes who believed himself the equal of Dingiswayo attacked Matiwane and drove the emaNgwaneni from their lands. This action precipitated the mfecane. Zwide then began hostilities against the Mtetwa by murdering Dingiswayo's son-in-law. In the ensuing campaign Dingiswayo was taken captive by Zwide and subsequently murdered. Without their leader, the Mtetwa army retreated. Shaka, whose forces arrived after Dingiswayo's death, could do nothing to reverse the Mtetwa defeat. However, the death of Dingiswayo meant that the Mtetwa nation was open for conquest by both Zwide and Shaka.

Meanwhile Matiwane, robbed of his cattle and lands, was blocked by the Tembu, Xosa, and Boers in the south, the Zulu and Mtetwa in the east, the Ndwandwes and Tonga in the north, and the Sotho in the Drakensberg and beyond in the west. Matiwane could sit quietly and watch his people starve or he could try to get cattle and food from his neighbors. Matiwane's desperate people fell on the amaHlubi, massacred the subclans, and took back their cattle. The remnants of the amaHlubi retreated across the Drakensberg, striking against the small unorganized Sotho clans. The mfecane had begun. Matiwane's people settled for about four years in the lands vacated by the amaHlubi. By 1822 the Zulu were dominant east of the Drakensberg and their impis had begun to raid into the emaNgwaneni territory. Matiwane then led his people through the Drakensberg passes in the wake of the amaHlubi who had been killing and pillaging the Sotho for years. In 1823 Matiwane's forces caught up with the amaHlubi remnants and in a five-day battle destroyed most of them. The seven-year period following this event was one of chaos, plundering, and killing which is nearly impossible to unscramble. It was a time of confused coalescing and breaking apart of numerable clans. Pillage and warfare became the way of life for the heretofore settled Sotho clans.

One example of this desperate reshuffling is the career of Mantatisi, the female ruler of the Sotho baTlokwa clan. They were among the first to be driven from their homes by the amaHlubi. As the baTlokwa moved in a generally southern direction, other scattered Sotho groups joined the migration. It is estimated that by the time they neared the northern borders of Cape Colony the "Mantatee horde" numbered over 50,000 people who literally ate up the country. Mantatisi's people were turned back from the Cape by a combination of settled Bantu led by missionaries and armed, mounted Griquas. Turning northward the horde began to disintegrate. However, elements of the baTlokwa under Mantatisi's son, Sikonyela, remained a threat to settled areas until destroyed by the Basuto in 1852.

Mantatisi's group on their northward retreat displaced a small Sotho

Approximate Bantu Movements during Mfecane, 1820–1835

clan led by a young chief, Mshweshwe. Instead of joining the landless pillagers, he led his people south to the western foothills of the Drakensberg. Here he found a flat-topped mountain, Thaba Bosiu, where he could locate his people and be able to defend them from the marauders. The area around Thaba Bosiu became an island of peace in the midst of disorder. In time other Sotho, sick of the wars and death, drifted to Mshweshwe. Out of such debris this remarkable man created the Basuto nation.

Matiwane, one of the chief architects of the mfecane, had by 1828 settled his people temporarily in Tembuland. Here misfortune continued to plague him. A Zulu impi that year had ranged far south into Xosa territory. Colonel Henry Somerset and a strong imperial force was dispatched to deal with this raiding column. Somerset's scouts confused the emaNgwaneni with the Zulu. Together with their Tembu allies they attacked and crushed Matiwane's force. The chief fled north where he was eventually captured, tortured, and killed by the Zulu.

After Dingiswayo's death an unquiet truce prevailed between Zwide and Shaka for a few months while the Mtetwa hegemony dissolved. Then in early 1819 Zwide moved his much larger army against Shaka. At Gqokoli Hill, Shaka abandoned his usual offensive tactics and fought a magnificent defensive battle. Zwide withdrew with most of the Zulu cattle. In the following months Shaka absorbed new elements into his armies, reorganized his regiments, and perfected his plans for the Ndwandwe invasion he knew was coming. When Zwide invaded Shaka's territory in May he found that Shaka had retreated, burning everything which could be used by the invaders. Shaka's supply corps kept the Zulu army well supplied with water and food while Zwide, without such a unit, could find little in the denuded country to assuage the hunger of his men. Shaka finally attacked and in two days of fierce battle destroyed the numerically superior Ndwandwe army. Shaka quickly followed up his advantage, invaded Zwide's territory, burned the chief's kraal, and ruthlessly smashed all possible future opposition. With this victory he had removed the only competitor to Zulu hegemony over the entire area of Natal. By 1820 Shaka could dispose of a finely tuned army of over 20,000 men and controlled directly over 10,000 square miles of territory. The later policy by which Shaka sent his impis to raid surrounding peoples made the Zulu power felt as far south as Xosaland. His regiments had humbled the Tembu and Cunu clans and cleared a hundred-mile-wide belt of all population south of the Tugela River.

The effects of Zulu nation building and the mfecane extended also far to the north. One of Zwide's generals, Soshangane, fleeing Shaka, drove the Portuguese out of the territory north of St. Lucia Bay and formed the basis there of the Shangan nation. The Ndwandwe refugees after the burning of Zwide's kraal retreated northward into the Transvaal area. Reorganized under Zwide's son, Zwangendaba, they scattered assorted northern Sotho tribes which added to the disorder of the mfecane. In the mid-1830s they crossed the Limpopo and cut their way across Rozwi territory destroying the Changamire empire. Eventually Zwangendaba's impis came to rest along the western shores of Lake Malawi. One of Shaka's generals, Mzilikazi, who had defied the great Zulu chief's orders, led approximately 300 Zulu warriors into the denuded central Transvaal area. There out of the scattered Sotho and his Zulu he created the militaristic Matabele nation. The Matabele remained dominant in this area until driven north across the Limpopo in 1837 by the Boers. The final northern offshoot of the mfecane was the Kalolo migration. They had been a part of Mantatisi's horde who found temporary safety in the area immediately south of the Limpopo River. By 1831 the Kalolo were a finely organized fighting force and had reached the confluence of the Zambesi and Chobe rivers. Their chief, Sebitwane, led them further into Luyi country and by 1838 they were masters of all Barotseland.

Shaka, the master of the Zulu, refused to relax the stringency of his rule after all his major enemies had been defeated. The armies were continually engaged in campaigns. Shaka, who had hundreds of wives with whom he had no contact, could not appreciate the attitudes of his warriors. The iron discipline of the Zulu military required them to remain celibate until given permission by Shaka to marry. Shaka in the past had rewarded victorious regiments with this permission. By 1828 it had been years since Shaka had waived his rules except for men too old to be of service in the field. In the security of his strength Shaka became unspeakably cruel. The death of his mother, Nandi, in October 1827, showed this trait more clearly than any other event. The people at the king's kraal taking their cue from Shaka began an orgy of grief which led to the indiscriminate killing of all those whose mourning did not seem genuine. Nandi was buried with ten live handmaidens whose arms and legs had been broken before burial. Shaka set an entire regiment to stand guard at her grave. He issued orders that in honor of his mother no crops were to be planted for the following year and no milk was to be used. Since sour milk was the main food of the Zulu this was tantamount to condemning the nation to a semistarvation diet. All women found to be pregnant in the period of mourning were to be killed. This blind, unreasoning reaction to Nandi's death continued for three months.

A plot to kill Shaka was devised in early 1828 by his two half brothers, Dingane and Mhlangana, and the chief of Shaka's household. In September the entire army was away on a campaign leaving only a small bodyguard at the king's kraal. The conspirators feigned illness and left the army. On September 22 while Shaka was receiving gifts from a delegation of Pondo, his brothers stabbed him to death. The assassins and people were so frightened by their deed that the scourge of the Zulu remained where he was killed for an entire night. The next morning he was dumped without ceremony into an empty grain pit.

After Shaka's murder there was a short period of joint rule of the brothers until Dingane, then thirty years old, determined that the army would be loyal to him. Most of the regiments which had been campaigning against Soshangane returned dispirited and low in morale. Dingane had already stopped the senseless slaughter at his court and he won the affection of the army by allowing a number of regiments to marry. As soon as he believed it safe he had his brother Mhlangana murdered along with a number of powerful nobles. The Zulu nation by 1829 was firmly in his hands. Dingane was for the Zulu an improvement over Shaka but his rule was still based on the strength of his army. He fought few major wars, but the regiments were kept busy since Dingane's normal response to problems was a violent one. Shaka had been an ascetic. Dingane was a hedonist who loved to eat, dance, and spend the majority of his time with his 300 wives. Dingane was not as consistent in the use of his power as was Shaka and was considered by Europeans to be more treacherous.

When the dissatisfied Boers began to leave Cape Colony for the north they found a largely depopulated land north of the Orange River. Only three major Bantu nations confronted them in their search for new land—the Basuto, the Matabele, and, most important, Dingane's Zulus.

The Great Trek

In 1823 following immediately after Captain Owen's survey of the coastline of southeastern Africa, a group of traders and adventurers first established themselves at Port Natal. They found the land surrounding the harbor to be good and relatively free of Bantu. The first settlers were, however, not primarily concerned with farming or cattle raising, but with trade into the interior. Men such as John Thompson, Francis Farewell, James King, and Henry Fynn believed it possible to establish profitable relations with Shaka who controlled all of the land surrounding Port Natal. In July 1824, Farewell and Fynn visited the king's kraal. Shaka welcomed them, paraded his wealth and power before them, and gave them permission to stay at Port Natal. In early August, Shaka was accidently stabbed and Fynn was instrumental in nursing him back to health. In gratitude he signed a treaty granting Port Natal and approximately 3,500 square miles of territory adjacent to it to the Farewell Trading Company. Shaka had no intention of permanently alienating this land. The treaty was merely a sign of his respect for the white men.

Until Shaka's death the European community at Port Natal had nothing to fear from the Zulu. They traded beads and other manufactured goods to the Zulu for ivory, cattle, hides, and grain. Henry Fynn was so respected that he became a chief of one of the smaller Zulu clans. Despite the respect given to individuals by the Bantu, the colony did not thrive. The number of settlers at Port Natal until the late 1830s seldom exceeded forty. There was also a drifting African population which numbered approximately 2,000 persons. There were few items of profitable trade which could lure men from more settled areas to a land of such hardship and potential danger. A sandbar blocked the full use of the harbor to all but very shallow draft ships. Despite all these negative factors Port Natal was an established tiny community when Petrus Uys and twenty-one men of a kommissie trek reached it in the winter of 1834. The reports given by these trekkers of the green open country, few natives, and a functioning port played a most important role in the history of the Great Trek. Many of the Boer leaders came to regard Natal as the logical end of their long journey.

The exodus of Boers from Cape Colony began slowly and did not reach maximum proportions until mid-1837. Boer families had to reach individual decisions of the greatest magnitude. They had to decide to give up a settled existence for the unknown. Heads of families who chose to trek placed all their possessions into ox wagons, trailed their herds behind, and committed their families to the rough life of the trek and the danger of death from many sources. Nevertheless, by the midpart of 1836 all of Cape Colony was in ferment as hundreds of families prepared to risk everything rather than continue to be governed by the British. The first party of a dozen families under the leadership of Louis Trigardt left the colony in November 1835 and was soon followed by another small party led by van Rensburg. Trigardt's party settled near the Zoutpansberg range but found this was too isolated for them to get supplies of gunpowder. Eventually Trigardt led them into Portuguese territory where they settled in a fever area near the coast. In 1839 only twenty-nine people of this party were left and they were evacuated to Port Natal. Van Rensburg's party of ten families were simply lost somewhere on the high veld.

The first of the large parties was that of Andries Potgieter and Sarel Cillers with sixty-five families in 1836. At their encampment at Vegkop they met the first Bantu resistance. Matabele impis attacked and, although driven off, the Boer party lost all their cattle. Potgieter and Cillers fell back to Basuto country and in the winter were joined by Gerrit Maritz's party of one hundred families. In January 1837 the combined party fielded one hundred men and forty Griquas against the Matabele. In the ensuing battle which gave portents of the future, the Boers killed over 400 Matabele and recaptured their cattle. In April 1837, Piet Retief left the Cape accompanied by 120 families and he was soon followed by Piet Uys and another large group. By the end of 1837 an estimated 4,000 people had left Cape Colony.

Individualism was the Boer's greatest weakness as well as his great strength. Strong leaders of single treks found it difficult to control the desires of those who followed them. When it became necessary for different parties to cooperate, it was all but impossible to decide on a common policy. This facet of the trek became apparent in June 1837 when representatives of all groups met on the Vet River to establish common planning and unified leadership. Although they formed the United Laagers, there was no common leadership except when extreme danger threatened all the groups. One question more than any other divided the leaders. Where were they going? Retief and Uys were greatly influenced by the reports of the kommissie trek to Natal. They believed they could obtain permission from the Zulu king to settle in the vacant lands. Once settled they would have the advantage of Port Natal for obtaining the necessary

The Great Trek

Legend:
- ╾┼╾┼╾ Trigardt & Van Rensburg
- ━·━·━· Potgeiter & Cillers
- ━━━━ Maritz
- ·········· Uys
- ━ ━ ━ Retief

Map labels:
- 30°
- Limpopo R.
- Zoutpansberg
- Olifants R.
- MATABELE
- Rustenberg
- Lydenburg
- Mosega
- SWAZI
- Lourenço Marques
- Harts R.
- Vaal R.
- Vaal R.
- Sand R.
- Winburg
- BASUTO
- Blood R.
- Umfolozi R.
- ZULU
- Modder R.
- Thaba Nchu
- Bloemfontein
- Weenen
- Tugela R.
- 30°
- Boomplats
- Caledon R.
- Orange
- Orange R.
- Umzilkulu R.
- Port Natal
- Colesburg
- Umzimbuvu R.
- POND O
- Bashee R.
- TEMBU R.
- INDIAN OCEAN
- Graaf Reneit
- XOSA
- Kei R.
- Gt. Fish R.
- Keiskamma R.
- Grahamstown
- Uitenhage
- Alagoa Bay
- 0 50 100 Miles

supplies which they could not produce themselves. Maritz and Potgieter were lured by the high veld north of the Vaal River. It would be nearly impossible for the British to follow them, the land was good and almost completely empty, and Boers had already confronted the major native group, the Matabele, and won.

On the question of direction there was no compromise. Potgieter and those who agreed with him moved north of the Vaal River. In early autumn a Boer commando of approximately 135 men moved against the Matabele beyond the Marico River. In a battle of movement the Boers, without losing a man, drove the Matabele off the inland plateau and chased them toward the Matopo hills. The way was thus cleared for the establishment of the town of Potchefstroom and the peaceful settlement of the Transvaal areas. Meanwhile Retief leading fifty wagons had moved eastward toward Natal. After leading them down the escarpment of the Drakensberg, Retief rode ahead to the newly renamed Durban which had been called Port Natal before 1835. He saw or heard nothing at Durban which would indicate that he had made a bad choice. The settlers at Durban were friendly. The Cape government, although still claiming jurisdiction over the Boers, was engaged in the sixth Kaffir war and in no mood to annex further territory. The harmonious relations between the Durban settlers and Dingane indicated to Retief that he would have few problems in arriving at a settlement with the Zulu king.

Retief and his small escort then proceeded to Dingane's kraal. They were treated well and there were days of feasting and celebration. Finally in a conference Dingane accused Retief of stealing Zulu cattle. Retief denied this and guaranteed to recapture the stolen animals from the real culprit, Sikonyela of the baTlokwa. Dingane promised to give the settlers land if the cattle were returned. Thus emboldened, Retief sent word to his people that Natal was soon to be opened up and went after Sikonyela. The campaign was successful. Sikonyela was captured and ransomed off for cattle. A jubilant Retief led his sixty-nine men back to Dingane's kraal.

Retief's optimism was illusory since Dingane had no intention of allowing a thousand Boers to settle in his territory. Dingane was afraid. He had allowed the settlers at Durban to remain unharmed because they were few in number and therefore weak. These Boers were not weak. The Matabele who had resisted Dingane's best attempts to destroy them had been driven out of their lands by fewer Boers than were already camped in Natal. Dingane had decided, therefore, to kill all the Boers even before Retief returned from the campaign against Sikonyela. On February 4, 1838, Dingane signed a treaty ceding to Retief as governor of the territory all the area from the Umzimvuku River to the Tugela River and from the mountains to the sea. On the morning of February 6, the unarmed Boers were watching a farewell dance given in their honor. At a signal from Dingane the Zulu threw themselves on Retief and his followers and killed them all. The massacre was witnessed by Francis Owen, an American missionary to the Zulu, who brought the news to Durban.

Before word of the tragedy reached the Boer encampments, three Zulu regiments fell upon the unprepared laagers. Some of the larger encampments beat off the attacks, but many were destroyed. The Boers lost forty-one men, fifty-six women, 185 children, and 250 Hottentot servants before the onslaughts were checked. The Zulu drove approximately 10,000 captured cattle back to the king's kraal. In the two months that followed the death of Retief, Boers drifted into Natal from all parts of the interior, and finally a commando of 350 men led by Maritz, Uys, and Potgieter invaded Zulu territory. After an indecisive battle in which Uys was killed, the Boers retreated back to the main laagers. In May the situation had become critical for all Europeans in Natal and the settlers at Durban were evaculated from the town.

At the main Boer laagers over 4,000 people were concentrated. Many were sick and wounded and, after the failure of the previous commando, leadership was more divided than ever before. Then in November Andries Pretorius of Graaf Reinet arrived with sixty men and a cannon. He was elected commandant and almost immediately began another offensive against the Zulu. After a few indecisive skirmishes Pretorius and his small army of 450 men arrived at the Ncome River on December 15. Scouts had reported the presence of the main Zulu army. Pretorius selected a strong defensive position at the junction of the Ncome and another small stream. He had brought along a number of heavy ox-driven wagons which were put into a defensive position every evening. The wagons were placed in such a position that, if the Zulu attacked, they would have to do so on a narrow front. Early the next morning the Boers awoke to see an army of over 10,000 Zulu confronting them. The battle was soon begun by Zulu charging directly at the Boer position. However, the Zulu ox-head formation could not be used and Boer firepower was directed against a restricted area. After a two-hour defensive battle, Pretorius ordered the Boers to mount their horses and charge the Zulu. The Zulu regiments broke and the Boers chased the scattered army for the rest of the day. The Zulu lost over 3,000 men killed while the Boers suffered only four men wounded. From this time forward the Boers would refer to the Ncome as Blood River.

Dingane burned his kraal and moved northward accompanied by a powerful army driving the Zulu and captured Boer cattle before them. Pretorious and his force moved quickly to the king's kraal, but could recover only about one-half of the cattle lost to the Zulu. The commando soon disbanded, some men to return to the high veld, but most to move their families to the now open area of southern Natal. In early 1839 these established their capital approximately thirty miles west of Durban and called it Pietermaritzburg after two of their dead leaders. They proceeded to establish a governing body, the volksraad, elected Pretorius commandant-general, and began the difficult task of apportioning land. The governor of Cape Colony, Sir George Napier, sent eighty men to garrison Durban in December 1838, but since he received no orders to annex the adjacent area, these were withdrawn in December of the following year. It appeared to many Boers that Retief had been correct. They had reached the end of their wandering.

Dingane returned to his area and rebuilt his kraal. Leaving the Boers alone, he directed his armies northward against the Swazi in 1839. Preparatory to this campaign he ordered his brother, Panda, to bring his forces and join the main Zulu force. Panda, instead, learning that Dingane planned to kill him, moved all his people south of the Tugela River into lands occupied by the Boers. Panda, unlike his brothers, was weak by Zulu standards. He was reasonable, passive, and honorable in a European sense. At this time and later he was ignored by his relatives and powerless unless his orders coincided with their desires. The people who followed him south of the Tugela did so not out of loyalty, but because of fear of Dingane. Panda and his entourage traveled to Pietermaritzburg and he appeared before the volksraad on October 15, 1839. The Boers were pleased with the demeanor and promises of this passive Zulu ruler. He promised to stop what Europeans considered to be certain barbaric practices, cease waging war, and submit the choice of his successor to the volksraad. In return the Boers recognized him as Reigning Prince of the Emigrant Zulu and granted him permission to remain south of the Tugela.

The problem of cattle taken by Dingane from the Boers in 1838 proved a continual irritant. Dingane had no intention of returning them, and finally in January 1840 a new Boer commando entered his territory to take them back. The commando was composed of two sections, one Boer and one Zulu hostile to Dingane. On January 30 the Zulu contingent under Nongalaza met Dingane's regiments and after a bloody battle drove them northward. Dingane once again fled north across the Pongola River. This time he had only a few loyal troops and even these began to desert him. Relatively defenseless, he was killed by the Nwayos whose country he was invading. Even before his brother's death, Panda had been recognized by the Boers as king of the Zulu in February 1840.

The Natal trekkers, now safe from the Zulu, turned to the problems of government. The major local problem concerned land allocation. Each Boer male of the 1838–1839 group was entitled to have from one to three farms of 6,000 acres each. Some of the leaders such as Pretorius claimed many more. Many of the veterans of the campaigns of 1838 had not received their second farm when new Boers of the recent campaigns against Dingane demanded land. The disputes over land further divided an already highly individualistic people. Government was also plagued by jealousies between the leading citizens and was chronically short of money. The fees for registering land which provided the bulk of revenue, however low, were still beyond the means of many Boers. The volksraad also confronted the same problem of control over interior people which had hampered the East Indies Company and the British in Cape Colony. It did not have the power to enforce its decrees.

In 1840 the Pietermaritzburg volksraad attempted to weld together all the trekkers in the high veld under its rule. These areas included those closest to Cape Colony which were called Trans-Orangia. Few Boers lived on these hot grassy plains. The southern portion of Trans-Orangia was inhabited by the Griquas organized under their own captains. Thus the Natalians were relatively unconcerned about this area. To the north the area between the Vet and Vaal rivers which came to be called Winburg was fairly well populated and organized. The third area of the high veld was Potchefstroom north of the Vaal. Although Natal appointed a land-drost for this area, the unquestioned leader was Potgieter.

In November 1840 an agreement between all factions created a single republic with the Pietermaritzburg volksraad the chief instrument of government. Pretorius was appointed commandant-general of all Boer forces. Potgieter was named administrator for the north and there was a subsidiary volksraad located at Potchefstroom. In September the Natal volksraad sent a proposal to Sir George Napier at Cape Town asking to be recognized as an independent state. Temporarily united, the Boers sent a more direct and specific request in January 1841. Boer policing actions against scattered Bantu people and the use of the prisoners as apprentices to ease the acute labor shortage in Natal had prejudiced the Cape government against the volksraad. Napier refused their request for recognition in March 1841 and dispatched Captain Thomas Smith and a detachment of regular troops to a position on the borders of Natal. The inability of the Pietermaritzburg government to solve its most acute problems became more obvious in the spring and fall of 1841. This led directly to Napier's proclamation of annexation in December 1841.

The volksraad was divided sharply between those elements which favored acceptance of the inevitable and those who were willing to fight the British. Even when their independence was threatened the Boers continued to pursue their own selfish private goals. It was soon apparent that the Natalians would receive little help from Winburg and Potchefstroom. In May 1842, Smith and 250 regulars arrived and without opposition took possession of Durban. The Boers under Pretorius began to build up their strength at Congella. Smith rashly moved against the Boers and lost forty-nine men. Soon thereafter Pretorius' men captured two British ships and carted away fifty-six wagon loads of booty. Pretorius, however, could not drive the British from their fortified positions and Smith was able to send out a rider for help. The almost unbroken ride of Dick Smith for help to Grahamstown has become a South African legend. In response to Smith's request for help, a fifty-gun frigate and imperial troops under Colonel Cleote raised the siege of Durban in June 1842. By this time many of Pretorius' men had left him, the volksraad was still bickering, and there were rumors that Panda was planning to attack. Therefore, a rump volksraad on July 15 admitted the supremacy of the queen. Although the volksraad lingered on until late 1843, the Republic of Natal was a dead issue. Large number of Boers retreated west across the Drakensberg to the high veld. The volksraad made final the transfer of sovereignty in August 1843, and British troops occupied Pietermaritzburg. The Great Trek was finished and the Natal Boers, despite their hardships and sacrifices, found themselves still controlled by the British. On the high veld British authority was reaching out toward the Boers of Winburg and the Transvaal.

Relationships between Boer, Briton, and Bantu through 1872

The Boer settlements in the high veld in the 1840s and 1850s reflected the individualistic, quarrelsome nature of their leaders. Potgieter who had dominated Potchefstroom moved to Zoutpansberg in 1846 leaving Pretorius as the leader of Potchefstroom and Winburg. In 1846 another republic was briefly created at Ohrigstad in the Transvaal area. The farmers showed few signs of cooperating with one another against the specter of British activity in Trans-Orangia. The weakness of the separate trekker republics, individual jealousies, and the Boer's harsh attitude toward their native neighbors made it easier for the triumph of Britain's expansionist policy in the 1840s.

The same forces in Britain and South Africa which had impelled Governor Napier to annex Natal also pushed Britain to a more expansive policy in Trans-Orangia. In 1845 the Hottentot Griqua leader, Adam Kok, in attempting to arrest a Boer, brought on the threat of a minor war. The new governor of Cape Colony, Sir Peregrine Maitland, led British troops into Griqualand to reestablish order. He made it clear that Britain supported the independence of the Griquas. However, before any further northward expansion took place the seventh Kaffir war diverted the total energies of the Cape military to the eastern frontier.

The seventh war is known as the War of the Axe because its ostensible immediate cause was the arrest of a Xosa charged with stealing an axe. He was liberated from the Grahamstown jail by friends, the British sent troops into Xosa territory, and the war was on. The actual cause was the failure of the Colonial Office to approve D'Urban's settlement after the sixth war. Stockenstrom's treaty system had broken down by 1840. After that date order was maintained on the frontier by Governors Napier and Maitland, forcing the Xosa to accept more direct British rule. The seventh war was a direct result of Xosa dissatisfaction with such a system. The war which lasted almost two years convinced the Colonial Office that a more forward policy beyond the Cape borders was needed. They supported the Cape government with imperial troops and designated the governor as a high commissioner with authority to treat with natives beyond the frontiers.

A new governor, Sir Harry Smith, who had the most distinguished military career of any previous British governor, arrived in Cape Town in December 1847. He brought the Kaffir war to a quick conclusion and sanctioned the selling to Europeans of much of the land between the Fish and Keiskamma rivers. The area between the Keiskamma and Kei rivers he annexed to the crown as a separate entity called British Kaffraria. In order to provide a land bridge to Natal, all chiefs beyond the Kei had to recognize British sovereignty. D'Urban's rejected policy had at last triumphed in a slightly altered form.

Smith immediately turned his attention to the troubled areas north of the Orange River. The constant bickering between Boers, Basuto, and

Griquas posed a continual threat to the stability of the Cape's northern frontier. In February 1848, Smith declared all territories between the Orange and Vaal rivers to be subject to the rule of the queen and sent Major Henry Warden as resident with a few troops into the area to secure the allegiance of the Boers. Although many Boers welcomed an end to the internecine squabbles, many others joined Pretorius who came down from Potchefstroom with a few Transvaalers to oppose the British action. They expelled Warden and began to prepare to defend the area. Retribution was not long coming. Smith marched north and defeated the recalcitrant Boers at the battle of Boomplaats in August 1848. He then constituted the Orange River Sovereignty. British authority by 1849 had thus been extended north to the Vaal. A united British South Africa seemed inevitable.

Smith's dreams, however, were to prove futile. The reduction of the power of the Xosa chiefs in Kaffraria brought on resentment which exploded in 1850 in the eighth Kaffir war. To the dismay of Smith, the Xosa were joined by many Hottentots who felt cheated because of lack of compensation for their support of the British in the previous war. The farmers and burghers on the frontier also found numerous excuses to avoid commando duty. Thus the brunt of the fighting fell on imperial troops. This meant increased expenditure from the British treasury. Major Warden, the British resident in the Orange River Sovereignty, became engaged in an ill-advised war with the Basuto at the same time that Smith was involved with the Xosa. The British government after 1848, dominated by the non-expansion corollary of free trade, began to question the advisability of further responsibilities in southern Africa. Two assistant commissioners who did not have to report through Smith's office were sent to investigate the problem of the northern and eastern Cape boundaries. Smith believed that if they recommended retention of the sovereignty he could still induce the Transvaal Boers to agree to British sovereignty. However, at Sand River in January 1852 the commissioners dashed this hope by recognizing the independence of the Boer territories across the Vaal. The retreat from Smith's policy was continued when in February 1854 another special commissioner, Sir George Clerk, signed the Bloemfontein Convention. This withdrew the British from the Orange River Sovereignty and recognized the independence of that state.

Sir George Grey who became governor of Cape Colony in 1854 recognized immediately the problems of such a reversion. To him a common native policy in southern Africa was of prime importance. In 1856 he inquired of the Colonial Office about the feasibility of revoking the Bloemfontein agreement and received a negative reply. Two years later when his opinion was asked concerning a federation of Cape Colony, Kaffraria, and Natal he exceeded his authority by having the Cape parliament vote to include the Orange Free State in the proposed federation. Grey was rebuked and recalled by the Colonial Office. Although he returned as governor the following year, his reappointment was contingent upon his agreement to forget about any absorption of the Boer states. When Grey left office in 1861 federation seemed far away.

The decade following the Sand River Convention was a stormy period for the Boer states. The Pretorius and Potgieter factions of the Transvaal came together briefly to assure the Sand River Convention in 1852. The truce was short-lived. Andries Pretorius' son, Marthinius, succeeded to the leadership of the Potchefstroom settlers on the death of his father in 1853. His attempt to create a unified republic was rebuffed by other factions who were responsible for creating three small competitive republics— Lydenburg, Utrecht, and Zoutpansberg. Within each of these polities their volksraads had little authority and they were continually without funds. The Boers were little more than a collection of clans constantly involved in small-scale warfare against the Bantu. The Orange Free State was more viable since it was not as wracked by personal quarrels between its leaders and the potential threat of the powerful Basuto forced a more unified government.

In 1857 Marthinius Pretorius attempted to unite the Free State with his South African Republic. President Boshof of the Orange Free State ordered Pretorius from the country, and war between the two areas was only narrowly averted. During the same year Zoutpansberg blended with the South African Republic and in 1860 Lydenburg and Utrecht joined to create a single polity north of the Vaal River. In 1860 Pretorius was elected president of the Orange Free State and thus became the chief executive of both areas. For over two stormy years he tried to bring the two polities together. Finally in 1863 he resigned as president of the Orange Free State in order to retain control of the South African Republic against the challenge of Commandant Paul Kruger.

British activity in the areas beyond the borders of Cape Colony and Natal was at a minimum during this period. Most of their involvement was in Kaffraria where Grey and his successors attempted to convert the Xosa into farmers ruled by white magistrates rather than by their chiefs. This task was made easier by the actions of the Xosa themselves. In 1856 a young girl, Nongquase, the niece of an influential witch doctor, had a series of visions. These promised that a hurricane would be sent to sweep the white man from southern Africa if the Xosa placated the gods by destroy- ing their grain and killing their cattle. If this were done the whites would disappear, all dead Xosa warriors would arise, and fat cattle and grain would be sent to them. Believing the vision, the Xosa launched upon a policy which led to their end as a major power in southern Africa. The vision did not prove true: The dead warriors did not rise and the cattle did not come. Instead an estimated 65,000 Xosa died of starvation.

Two unrelated factors propelled Britain more directly into interior affairs after 1865. Msheshwe of the Basuto had been under pressure from the Boers of the Orange Free State for years. There had been a number of wars between the two polities but none as serious as that of 1865–1867. Fearing the destruction of the Basuto nation, Msheshwe appealed to Sir Philip Wodehouse, the Cape governor, for protection. Not wishing to stand by and do nothing while the Basuto were destroyed, Sir Philip exceeded his instructions and granted Msheshwe's request. The Colonial Office, although displeased, concurred. However, in 1871 the Cape government

Southern African Polities, 1860

was cajoled into taking over the responsibility of the Basuto. The other event which more profoundly altered British attitudes was the discovery of diamonds in 1867 near the junction of the Vaal and the Orange rivers in Griqualand West. Men from all over the world poured into the diamond areas. By the time the river diggings had been exhausted in 1871, over £300,000 worth of diamonds had been retrieved. The newly founded Kimberley soon became the second largest city in southern Africa.

The area of the diamond fields was claimed by the Griqua chief, Waterboer, and the Orange Free State. The South African Republic also maintained that a portion of the territory was under its jurisdiction. The British government at the Cape supported the Griqua claim. With thousands of miners in the area, some type of government beyond that which the Griquas could provide was necessary. Sir Henry Barkly, governor of the Cape, favored a settlement with Waterboer and direct annexation. Prime Minister Gladstone demurred because of the expense of governing unwanted territory, but agreed that it could be annexed to the Cape. On October 31, 1871, Barkly raised the flag and the area became British territory. However, the Cape parliament refused the honor of bearing the cost of administration and despite Gladstone's objections, Britain had to assume direct control. The British throughout the period prior to annexation had staunchly repudiated the claim of the Orange Free State and had refused to arbitrate the matter. At a time when British interests turned once more toward a peaceful federation of all of southern Africa they had by their stand on the diamond fields alienated one of the necessary units to such a federation.

The fifty-year period after the landing of the Albany settlers witnessed the rapid economic development of Cape Colony. In 1820 there were a few thousand Europeans scattered thinly into the interior. By 1870 the population had grown to over 200,000. The prosperous Boer farmers of the western Cape were being matched by the primarily British farmers in the east. The passing of the Xosa threat in the 1850s expedited the development of the eastern regions. Despite prolonged drought in the 1860s, the Cape farmer was a rich man by comparison to his counterpart in the republics. The wine industry was falling off, but wool exports were worth almost two million pounds. There were banks, schools, and churches in all the major towns and even sixty-three miles of railway between Cape Town and Wellington. Though there was little industry except small firms which catered to specific services, Cape Colony had reached a point where a major infusion of capital could convert it from an agricultural to a proto-industrial society. The discovery of diamonds and less than two decades later, gold, provided the necessary impetus for this change.

The government of the colony had changed radically since the auto-cratic rule of Lord Charles Somerset. In 1834 there had been created a legislative council nominated by the governors to aid in policy making. Agitation in other colonial areas, particularly in Canada and Nova Scotia, for the colonists to have more voice in their own affairs had an effect on Cape Colony also. In 1842 the Colonial Office turned down the request by

Cape petitioners for representative government. The reason given for this action was the nature of the Cape community and the Colonial Office's fear that an elected government would lead to the oppression of the blacks. This and the jealousy between eastern and western areas of the Cape postponed representative government until 1853, five years after Canada had received responsible government. The tensions between British eastern farmers and their Boer western counterparts, combind with almost a decade of drought, delayed the grant of responsible government to the Cape. In the 1860s the British government had enunciated the principle that with self-government came self-defense. The Cape was in no position to assume the burden of funding the armed forces necessary to guard its frontiers. Finally in the 1870s eastern and western politicians agreed to cooperate with one another, the drought ended, and Britain agreed to maintain imperial troops in Cape Colony. On this basis a formula was worked out whereby the Cape received responsible government beginning in 1873. From this time forward the prime minister of Cape Colony and his ministry had a most important role to play in the development of southern Africa.

The colony of Natal lagged far behind the Cape. Plantation-type agriculture in sugar and tea was not developed until the 1870s. There was a continual labor shortage throughout Natal and the European population in 1870 was only 18,000. Therefore the grant of more self-government to the Natalians was understandably slower than to Cape Colony. Until 1856 Natal was administered as a part of Cape Colony with the chief executive being a lieutenant-governor. In that year Natal was separated from the Cape and given autonomous representative government with a small elected legislative council of sixteen members. Some citizens attempted to gain responsible government for Natal at the same time it was given to the Cape. However, the smallness of the population, lack of revenue, and the threat of the Zulu north of the Tugela River meant that Britain did not seriously consider such proposals. Natal did not receive responsible government until 1893.

Native policy in Natal followed to a large degree the ideas of one man, Theophilus Shepstone. Instead of attempting to westernize the Bantu as Smith and Grey were trying in Kaffraria, the people were segregated into special native reserves. This was done partially to keep them divided, but Shepstone also sincerely believed that their own chiefs could govern them best. The lieutenant-governor of Natal was declared the paramount chief of the Bantu south of the Tugela River. Thus government orders passed to the tribes from the white paramount chief through African leaders. This system kept order and prevented alienation of native lands, but it also created for the native a position as second-class citizen in Natal where there were few attempts made to give him equality with the whites.

North of the Tugela River lived the Zulu who might have remembered Blood River but certainly were not a conquered people. Panda could not control the Zulu in the same way his brother had and there evolved a loose system of government with each chief obeying the king when it seemed to his advantage to do so. Nevertheless, the foundation of the state still rested upon the military. Panda could not have destroyed the warrior system even had he wished to do so. It remained intact although little used during his reign. He sincerely pursued a policy of peace toward the Europeans south of the Tugela. Because of this and partly because of the small numbers of whites in Natal and the native policy of Shepstone, there were few examples of conflict between the Zulu and the settlers.

The somnolent Zulu were, however, revived by one of Panda's sons, Cetewayo. Panda had intended another son, Umbulazi, to succeed him, but Cetewayo gained the allegiance of a large portion of the Zulu and in 1856 declared war on his younger brother. In December of that year Cetewayo's regiments defeated his rival's armies and Umbulazi was killed. At an assembly the following year, Cetewayo was confirmed as the decision maker in the Zulu nation while Panda remained only the titular paramount chief. Cetewayo was more in the mold of his uncles, Shaka and Dingane. He revitalized the army and turned them loose on his native neighbors to the north. When he succeeded to his father's ceremonial title in 1872, he had managed to frighten a large portion of the European settlers in Natal and the South African Republic. Their misreading of Cetewayo's actions led to a disastrous Zulu war in less than a decade.

FOUR
Northeastern Africa

The Egyptian problem

Khedive Ismail who came to power in 1863 could not escape from the pressures of an affluent, expansive Europe. The French and British had long had sizable investments in the Middle East. Britain's support of the tottering Ottoman Empire, because of India, had great ramifications for Egypt. British intervention had already prevented Muhammad Ali from extending his influence into Syria at the expense of the sultan, his nominal suzerain. British entrepreneurs, urged on by their government, which was committed to Ottoman hegemony brought their new skills of building railroads, roads, and irrigation systems to Egypt. They were countered by entrenched French political and economic interests. Ismail's predecessor had in 1858 succumbed to Fernand de Lessep's scheme to build a canal linking the Mediterranean and Red seas. This was a diplomatic defeat for Britain which had wanted instead an interlocking system of British-built railroads for the Middle East.

Ismail saw no threat from the Europeans since he wanted for Egypt many of the things which only Europe could provide. He wanted to improve trade, the irrigation system, and with it agriculture. He was concerned with beginning European-style schools to provide a technically competent group as well as a Western-oriented elite. All of these schemes for internal betterment, added to his dreams of a great Egyptian empire, demanded a great amount of money. The Suez Canal by the time it was completed in 1869 cost twenty-six million pounds. The bulk of this had been borrowed by the khedive at high interest rates in the name of the Canal Company. Modernization of his army required large amounts as did his ventures in the Sudan and Ethiopia. In his borrowings he was urged on by French, German, Austrian, Italian, and British bankers who sadly miscalculated Egypt's ability to repay. The 1860s were good years for Egypt. There was a worldwide trade boom and the stoppage of American raw cotton for European mills increased tremendously the demand for Egyptian cotton. However, the good years of the 1860s gave way to the troubled 1870s. The reentry of American cotton on the market and a general worldwide trade depression meant that Egyptian expeditures could not continue at a high level without causing economic disturbances. Despite this the tempo of Egyptian spending and borrowing did not abate. Within a year of its opening the Suez Canal was making profits for its shareholders. Otherwise by the mid-1870s the finances of the khedive were in a chaotic state. The public debt which stood at four million pounds at the beginning of Ismail's rule had risen to ninety-one million pounds by 1879.

In November 1875, Ismail was forced to sell his 176,000 shares of the total of 400,000 shares in the Canal Company. The British prime minister, Benjamin Disraeli, by a combination of luck and skill managed to secure these and Britain thus became the largest stockholder in the Canal Company. Ismail's troubles were only beginning since the European bondholders began more stridently to pressure their governments to demand payment from the khedive. In 1876 the management of Egyptian finances passed to a European consortium called the *Caisse de le Dette*. The chief figures of the Caisse were the two secretaries, one French and one British. This dual control brought about only slight improvement in financial affairs and in 1879 when it was discovered that Ismail was plotting against the Europeans he was deposed by the Turkish sultan on the advice of the British.

The new khedive, Tewfik, obviously could not succeed where his predecessor had failed. Europeans kept demanding their money and Egyptians came to believe that they were the cause of all the evils which had befallen the country. The numbers of Europeans resident in Egypt had grown from only 6,000 in 1853 to almost 100,000 by 1882. Egyptian nationalism posed a considerable threat to the security of these Europeans. Arabi Pasha, the minister of war, put himself at the head of the Egyptian nationalists and demanded that Egypt be permitted to rule itself without outside interference. The French premier Gambetta became so perturbed over the danger to French nationals and the specter of Arabi becoming dictator that he proposed to Britain a joint occupation of the country. At first Prime Minister Gladstone refused, but continuing disorders threatening the lives of Europeans compelled him to agree to a joint naval force to overawe the Egyptians. After the killing of Europeans in June 1882 the decision was made to invade Egypt, if necessary, to restore order and rid the country of Arabi. A change in government in France resulted in a reversion of their aggressive policy. Gambetta's successor, Charles Louis Freycinet, refused to authorize the use of French armed forces. Without French assistance the British bombarded Alexandria in July 1882. In August British troops under the command of Sir Garnet Wolseley landed at Ismalia and in the following month defeated Arabi's forces at Tel-el-Kebir. Tewfik was restored to the throne by a British army of occupation and dual control was declared to be ended.

The internal history of Egypt after 1882 is beyond the scope of this work. However, because Egypt was such a key factor in the scramble for Africa it is necessary to outline briefly the international implications of the British occupation. The report of 1883 submitted by Lord Dufferin indicated how archaic and corrupt the Egyptian administration was. The British position then became one of reconstructing the government, employing honest, efficient men in the offices of the state and rebuilding the army around a cadre of British noncommissioned and commissioned officers. Britain contemplated that the reforms would take years to effect and would thus drain away large sums for reconstruction which otherwise would have been applied to pay the bondholders.

The French government, despite involvement in planning for the occupation, assumed that Britain was in Egypt only as agent for the bondholders. Their concept was that the occupying force should not commit itself to any long-term rebuilding. It was merely to act as a means of forcing the money from Egypt to meet the obligations to European investors. As soon as this was done all British troops should be withdrawn. Obviously the French posture was dictated by factors other than merely concern for the bondholders or for Egyptian independence. French financial interests in Egypt were greater than Britain's, and France was beginning to expand its territorial empire throughout Africa. In Egypt, Britain blocked French plans for extension of their own empire. The *Caisse de la Dette* which still functioned was one of the major mechanisms the French used to block Britain's proposed activities in Egypt. British plans for reconstruction of Egypt were saved by the support which they received from Germany. German chancellor Otto von Bismarck was at first relatively uninterested in a territorial empire in Africa. One of his major concerns was to force Britain from its "splendid isolation" into a definite alliance with Germany. In the mid-1880s this long-range German goal dictated support of Britain's Egyptian plans. Therefore by 1887 there came to be a de facto recognition of Britain's premier position in Egypt by all European powers. This concession carried certain disabilities for Britain elsewhere in Africa. As a price for such recognition, France and Germany expected and received little opposition to the expansion of their territorial empires in West and East Africa. In assessing Britain's attitudes toward European encroachment in areas previously considered British spheres, one is led back again and again to its fixed position in Egypt.

Britain's reorganization of Egypt did not at first touch the structure of government. The khedive as a vassal of the Ottoman sultan remained the head of state. An Egyptian ministry was allowed to continue as well as the local government structure. The British merely interposed themselves in the operation of government at all levels. British officials replaced Egyptians on the intermediate levels particularly in offices concerned with finance. The Egyptian army was reorganized according to the British model with the most important positions being filled by British officers. Undoubtedly the most important official in the Egyptian government was

Sir Evelyn Baring (later Lord Cromer) who from 1883 to 1906 was the British consul. Through him the British Foreign Office channeled its high-level decisions which became binding on the khedive's government.

Egypt in the Sudan to 1885

Egypt's dominant position in the Sudan dated from the early days of the rule of Muhammad Ali. This Albanian adventurer, one of the most astute rulers of his day, saw many opportunities in the troubled Sudan. The southern frontier of Egypt was vulnerable to attack from the displaced Mamluks who had fled south after Muhammad's seizure of power. More important than this strategic consideration was the economic factor. Possession of the Sudan would greatly increase the animal and agricultural potential of Egypt. There were also rumors of ancient gold mines in the Sudan which, with the proper care, could be made productive. Then there were slaves which could be taken in the extreme south and either sold or retained as soldiers or forced workers for the state. Obviously an important consideration in the viceroy's planning was the defenseless position of a large portion of the most valuable riverine territory. The Funj rulers no longer exercised any real power over the bulk of territory which had once been their empire. Real power resided in the hands of individual sheikhs who were most concerned with maintaining their privileges against interlopers. It was unlikely that Egyptian forces would meet much opposition if they chose to invade the southern territory.

In 1820 Muhammad Ali dispatched two columns of over 9,000 men into the Sudan. One was under the command of his third son, Ismail, and the other of his son-in-law, Muhammad Bey al Daftardar. Both armies were equipped with the latest in European weapons. As expected, the only effective resistance to this invasion came from the Shukriya. After their surrender the rulers of Shendi capitulated, the Abdullah chiefs surrendered, and Ismail occupied Sennar without difficulty. Al Daftardar's forces immediately invaded Kordofan and in a fierce battle defeated the armies of the representative of the Fur sultan, and this part of the Mussabbaat territory became a part of Muhammad Ali's empire.

Even before the initial conquest had been completed Ismail, assisted briefly by his brother, Ibrahim, began to exploit the territory. Troops were dispatched southward to raid for slaves and a tax levy was imposed many times that which had previously been paid. Despite the fear engendered in the Sudanese by the "Turks" many refused to pay the tax and some fled their homes rather than submit. Ismail's government, although hastily constructed and designed to exploit the territory to the maximum, was not otherwise cruelly oppressive. In most conquered areas the traditional rulers continued to function although under the surveillance of Egyptian officials.

The murder of Ismail changed briefly, but decisively, Egyptian policy to one of direct, violent, oppressive actions against the Sudanese. Ismail in October 1822 paused at Shendi on his way to Egypt after almost two years in the Sudan. At an audience with the local ruler, Ismail demanded the payment of approximately $30,000 and 6,000 slaves. This payment was to be delivered within two days. A brief quarrel ensued over the impossibility of these demands and Ismail struck the ruler with his pipe. Later retainers of the sheikh set fire to the house where Ismail slept and he died in the fire. When news reached al Daftardar of the details of Ismail's death, the reaction was swift and generalized. He sought not to punish those responsible, but to make all Sudanese pay for the action. His armies pillaged and killed from Sennar north to Metemma. Thus the Sudanese learned very early that the "Turks" were violent oppressors, a view which later benevolent actions of Egyptian rulers could not remove.

Following the conquest, Muhammad Ali proceeded to organize a centralized government for the Sudan. The entire area was ruled by a governor-general (hikimdar) who was appointed directly by Muhammad Ali. The governor-general possessed military as well as civil authority and his decisions could be reversed only by Muhammad Ali. In a short time the Sudan was further divided into a number of provinces, each ruled by a governor (murdir) responsible to the governor-general. By the time of Ali's death in 1849 there were seven provinces—Dongola, Kordofan, Berber, Khartoum, Fazughli, Taka, and Sennar. Although there were various experiments by Ali's successors, the provincial type of government remained the basic pattern throughout the period of Egyptian rule. Since it would have been nearly impossible to staff all administrative offices with Egyptians, each province was further subdivided into districts over which traditional rulers presided, subject to control by the governor.

Egyptian rule in the Sudan in the nineteenth century was based upon its exploitation for the benefit of Egypt. The chief administrators were foreigners who generally did not understand or appreciate the cultures of the indigenous people. All Sudanese were taxed heavily and when Egyptian authority spread southward into the Bahr al Ghazal and Equatoria the tribal structure of the people was directly undermined by incessant slave raiding. Government at all higher levels was characterized by corruption, lack of administrative continuity, and open insubordination of officials who could take advantage of the vast distances and poor communications in the Sudan. Other factors must be mentioned in connection with Sudanese misrule. The gold mines proved not to be worth much, agriculture was slow to develop, and therefore the Sudan remained a poor area. Despite high taxes even in years of peace, it was always a drain on the Egyptian treasury. Therefore there was extreme reluctance in Cairo to approve expenditure of funds for improvements in the Sudan.

From the beginning of Egyptian rule the slave trade occupied a prominent position in the affairs of the Sudan. The government until the reign of Abbas Pasha (1849–1854) in Egypt maintained a monopoly of all trade and therefore also of the slave trade. Muhammad Ali's reorganization of the army of occupation in the Sudan was based upon captured slaves trained by European officers. During the entire period of Egyptian rule there was a steady demand for slaves in the northern Sudan, Egypt, and in Muslim territories across the Red Sea. After the late 1850s private companies were organized to tap the human riches of the areas south of Gondokoro. Slaver entrepreneurs such as Zubeir Pasha maintained their own forts and private armies and were laws unto themselves in the frontier areas of the Sudan.

More as a concession to British antislavery pressure than from real conviction, Khedive Muhammad Said (1854–1863) in 1854 issued orders to all his officials in the Sudan to stop the traffic in slaves. A new post was established at Fashoda ostensibly to control the southern trade, but officials in the Sudan merely ignored the khedive's strictures on the trade. By the opening of Khedive Ismail's reign (1863–1879) the only real Egyptian authority in the area south of Gondokoro to the borders of Bunyoro were the slavers.

In the early years of Ismail's term, Egypt's economy improved greatly. This improvement, largely caused by the increased demand for cotton, led Ismail to overcommit himself to European financiers. A substantial portion of the extra funds available to Egypt were spent in furthering the imperialistic ambitions of the khedive. Ismail brought to Egypt many foreigners whom he believed would help him create a modern Western-style army. Many ex-confederate and northern officers from the United States were employed in this task. One, General Charles Stone, became chief of staff of the army. Ismail greatly expanded the size of the army and stationed between seven and ten thousand men permanently in the Sudan during the 1860s. Most of these troops were armed with the latest rifles and, beginning in the 1870s, the army also relied upon various caliber of cannon from Germany.

One of the earliest areas of attempted Egyptian expansion was Ethiopia. In December 1862, Governor-General Musa Hamdi led an expedition of over 7,000 men well into Ethiopia. In 1866 Ismail leased Suakin and Massawa from his Ottoman overlord and in 1870 the coast of Somalia from Bulhar to Berbera was acquired in the same way. In 1874 the Egyptians under Raul Pasha occupied Harar. Two years later the main Egyptian thrust into Ethiopia was permanently damaged when Emperor Johannes IV at Gura defeated an Egyptian army of 12,000 men commanded by the American general Loring and the sirdar Ratib Pasha. Although not abandoning completely the Ethiopian arena, Egypt was forced by internal problems to curtail any further ambitious schemes in this direction after 1877.

The area of Egyptian control over the Sudan was increased in the early 1870s largely by the efforts of the greatest of the Sudanese slavers, Zubeir Pasha. In 1872 his independence and power in the Bahr al Ghazal was challenged by the government. Zubeir's private army defeated the government forces. Instead of being punished for his action Zubeir, after convincing the khedive of his loyalty, was rewarded by being appointed governor of the territory. In 1874 Zubeir's forces, preceding the army of the governor-general, invaded the Fur kingdom, defeated its armies, and occupied El Fasher. Soon afterward, however, the governor-general who feared Zubeir's power convinced the khedive to banish the slaver-captain from the Sudan. Nevertheless, Zubeir's interests were guarded by his son, Suliaman, who reigned supreme in the Bahr al Ghazal.

Another area of great expense which yielded Egypt very few tangible imperialistic gains was the Upper Nile. Sir Samuel Baker, the explorer whom Ismail had first met in 1869, was employed by the khedive and given a twofold task. The first and most important charge was to extend Egyptian influence into the interlacustrine areas of East Africa. Secondly, Baker was to use all means at his disposal to end the slave trade. Baker was well provided with troops and had at his disposal six river steamers and a fleet of sailboats. Almost immediately after his arrival at Gondokoro in April 1871, he set the tone for his relations with the local people by quarreling with Egyptian merchants and confiscating large amounts of cattle from the Bari tribesmen. Baker was henceforth viewed as a danger to the Bari and it took his successor, Charles Gordon, years to gain their confidence. Baker soon moved southward and established a fort at Masiudi from whence he declared Bunyoro an Egyptian protectorate. However, Kabarega, the ruler of Bunyoro, was not favorably impressed by Baker's plans for his kingdom and eventually Bunyoro armies forced Baker to withdraw from Masiudi. Baker also contacted Mutesa, ruler of Buganda, with no more satisfactory results for Egyptian plans. Ultimately Baker had to be satisfied with garrisoning such small places as Fatiko and Folero. Baker left Gondokoro for Egypt in April 1873 with little to show for his two years as governor of Equatoria.

Not warned by his experience with Baker, Ismail employed the hero of the Taiping rebellion in China, Colonel Charles Gordon, to finish the tasks outlined to Baker. Gordon was much more successful than Baker in mollifying the feelings of Africans. Working tirelessly after early 1874, Gordon from his administrative center at Lado extended Egyptian influence deep into Bunyoro. He established a series of military posts between Rejaf and Dufile from whence his boats could travel to Lake Albert. Nevertheless, Gordon's resources were not sufficient for the tasks assigned him. His personality alienated many of his European lieutenants and disease also took a heavy toll of his subordinates. Finally in 1876, near exhaustion himself, he resigned and returned to England. The results of Baker's and Gordon's efforts taken in conjunction with Egyptian failures of the same period in Ethiopia certainly justified the critics of Ismail's government who accused him of spending lavishly without achieving any definite advantage.

Gordon's connection with the Sudan, however, had not ended. There were to be two other acts in the tragedy before his death, at Khartoum, in January 1885. The first of these was when he decided in 1877 to return to his post as governor of Equatoria. By the time he arrived in Cairo he had decided that his major function should be the suppression of the slave trade. To accomplish this aim he demanded that he be appointed governor-general. Surprisingly, Ismail concurred in this request. For almost three years Gordon devoted himself unsparingly to the eradication of the trade. He quelled a revolt against the government in Darfur, and defeated and executed the slaver Suliaman in the Bahr al Ghazal. When he resigned in 1880 in loyalty to his deposed chief, Ismail, Gordon had made severe inroads into the slave trade. However, he had not succeeded in infusing efficiency into the government of the Sudan nor had he taught the Egyptian staff the dangers of a corrupt government.

Egyptian misgovernment brought on a reaction against foreign rule which, coinciding with the British occupation, swept Egyptian authority from the Sudan. The leader of this revolt was Muhammad Ahmed, a religious teacher who in his mid-thirties proclaimed himself the Mahdi. To the Sudanese who are Sunni Muslims this term means the "guided one" who would bring justice to society as the head of the Islamic community. Muhammad Ahmed, the son of a boat builder, had early distinguished himself by his piety and learning. After his studies under a number of famous Sudanese holy men were completed, he became a religious teacher of the Sammaniya sect. From his base at Abba Island in the Nile he began to carry his message of self-denial and purity throughout the central Sudan. One such trip through the Kordofan in 1879 was particularly fruitful in gaining converts and spreading his fame. Sometime before 1881 Muhammad Ahmed began to believe himself the Mahdi. Aided by the Sudanese expectations of the appearance of the chosen one, he soon gathered about him a number of persons who believed him. Among these early converts was Abdullah, the future khalifa.

Muhammad Ahmed spent most of 1881 in Kordofan preaching the need for purity and criticizing the activities of the Egyptian rulers. By mid-1881 he had openly declared himself the Mahdi. In August Governor-General Rauf Pasha sent two companies of troops to Abba Island to arrest the troublemaker. A series of tragicomic events culminated in the Mahdists, with sticks and spears, routing the better-armed soldiers. Muhammad Ahmed then retired to Kordofan. The Egyptian commander at Fashoda, ignoring orders, dispatched 400 regular troops and 1,000 Shilluk to pursue him. On December 9, 1881, the troops were ambushed by Abdullah's irregular forces. Egyptian losses were heavy. These triumphs over established authority earned the Mahdi prestige and gained him many more volunteers.

Governor-General Rauf Pasha was recalled by Tewfik and before his replacement arrived the acting governor-general decided to crush the Mahdi. In the spring of 1882 a military expedition of over 4,000 troops left Fashoda for Kordofan. The Egyptian military commanders took no defensive precautions and they too were ambushed by the Mahdists. Very few Egyptian troops escaped and the Mahdists for the first time secured large stores of modern arms. More important, most of the tribes of the Western Sudan, the Fur, and the Beja joined Muhammad Ahmed. He declared a jihad against the Sudan's Egyptian rulers and his forces immediately laid seige to the towns of El Obeid and Bara.

The Mahdist success was due to more than Muhammad Ahmed's charismatic personality or the ineptitude of the Egyptian authorities. The various crises which led eventually to the British occupation engaged the attention as well of the Egyptian leaders. Even had there been good leader-ship in the Sudan, Arabi Pasha was not likely to send any significant reinforcements to the Sudan in 1882. The defeat of the Egyptian army at Tel-el-Kebir further reduced the ability of the Egyptians to crush the Mahdi. Nevertheless, the British advisers to the khedive gave their consent to sending another large army in pursuit of the Mahdi. A pickup army was formed and concentrated at Khartoum in the early months of 1883. Winston Churchill writing a few years later called this army "perhaps the worst army that has ever marched to war." General Hicks, a retired officer of the Indian Staff Corps, commanded this force of slightly over 7,000 men. Ostensibly they were to relieve El Obeid, but this city fell to the Mahdi before Hicks left Khartoum. However, Hicks' force still left for that area presumably to relieve pressure upon the governor of Darfur, Slatin Pasha, who was still resisting the Mahdists. Plagued by dissension, bad leadership, and poor knowledge of the terrain, Hicks' army met the Mahdist's forces on November 3, 1883. In a series of confrontations over the next two days the Egyptian army was almost completely destroyed. Only about 500 Egyptians escaped and Hicks and the European officers were killed.

The fate of the Sudan was sealed after this battle. Slatin surrendered in Darfur, the riverine tribes joined the Mahdi, and leaders of the eastern Sudan such as Osman Digna also joined. At this juncture the British advisers to the khedive, faced with the shambles of the Egyptian economy, persuaded Tewfik to abandon the Sudan. Prime Minister Gladstone's government refused to commit any more British troops than absolutely necessary to hold Suakin and the southern approach to Egypt. Two courses were open to the khedive. He could follow the stern advice of the British and evacuate the Sudan or he could attempt to reestablish government in the Sudan under a strong dynamic leader such as the slave entrepreneur Zubeir Pasha. The decision was made to withdraw all Egyptians from various garrisons still holding out. Most of them were concentrated in the capital city of Khartoum. The final decisions were made in London in January 1884. Gladstone, against his better judgment, bowed to public opinion and asked the popular hero, General Gordon, to return to the Sudan to effect the pullback of Egyptian forces. Only Wadi Halfa and Suakin were to be kept as military bases to check the further expansion of Mahdism. The instructions given Gordon in London remain something of a mystery, but it appears that the ministry was convinced that Gordon's objectives were clear and that he would carry them out.

On his arrival in Egypt, however, Gordon had developed a counter-proposal which he felt would continue Egyptian hegemony over some of the Sudan. This scheme involved the establishment of his old enemy, Zubeir Pasha, as a counterforce to the Mahdi in the Sudan. The British Foreign Office, appalled at the idea of using such a notorious slaver, refused and Gordon left for the Sudan. From Berber in February he sent gifts to the Mahdi, named him the king of Kordofan, and declared the government's intention of evacuating the Sudan. Arriving at Khartoum, Gordon effected a number of changes designed to placate the Sudanese such as reform of the taxing system and abolishment of the new laws relating to the slave trade. Finally he announced the separation of the Sudan from Egypt. He began to send officials, civilians, and sick soldiers down the river. However, the Mahdists, flushed with success, had no intention of accepting from Gordon favors which were theirs for the taking anyway. The active operations of the British and Egyptians in the eastern Sudan against Osman Digna seemed to cast doubt on Gordon's sincerity.

By the end of March 1884, Khartoum was heavily besieged by the Mahdists. Only steamers operating under hazardous conditions gave Gordon a link with the north. Even this link was severed when Berber fell to the Mahdists in May. The future of Khartoum became a foregone conclusion unless the British intervened. Muhammad Ahmed arrived at Khartoum with over 60,000 men in October. Gordon held on to Khartoum doggedly with approximately 7,000 troops, expecting that a relief column would be sent to relieve him as soon as his plight became known. However, the British government procrastinated during the summer and it was not until late August that the decision was made to rescue Gordon. The commander of the relief expedition, Sir Garnet Wolseley, spent almost two months preparing for the campaign and his main army did not leave Cairo until October. When it became apparent in December that the army would not reach Khartoum in time, a specially organized camel column raced ahead of the main body, cutting across the desert from Korti to Shendi. They fought two major battles with the Sudanese and arrived within sight of Khartoum on January 27, 1885, where they learned that the city had been stormed the day before and Gordon had been killed.

British public reaction to the death of Gordon, predictably, was bellicose. It is doubtful whether Prime Minister Gladstone could have long resisted public demands for revenge. However, the Russian occupation of Penjdeh in Afghanistan in March 1885, which resulted in a brief war scare in Britain, gave him an excuse for withdrawing Wolseley's troops from the Sudan. Nevertheless, the shame of Gordon's death going unrevenged rankled a growing imperialistic Britain. As the scramble for Africa increased in intensity it became only a matter of time before Britain in conjunction with Egypt attempted the reconquest of the Sudan.

The Mahdi, after establishing a new capital city at Omdurman across the Nile from Khartoum, began to consolidate his power. He called upon other Islamic rulers to recognize him as the Mahdi and join him in his jihad. However, he died less than six months after his forces had captured Khartoum. On his recommendation he was succeeded by Khalifa Abdullah. In the twelve years respite given him before direct European intervention, Abdullah wasted much of the potential of the Mahdist movement by internal purges and a series of conflicts with Ethiopia. This latter interest of the khalifa directed the full force of his armies away from Egypt and in the direction of Ethiopia. This gave the British time to rebuild the Egyptian army. The death of Johannes IV of Ethiopia in battle against the khalifa in 1889 was crucial to the developing expansion of Europe in Africa.

Ethiopia through the reign of Theodore

After the death of Yasu II in 1730 Ethiopia quickly drifted into a type of anarchy whose closest European analogy was Merovingian France. The great nobles of the state quarreled with one another and the leaders of the church used their considerable influence on one side and then on another. Emperors came to be figureheads controlled by kingmakers. Warfare between factions continued intermittently and the military literally "ate up the land." The emperors once more abandoned a stationary capital and moved with their courts and followers from one part of the kingdom to another. The glorious palaces at Gondar and Debra Tabor, like the stable dynasty they represented, began to fall apart. In this troubled period the Galla leaders assumed more power than ever before. There is considerable knowledge of a portion of this period because the explorer James Bruce visited Ethiopia in 1769 and much later wrote of the reign of Emperor Takla Haimanot II. The young emperor was controlled by Ras Michael Sehul, the strongest of the Ethiopian nobles. Ras Michael and the imperial armies were continually at war with competitive forces. Eventually in 1779 Takla Haimanot was killed and the central authority broke down completely.

The period between 1779 and 1855 has been called somewhat euphemistically "the era of judges." In actuality this was a time when the emperors had little power, the church declined, and the united kingdom was split into powerful substates. Shoa cut off from the northern provinces by the Wollo Galla obtained almost total independence under the rule of Sahale Selassie (1813–1847). In some of the provinces many of the rulers were either Galla or Muslims. By 1840 there were four main competitive states—Shoa, Gojjam, Tigre, and Begameder. A puppet emperor, Sahela Dengel, presided ineffectually and impotently over all these.

In the late 1830s a young leader with all the attributes of a tillak sew, a strong man, first made his appearance on the political scene. This was Ras Kassa who had originally been destined for the church. However, in one of the many skirmishes his monastery was burned and he was forced to take refuge with his uncle who was one of the emperor's officials. This was the period when Muhammad Ali, the Egyptian khedive, was seeking to expand his control over areas adjacent to the Nile Valley. Ras Kassa became a leader of irregular troops which made raids into the Sudan. His success in boldly raiding as far as Metemma gained him fame and many adherents. The widow of Emperor Johannes III, Manon, became fearful that such a popular powerful figure would upset the control her son, Ras Ali II, exerted over Begameder. However, Ras Kassa defeated her armies and forced a marriage with Tawabatch, the daughter of Ras Ali.

Ras Kassa briefly joined forces with Ras Ali and Ubye of Tigre to meet the further attacks of the Egyptians. After the British brought pressure upon Muhammad Ali to abandon his plans of conquering Ethiopia, Ras Kassa found that he had a parity of power with the other leaders of divided Ethiopia. He then compelled Ras Ali to recognize his authority

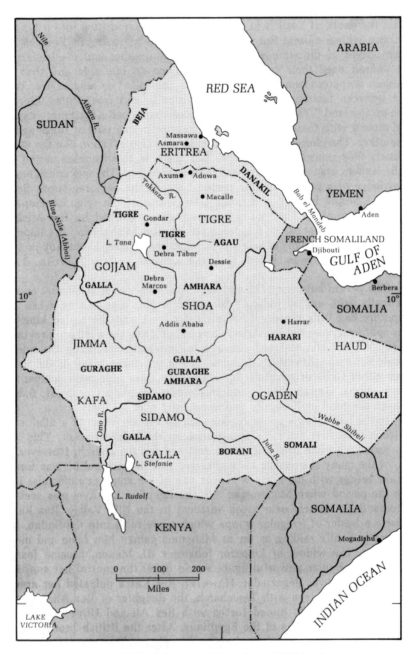

Political Divisions and Peoples of Ethiopia

over his uncle's lands, imprisoned Empress Manon, and established himself at Gondar. In the early 1850s Ras Kassa was in a position finally to attempt to dominate his competitors. He demanded that the ruler of Gojjam, Ras Goshu, submit to his overlordship. When this was refused, Kassa invaded Gojjam and in November 1852 defeated and killed the ras. Moving swiftly he forced Ras Ali from the throne in Begameder. In 1855 Ras Kassa's armies overran Tigre and Ubye was captured. Soon afterward Malakot, king of Shoa, was deposed and sent to a monastery. His son, the young Menelik, was kept as a hostage at Ras Kassa's court. Thus by the mid-1850s through military skill, cunning, and ferocity, Ras Kassa reimposed unity on Ethiopia after over a hundred years of disorder and schism.

The puppet Emperor Sahela Dengel was forced to abdicate even the shadow of authority which he had. Ras Kassa, although not of the Solomonic line, justified his seizure of power by referring to an ancient prophecy that a new ruler, blessed by God, would arise to deliver Ethiopia from its bondage. Kassa took the royal name Theodore which betrayed his sense of divine mission. He was the last ruler to be crowned at the old capital of Gondar even though he did not like the city. The city had been allowed to decay. Only the castle of Ras Michael Sehul and part of the palace of Fasilidas were in livable condition. Theodore preferred Debra Tabor and very early in his reign decided to build a new city which would reflect the glory of his rule.

European interest in northeastern Africa was just beginning to develop when Theodore came to power. The focal point of this interest was Egypt, the Sudan, and the Red Sea. Specific interest in and knowledge of Ethiopia were slow in developing. In 1843 two British travelers, Walter Plowden and John Bell, visited the highlands. Five years later they returned with Plowden as British consul. These two men became close friends of Theodore. They told him of the wonders of European technology and tried to obtain for the emperor some share of these wonders. He trusted them and they, together with his wife, helped to stabilize the brilliant but emotionally erratic ruler. In retrospect what the "mad" ruler of Ethiopia wanted does not seem unreasonable or much different from what the khedive Ismail of Egypt was planning. Theodore wanted a commercial treaty with Britain and more than anything else he wanted modern equipment of war and European instructors. With this equipment Ethiopia could take the offensive against the unbelievers and Theodore could give Britain, his ally, the friendship of a power which controlled all of northeastern Africa from the Nile to the Red Sea. Unfortunately the only section of the British government really concerned with events in Ethiopia was the India Office and they did not approve of any expansion by a powerful Ethiopia. It is doubtful whether anyone above the rank of a junior clerk in the Foreign Office paid any attention to Plowden's extremely detailed account of Ethiopia and the plans of its ruler.

Theodore, master of an Ethiopia he had welded together by force, believed with considerable justification that he was surrounded by enemies. He had taken steps to limit the power of local nobles and to centralize control of the government and the army. In his need for a larger state income, Theodore had undermined the privileged position of the landowning church. Always unstable, Theodore, further, felt isolated with no one he could trust. His first wife had died in 1859 and in the following year both Plowden and Bell were killed by bandits. Theodore became more cruel and erratic and began to harbor deep suspicions of European intentions. The French had established themselves at Oback in 1862 and in 1865 the khedive had negotiated the cession of Massawa to Egypt. From these bases the French and Egyptian consular agents were attempting to extend their authority into Ethiopia. Theodore expelled all Catholic missionaries from Ethiopia, believing them to be French agents, and began to spy upon the activities of all other missionaries.

Whether or not the British consul, Charles Duncan Cameron, who arrived in 1861, was the fool Lord Palmerston called him, he did nothing to calm Theodore's fears and the emperor began to dislike him intensely. In 1862 Theodore attempted to awaken British and French interest in cooperating with him in a projected war against Egypt. The government of Napoleon III avoided Theodore's plea for military assistance and instead reproached him for excluding Catholic missionaries from Ethiopia. From the British government he received no reply. Attributing this to Cameron's actions, he had the consul arrested and placed almost all Europeans under custody. When this information reached Britain the government dispatched two political officers, Hormuz Rassam and Dr. Henry Blanc, to Ethiopia to negotiate the release of the prisoners. The diplomats reached the imperial camp in January 1866. At first Theodore treated them well, although he was disappointed that they had not brought him artisans and gunsmiths. Very soon he arrested them both. In April he directed Rassam to write the British government asking formally for workmen and machinery to help him make guns.

Beginning in the early 1860s Theodore's attention turned more and more toward Magdala. This was a stone outcrop located approximately seventy miles west of modern-day Desse. It was an extremely defensible position and its one-mile-square flat top provided the necessary land for the emperor's followers. As he worked to strengthen his fortress and as his attention was diverted by the Egyptians and the perfidy of Europeans, his kingdom began to fall apart. In 1865 Menelik escaped from Magdala and soon Shoa's loyalty to Theodore was negligible. In 1866 Theodore was forced to take the field against rebels in Gondar. As punishment the churches of the city were plundered of their art treasures, the inhabitants were driven out, and the city was set on fire.

In the autumn of 1867 the British government finally took notice of Theodore. Parliament appropriated two million pounds to support an invasion force to release the prisoners. Sir Robert Napier in command of 62,000 men of the Bombay army landed in Ethiopia in December. Napier marched inland across the Danakil plains and up the escarpment arriving before Magdala with 4,000 effectives in early April 1868. On his march he met no resistance. Kassai, the future Johannes IV, ruler of Tigre, met with

Napier and agreed not to oppose the invasion. Gojjam and Shoa rose against the emperor. At Magdala hundreds of Theodore's troops deserted him. Accepting the inevitable with his typical dual attitude toward reality, Theodore dismissed his European prisoners after massacring hundreds of Ethiopians who were also captives. On April 13 the final British assault began. The gates were easily forced and Magdala was taken, with the British suffering only fifteen wounded. Theodore committed suicide before his fortress fell.

With Theodore's death Ethiopia reverted to the same divided condition as before his imposed unification. General Napier had accomplished his mission and did not mean to become involved in the morass of trying to reestablish order. He installed the queen of the local Gallas as ruler of Magdala, blew up the fortress, and retreated to the coast where the last British troops were evacuated before mid-June 1868. Ethiopia in the 1870s was thus left to two strong competitors for power—Kassai of Tigre and Menelik of Shoa. Kassai had by 1872 negated his major foes in the northern provinces and was crowned as Johannes IV. Shoa became, in theory, a part of a united empire. In fact Menelik, like a medieval European feudal vassal, obeyed the emperor only when it was to his distinct advantage to do so. Ultimately more important to Ethiopia than this rivalry during the reign of Johannes IV was the loss of Ethiopian isolation. Egyptian imperialism, the Mahdist revolt in the Sudan, and the establishment of European bases on the Red Sea coast threatened the independence of the state. Ethiopia thus became enmeshed in the complicated politics of the scramble for Africa.

Ethiopia and the scramble to 1945

Johannes IV was too occupied with consolidating his power in the north and meeting the threat of Egyptian invasions to bring Menelik under control in the decade following his coronation. Finally in 1882 on the eve of the Mahdist uprising in the Sudan, Johannes reached an agreement with Menelik which recognized the local autonomy of Shoa in exchange for Menelik's promise to support the emperor. In return Johannes recognized Menelik as the heir apparent to the Ethiopian throne. To seal the bargain Ras Area Selassie, Johannes' son, was married to Menelik's daughter, Zauditu. The eventual path to the throne seemed clear for Menelik, particularly after the death of Ras Area in 1885.

The reign of Johannes was marked by the growing intrusion of foreign influence in Ethiopia. The kingdom was subjected to increasing pressure from three different but closely interconnected sources—Egypt, Europeans along the Red Sea, and the Mahdists in the Sudan. Khedive Ismail, as a part of his dream of a greater southern empire, attempted for fifteen years to expand into Ethiopia. In 1866 he purchased the port of Massawa from his suzerain, the Ottoman emperor. Four years later, by the same process, he acquired the Somali coastline between the ports of Bulhar and Berbera. An even more aggressive Egyptian policy began in 1874 when Rauf Pasha's troops occupied Harar. In the following year Egyptian forces under Werner

Münzinger Bey attacked and occupied Bogos province and its capital
Keren. By then Johannes had gained sufficient control over Ethiopia to
thwart further Egyptian advances. In 1875 Münzinger's forces were routed
at Awassa. In the following year a much larger Egyptian army was cut to
pieces at Gura. These victories halted Egypt's immediate plans of conquest.
Internal problems in Egypt and the development of the rebellion in the
Sudan finally ended Egypt's threat. However, Egyptian forces continued
to hold Bogos, Harar, and Massawa.

Muhammad Ahmed's success against the Egyptians in the Sudan
which culminated in the taking of Khartoum and the death of General
Gordon had profound effects upon Ethiopia. Western Begameder and
Gojjam, abutting upon the Sudan, were areas of increasing conflict with
the Mahdi's successor, Khalifa Abdullah. In the crucial five-year period
after 1884 Johannes' attention was diverted from Italian activities along the
Red Sea coast by the operations of the khalifa's armies. In 1889 Johannes
gathered a large army to counter the Mahdist forces which had penetrated
Ethiopia as far as Gondar. Menelik did not contribute to the emperor's
army. At Metemma the Ethiopians won a decisive victory but a Sudanese
sniper mortally wounded Johannes. Before his death he summoned Ras
Aloula and other powerful nobles and proclaimed that Ras Mangasha,
ostensibly his nephew, was in reality his natural son. Johannes asked that
they recognize his son as the next emperor. Although no agreement had
been reached or oath sworn to Ras Mangasha before Johannes' death, it
was obvious that the emperor had repudiated the 1882 agreement with
Menelik.

The struggle for supreme power between the king of Shoa and Ras
Mangasha came at a crucial period in the attempted consolidation of
European control over the Red Sea coast and its immediate hinterland. The
French had been the first European power to acquire territory there when
they purchased the small port of Obock in 1862. They planned to use it as
a coaling station for their ships en route to their newly opened possessions
in Indochina. Later they moved their main base to Djibouti. The opening
of the Suez Canal in 1869 increased the importance of Obock and the
British station at Aden. In the same year the Italian firm, the *Societa di
Navigazione Rubbattino,* leased the port of Assab in an attempt to increase
Italy's share of the Red Sea trade. In 1882 the Italian government purchased the port from the company. This was the modest beginning for the
later Italian ventures in Ethiopia. For almost fifteen years after this action
Ethiopia became the focal point of Italian activities during the scramble.

The failure of Egypt to meet its debts brought about a major crisis
there in the late 1870s and finally the forcible British occupation in 1882.
The British consul, Sir Evelyn Baring, subsequently became the actual
fulcrum of power in Egypt. Confronted with a bankrupt government which
had greatly overextended itself, he sought to reduce all unnecessary
expenses. The increase in the Mahdi's power in the Sudan was a closely
related problem. Britain's solution to the unnecessary expense of the
Egyptian empire was to force the new khedive, Tewfik, to abandon any

plans for further expansion. In pursuance of this policy Gordon was sent to evacuate the Egyptian garrisons from the Sudan. At the same time Egypt decided to abandon its enclaves in Ethiopia. In May 1884, Britain sent Admiral Sir William Hewett as head of a mission to inform Johannes that Egypt was withdrawing its forces from Keren, Massawa, and Harar. An agreement between the emperor and Hewett formalized Ethiopia's right to use Massawa. In return for this open invitation to reoccupy these former Ethiopian areas Johannes promised to take the field against the Mahdi with a great army.

British foreign policy in regard to northeastern Africa in the decade following Hewett's mission was not simple. The essence of that policy was to assure that no unfriendly power could gain control of the Upper Nile or the Red Sea. Since Britain did not wish to assume the financial burdens of reconstituting the old Egyptian empire, its policy had to be directed toward allowing other states to provide the necessary stability. The obvious inheritor of this role was Ethiopia. However, its history of political instability and factionalism seemed to make it a poor choice to defend British interests. Most qualified observers expected Ethiopia to be continually wracked by civil war and then eventually become easy prey for some expansive European state. France then committed everywhere in Africa to a militant imperialism was the greatest threat to Britain's aims in northeastern Africa. If Ethiopia fell into chaos France would certainly gain strategic territory. To block this, Britain began to support Italy's claims to larger areas of the Red Sea hinterland adjacent to Ethiopia. By encouraging Italian ambitions while maintaining friendly relations with the emperor, Britain hoped to achieve the kind of stability necessary for the maintenance of her interests, whatever developed.

In February 1885, an Italian expedition led by Admiral Caimi occupied the port of Massawa. This action denied Ethiopia the use of the port and therefore was a violation of the agreement made by Admiral Hewett. Nevertheless, Britain openly supported the Italian move. The Italians after consolidating their position at Massawa, took advantage of Johannes' growing preoccupation with the Mahdists on his western frontier. Italian forces occupied Saati, a village on a major caravan route located a few miles inland. Saati was important primarily for its wells. Johannes protested this action as he had earlier the occupation of Massawa. He had never agreed in any manner to the cession of land to any foreign power. The first setback to Italian plans and a portent of future actions occurred in January 1887, when a 460 man column of Italian military on their way to Saati were intercepted by the most powerful Ethiopian chief in northern Tigre, Ras Aloula. Less than a dozen of the reinforcements survived the so-called battle of Dogali. Ras Aloula with over 16,000 men at his command, many armed with the latest rifles, was restrained from further advances toward Massawa only by the direct order of the emperor.

Italian pride, wounded by the massacre, called for revenge and in the months following Dogali they began to build up their forces at Massawa. This threatening situation called forth British efforts to mediate. Sir Gerald

Portal was sent to Ethiopia late in 1887 to visit Johannes with proposals which, if accepted, would end the possibility of war and give Italy a demarcated bloc of territory in the Massawa hinterland. Portal's party was halted by Ras Aloula at Asmara. Johannes refused Aloula's request that he be allowed to kill the British visitors. Portal finally met the emperor on December 6 and proposed that Saati and Keren be ceded to Italy and that Johannes recognize an Italian protectorate over territory one-day's-march inland from Massawa. In return Portal promised continuing British and Italian friendship. Johannes' reply was succinct. He would not give the Italians "an inch of land."

After the failure of Sir Gerald Portal's mission the British restrained the Italians and there were no further confrontations during Johannes' reign. However, after Johannes' death the Italians took advantage of the disorders within Ethiopia to occupy Keren. In 1890 they officially proclaimed the colony of Eritrea. Although the extent of the colony was not definitely stated, it marked a further step toward isolating Ethiopia. In the previous year the Italians had, they believed, gained the support of Menelik of Shoa who had just proclaimed himself emperor. In May 1889, in return for a gift of twenty-eight cannons and 38,000 rifles, Menelik signed the Treaty of Uccialli. Menelik had recognized the Italians' occupation of Massawa and by implication also their ambitions in the interior. The Italian foreign minister Crispi chose to interpret Article Seventeen of the treaty as giving Italy a protectorate over Ethiopia. There were two versions of the treaty, one rendered in Amharic and the other in Italian. The Italian version stated that Ethiopian foreign policy "shall" be conducted through the Italian government. The Amharic text, however, stated that the emperor "might" avail himself of the services of Italy. Despite their knowledge of Menelik and Ethiopia, the Italians in the early 1890s, using the treaty as an excuse, attempted to convert the theory of a protectorate into a reality.

With a greater power base in Shoa and the central areas, Menelik disregarded the deathbed wish of Johannes to be succeeded by Ras Mangasha and was proclaimed emperor in spite of the opposition of the majority of the nobles of Tigre. Although contacts continued between Menelik and Mangasha, the northern areas acted as if they were independent of the emperor. The Italians led Mangasha to believe that they supported him while at the the same time they continued their ostensibly good relations with the emperor. In the early period of Menelik's reign the centrum of the state shifted southward and Shoan affairs overshadowed those of Tigre. This shift was exemplified by Menelik's establishment of his capital at the old town of Entoto newly renamed Addis Ababa.

Italian troops took up the responsibility of campaigning against the Sudanese in the north. In 1893 they defeated the Mahdists and occupied Agordot; and in the following year the new commander, General Baratieri, took Kassala in the Sudan. They also pushed their occupation southward toward Axum as far as the Mareb River. From this point Baratieri began his disastrous forward policy against Tigre. This decision in 1894 was caused primarily by a series of uprisings against Italian authority in Eritrea.

Captured letters written by the leader of one major revolt, Batha Agos, revealed him to be in close contact with Mangasha. The Italians then determined to end the Tigrean threat to their supremacy and authorized the occupation of Tigre. They had received tacit British approval for this action by an agreement in 1891 which designated the bulk of Ethiopia an Italian sphere of influence. Communications with many powerful Ethiopian leaders such as Ras Michael of Wollo and Ras Makonnen of Harar led the Italian command to believe that they would gain the active support for their occupation from many Ethiopian leaders. Thus in the spring of 1895, Baratieri's forces established themselves at Adigrat in Tigre. Later that year they took Macalle and the strategic pass of Alagi. However, the force of 2,000 men detailed to hold this pass was inadequate given the strategic importance of Alagi which barred the main route into Tigre from the south.

Menelik had meanwhile, in 1893, repudiated the Treaty of Uccialli and had settled most of his differences with Ras Mangasha, and the ruler of Tigre had agreed to recognize him as emperor. Thus the disunity which the Italians had hoped for in 1895 was more apparent than real. Menelik and his lieutenants throughout the rest of the year were busy with their preparations to drive the Italians from Tigre. Ras Makonnen's troops from Harar were the first to arrive in the contested area and on December 7 they cleared the Italians from Alagi Pass. Italian Askari casualties were over 1,300 of the 2,000 man force. Makonnen's army then joined with other units from the south and Mangasha's forces to besiege Macalle. After a forty-five day siege the Italian garrison surrendered. They were escorted northward by a large segment of Makonnen's army which also screened the slow parallel movement of Menelik's main force.

Baratieri had gathered all his forces in Tigre and the reinforcements from Massawa at the town of Sawria, sixteen miles northeast of Adowa. Had the general understood the organization of Ethiopian armies he could have won the campaign by avoiding battle. Menelik's army was literally eating up the countryside. With time and this lack of supply, the divisive pressures within the Ethiopian army would have forced a retreat. Baratieri, however, pressured from Rome for a quick victory and having little respect for the Ethiopian army, decided to risk a battle. Baratieri's intelligence service was poor and he had no good maps of the area. He believed the Ethiopian army to number approximately 40,000. Since he had almost 18,000 men of whom 10,500 were European and his army possessed superior weapons, it was not unnatural to believe in the positive outcome of the campaign. On February 29, 1896, Baratieri's army, divided into three brigades, moved southward. On the morning of the next day it was discovered that one brigade was separated from the main body by four miles. Before the error could be adjusted, the Ethiopian army of over 100,000 began the battle of Adowa. By the end of the day Baratieri's army was destroyed. Italian losses were over 6,000 dead and 2,000 wounded while their Askari troops had lost over 4,000 dead. The stragglers retreated northward with their general toward Massawa. The Italians had lost more men in a single day than in all the wars of unification (risorgimento) and Europeans had suffered their greatest defeat at the hands of Africans. The

Ethiopians could sing in triumph. "The Corn of Italy, that was sown in Tigre, has been reaped by Abba Dagno [Menelik's horse] and he has given it to the birds."

Why did Menelik not drive the Italians from their coastal possessions after Adowa? Although no final answer can be given, there were a number of factors which contributed to his decision not to pursue the defeated Baratieri. The state of his own army was such that he could probably not have held it together very long. To the already mentioned problems of supply and dissension had to be added the very heavy losses sustained by the Ethiopians at Adowa. Menelik, always sagacious, probably realized that new Italian troops could be sent to defend Massawa and that in all probability Britain would have intervened on behalf of Italy. Finally, Menelik was at that time more concerned with expanding his influence over the areas immediately adjacent to Shoa. Thus he was magnanimous in the Treaty of Addis Adaba which ended the war. It repealed the Treaty of Uccialli but confirmed the Italians in possession of Eritrea. This included the area up to the Mareb River which the Italians had occupied at the beginning of the campaign. The new Italian foreign minister, Rudini, who had replaced Crispi after Adowa, recognized Ethiopia as an independent, sovereign state.

In the years immediately following Adowa, Menelik's armies brought under control the western areas of Wollega. The king of Kaffa was conquered and Ethiopian authority extended south and southeast toward Lake Rudolf and in the Sidamo Borana area bordering upon Kenya. In the north the death of Takla Haimanot, ruler of Gojjam until 1901, brought that troublesome area firmly under imperial control. Ras Mangasha continued to rule unimpeded in Tigre until he became involved in a small conflict with Menelik's favorite, Ras Makonnen, in 1899. Mangasha was defeated and forced to appear before Menelik with a stone upon his head as a token of submission in order to have the emperor spare his life. By 1901 Menelik had filled out of the borders of Ethiopia by conquering large numbers of non-Amharic, non-Christian people. In a series of agreements from 1897 to 1908 he made treaties with European powers in which they recognized the new, fixed, expanded boundaries of Ethiopia. Only the border of Italian Somaliland remained undelineated, a fact which gave rise to the incident that began the new war with Italy in 1935.

Before the emperor became incapacitated in 1906, he successfully played off the European powers against one another. He tended to favor the French who had received the right to build a railroad from Djibouti to Addis Ababa. The French *Compagnie Franco-Africaine* brought to Addis Ababa electricity, the telegraph, and telephone. Menelik's capital, sheltered by newly introduced eucalyptus trees, was an outpost of modernity in an otherwise conservative, highly formalized, Ethiopian state. Menelik for all his success had managed to create only a veneer of a modern nation state. When Menelik, the tillak sew, could no longer function adequately the old schisms rose and again threatened the destruction of Ethiopia.

The Emperor Menelik suffered his first cerebral hemorrhage in early 1906 and the next year his most trusted lieutenant, Ras Makonnen of Harar, died. The seven-year interval between Menelik's stroke and his death was a period when the various factions in Ethiopia maneuvered for power. This factionalism, so typical of Ethiopia, was not halted by Menelik's creation of a council of ministers in 1907 to aid him in governing. In June 1908, he proclaimed before a meeting of the great nobles of Ethiopia that his successor would be his grandson, Lij Iyasu. Later that year another stroke completely immobilized the emperor. However, he formalized the recognition of Lij Iyasu under the regency of Ras Tamara. With the emperor unable to act, the Empress T'aitu tried to maintain the centralized state by attempting to gain power herself at the expense of the powerful feudal nobles. Bribery and corruption increased alarmingly. By 1911 the major factions in the country were those who supported the empress and the traditional church, and those who supported Lij Iyasu and his powerful father, Ras Michael of Wollo. Ras Michael supplanted Ras Tamara as regent in 1911. The young emperor-designate had shown a decided preference for Islam and many of his most ardent supporters were Muslim.

In 1906 British, French, and Italian representatives, concerned over a return to anarchy in Ethiopia which might threaten their separate interests, concluded the Tripartite Treaty. This divided Ethiopia into spheres of influence and each European power agreed to protect the spheres of the other parties. If a given situation in the future necessitated a military expedition this would be undertaken jointly. Britain's sphere included the area around Lake Tana and the headwaters of the Blue Nile. Italy's area was the largest and was described by an arc stretching from Eritrea to Somaliland. The westward limits of the arc were beyond Addis Ababa. The French sphere was over the area traversed by the railway from Addis Ababa to Djibouti. It is perhaps fortunate for Ethiopia that the collapse of central authority in Ethiopia coincided with the coming of World War I. The major energies of the contracting powers were thus diverted elsewhere and no serious attempt was made to put into effect the Tripartite Treaty. However, France and Britain had agreed officially to Italy's premier position in Ethiopia. One Italian official in 1932 could, therefore, state that the Tripartite Treaty was Italy's "Magna Charta" in Ethiopia.

Lij Iyasu was not a strong man (tillak sew) who could force his will upon all factions in Ethiopia. His sympathy for Islam and his association with German and Turkish interests during the early stages of World War I also undercut his authority. The Allied powers welcomed the coalition against Lij Iyasu formed mainly by the church and Shoan nobles. The emperor's fortunes dipped low in 1916 and he abandoned the capital for the city of Jijiga in eastern Harar where he attempted to gain more Muslim supporters for his cause. The Shoan nobility took Addis Ababa in September and proclaimed Zauditu, Menelik's daughter, as empress. They declared the twenty-five year old governor of Harar, Ras Tafari, the son of Ras Makonnen, as heir presumptive. Zauditu was crowned in February 1917. However, Tafari, because of his youth and his progressive views, was not included in the triumvirate which ruled Ethiopia. This included the empress, Ras Wolde Giorgis, the negus (highest rank below emperor), and Habta Giorgis, the Minister of War. Lij Iyasu's forces continued an intermittent war against Zauditu which was only ended with his capture in 1921. He was confined in Harar until his death in 1935.

In the decade following World War I, Ras Tafari slowly built up his power base in Harar and also at the court in Addis Ababa. He emerged as a tillak sew who had the loyalty of a large segment of the army. Some of his more conservative opponents died and he was able to replace others with men loyal to him. The empress and her major advisers, Ras Kassa of Tigre and Dejazmach Balcha of Sidamo, were finally negated after the failure of an abortive palace coup in 1928. The last active violent opposition to Tafari was in 1929 when his forces surrounded those of the major rebels and compelled their surrender. Secure finally as the most powerful man in Ethiopia, he had been crowned negus in 1928, and on the death of Zauditu in 1930 he was proclaimed Emperor Haile Selassie I.

Long before he was crowned, Ras Tafari had attempted to associate Ethiopia more closely with other states. He had visited Europe in 1925 and brought back Theodore's crown from Britain which had been taken by General Napier in 1867. He was the leader in the abortive move to join the League of Nations in 1919. However, the practice of slavery in Ethiopia blocked this attempt. Four years later Zanditu under pressure proclaimed the death penalty for trading in slaves and in the same year Ethiopia was admitted to the League. Italy supported Ethiopia's request; only Britain had reservations about the weak central institutions of Ethiopia. In 1925 Britain sought to revive the Tripartite Treaty by securing Italy's support for a plan to build a dam on the Blue Nile below Lake Tana. Ras Tafari, immediately upon being appraised of this scheme, protested to the League of Nations. Italy and Britain did not attempt to defend their actions, and finally, in 1928, he concluded a twenty-year Treaty of Friendship with Italy.

Haile Selassie's role in Ethiopia after his coronation was that of the strong man who supported reforms considered by many of the nobles as extremely radical. An analysis of the reforms instigated by the emperor since 1930 shows that measured by Western standards he remained an autocrat. However, it was the emperor who promulgated the Constitution of 1931 against the desires of the majority of the ruling classes. This was duplicated again in 1955 by Haile Selassie's sponsorship of a much more liberal instrument of government. It was the emperor who encouraged the reorganization of government agencies according to Western patterns, sent students overseas for education, and brought in European technical, government, and military advisers. Even had the emperor been more radical, the modernization of Ethiopia's government would have been delayed for years by the Italian invasion and the disorders attendant upon the campaigns of World War II.

The European situation in 1934 was such that Mussolini's government believed the time had finally come to bring Ethiopia completely under Italian control. The rise of Hitler, the quiescence and pacifism of France, Britain, and the United States, and the weakness of the League of Nations made Mussolini believe that no major power would intervene on behalf of Ethiopia. Colonel Vittorio Ruggero, the Italian consul at Addis Ababa, was ordered in early 1934 to begin a program of political subversion in Ethiopia. In February the Undersecretary of War was instructed to begin plans for the quick subjection of Ethiopia. Despite this decision to exploit latent border problems with Ethiopia to bring on the war, Italy reaffirmed the 1928 Treaty of Friendship. Mussolini found his reason for war two months later in the Wal Wal incident.

Wal Wal was the site of wells used by Ethiopians and Somali tribesmen in the sparsely populated desert area of eastern Ogaden province. Although the border with Italian Somaliland had never been clearly defined in this area, Wal Wal was well within Ethiopian territory. But in 1930 the Italians established themselves there and built fortifications. They assumed that since no official protests had been lodged their position was recognized by Ethiopia. In 1934 a joint British-Ethiopian commission was formed to survey the Ogaden since the emperor had been considering ceding part of it to Britain in return for territorial concession elsewhere. In November the commission arrived at Wal Wal, but withdrew after the Italians had made clear they considered Wal Wal to be Italian. However, the commission's Ethiopian military escort of approximately 400 men under Fitaurari Shiferra remained behind. Later reinforcements brought the number of Ethiopian troops to approximately 550 men. The Italian garrison at Wal Wal numbered approximately 430 men. The two sides faced each other without particular incident until the afternoon of December 5 when firing commenced. When the battle was over the Ethiopians had lost 107 dead and forty-five wounded while the losses of native troops under Italian command were approximately thirty dead and one hundred wounded.

The Italian government immediately demanded redress. Ethiopia on December 9, 1934, invoked the clause in the 1928 agreement which called for arbitration of disputes between the powers. Italy ignored this and demanded formal recognition of their right to Wal Wal, the payment of 200,000 Maria Theresa dollars, and the surrender of the Ethiopian commander. Britain and France both suggested to the emperor that he accept Italy's demands, but Haile Selassie refused. On December 14, Italy rejected the arbitration clause of the treaty whereupon the emperor brought the matter before the League of Nations. On December 20, Mussolini drew up a directive which ordered the Italian military to be prepared to move at least 100,000 metropolitan soldiers and sufficient numbers of allied native troops into Ethiopia not later than October 1935.

The discussions on the Ethiopian crisis in the League were conducted against the background of worsening conditions in Europe. France, concerned primarily with the German question, did not wish to alienate the Italians. The United States wanted nothing to do with problems beyond its borders and reflected this by the passage of the Neutrality Act in August 1935. Only Britain of all the great powers seemed to be committed to opposing Italy. In June 1935, Britain offered the League a compromise solution which would have given a large part of the Ogaden and the

British port of Zeila to Italy. In August a three-power conference promised Italy what amounted to a full economic protectorate over Ethiopia. Mussolini rejected both offers, and it is doubtful whether Haile Selassie would have accepted either alternative. Later in August a League committee of five recommended much the same solution as had the three power conference. This, too, was rejected by Mussolini. His war plans were by then almost complete. The modern warriors of a revived Italy would avenge the shame and defeat suffered by the Italian army at Adowa in 1896.

Haile Selassie ordered mobilization of Ethiopian forces on September 29, 1935. This was followed on October 2 by Italian mobilization. The next day the Italian army under the command of the high commissioner for Eritrea and Somaliland. Emilo De Bono, crossed the Mareb River and the Ethiopian War began. Nine Italian divisions with the latest in modern equipment, first under De Bono and later under Marshal Pietro Badoglio, operated on the northern front. General Rudolpho Graziani invaded the south with an additional division. Despite the previous Italian planning and the Ethiopians' poor equipment, the campaign did not add to the repute of the Italian army. De Bono was replaced on November 28 because of the slowness of his advance. His successor, Marshal Badoglio, utilizing more energetic tactics and freely using poison gas, advanced more quickly. Between January and March 1936, the Ethiopian armies were shattered. On May 2 the emperor left Djibouti on a British ship. Three days later the Italians entered Addis Ababa and the main campaign ended.

In adding Ethiopia as a new colony to the Italian empire, Italy had broken the Tripartite Treaty of 1906, the Gas Protocol of 1925, the Italo-Ethiopian Treaty of 1928, the Pact of Paris of 1928, and openly flaunted the League of Nations. It would seem that this list of accomplishments would have brought some measure of assistance for Ethiopia from other states. The League immediately after the war began declared Italy an aggressor and, in November 1935, voted sanctions against it. However, only Britain seemed prepared to enforce sanctions and this position was later modified by the Hoare-Laval agreement of early December. This plan, evolved by the British Foreign Secretary and the French Premier, proposed an exchange of territory which would have given to Italy northern Tigre, most of the Danakil, and Ogaden. After Laval disclosed the details of this agreement to the press it was obvious that no major power would aid Ethiopia and the oil sanctions imposed by the League against Italy became a dead issue. It is ironic that despite this appeasement on the part of all the democracies, Italy decided in 1936 to cast its lot with Germany, and Laval's grand scheme for an Italo-French front against Hitler collapsed. A further example of the comic-opera nature of the latter years of the League was the fact that Ethiopia continued to be a member of the organization which had proved so impotent in defending Ethiopian territory against Italian ambitions.

In June 1936, a new constitution was issued by Italy which joined Ethiopia to the other Italian territories in northeastern Africa. Italy's African empire was then divided into six provinces. The new viceroy,

General Graziani, instituted policies aimed at continuing the animosities between different tribes in Ethiopia. Many of the Galla and Somali people had supported the Italians during the war and they were favored by the Graziani regime. However, the Ethiopian unity forged by the war continued during the occupation and active resistance was endemic throughout the country. After an attempt to assassinate Graziani in February 1937, there were reprisals against the younger, educated Ethiopians. These harsh policies were, in a sense, repudiated when Graziani was replaced as viceroy by the Duke of Aosta.

By 1938 Italy had decided upon a conciliatory policy toward Ethiopia. This was evidenced by its generous allocation of funds for public works projects. Many Italian farmers were also sent there as colonists to attempt to increase the export potential of the territory. During its short occupation, Italy expended great sums and continuous effort to modernize their new imperial appendage. New roads, telegraph lines, hospitals, clinics, and agricultural stations became the positive heritage of the Italian occupation.

Italy's entry into World War II against the Allies in June 1940 was followed initially by success in northeastern Africa. British Somaliland was early overrun by the Italians. British leaders in the Middle East, however, could not afford to allow a large Italian force to remain in a position to threaten Egypt and the Red Sea route. Haile Selassie joined the British at Khartoum and, in January 1941, two British divisions invaded Ethiopia and were so successful that the major portion of the campaign was over in six months. The Duke of Aosta finally surrendered on May 18, 1941, at Amba Alage. This short campaign resulted in the destruction or surrender of the greater part of the 220,000 man Italian force in Ethiopia. In Gondar the last Italian force surrendered to the British and Ethiopians in January 1942. The emperor had reentered Addis Ababa on May 5, 1941, five years to the day after the city had fallen to the Italians, and began immediately to restore his authority throughout the kingdom. British military and civil personnel on all levels cooperated with him and his government. These ad hoc wartime arrangements were regularized by a convention between the two countries on January 31, 1942. The terminology of the convention and the attitude of Britain indicated clearly that she supported Ethiopian independence. A further agreement between the powers in December 1944 placed Britain and Ethiopia on a level of complete equality.

Eritrea was administered by Britain after its conquest in 1941 and continued even after the territory was placed under the general supervision of the United Nations. In 1952 Britain and the United Nations agreed to the federal incorporation of Eritrea into the Ethiopian state. This gave Ethiopia direct access to the Red Sea and the excellent port at Massawa, which Italy had in the course of sixty years converted into a Westernized city. Their expenditures upon roads, wharves, and general agricultural and training facilities had made Eritrea far more prosperous, and from a Western point of view, more advanced than Ethiopia. The Eritrean population, early influenced by Islam and then later by contact with the Italians, are an alien people within the state. Eritrean social, political, and cultural values are far different from those of the dominant Amhara and since 1952 this increasingly became the centrum of discontent against the rule of the emperor.

FIVE
The scramble for Africa

Introduction

Direct European involvement in Africa had been minimal during the first three-quarters of the nineteenth century. As detailed elsewhere, Britain, France, and Portugal were the only European states which could have followed a policy of territorial expansion in this period. The rest were either too small, too divided, or concerned primarily with imperial ambitions on the European continent. Portugal was politically moribund and its economy was such that it could have supported large scale military campaigns or the staff necessary to rule a vast territory only with great difficulty. Its coastal possessions from Benguela to Luanda in Angola and near the mouth of the Zambesi River in East Africa suffered from lack of money and enterprise. France in this period was rent by civil dissension. The Bourbon restoration in 1815 had been followed by the revolution of 1830 which brought the Orleanist king Louis Philippe to power. He was unseated by a revolution in 1848 and the short-lived Second Republic gave way to the era of Napoleon III whose ambition except for his brief venture in Mexico was to make France dominant in Europe. The ill-timed war with Prussia destroyed his regime. The pent-up fury of the liberal and working classes then led to the fractricidal Commune of 1871. With such a stormy domestic history it is not surprising that France did not actively seek an overseas empire. Only Britain could have easily carried out territorial expansion during this period. However, both conservative and liberal governments rejected such costly ventures. During the first seventy-five years of the nineteenth century Britain was actively imperialistic, but in an economic not a territorial sense. Possession of African land would not have increased the wealth of Britain. On the contrary, it would have subtracted from the total wealth of the nation.

Why, then, did European states change their attitudes

toward acquiring African empires in the period after 1875? The answers to this question are complex and can, in most cases, be examined best by observing the events in individual territories. However, it is necessary to understand some general principles which tended to determine the timing, direction, and degree of European imperialism in the various sections of Africa. First, the reasons for the change of attitude toward Africa were primarily concerned with Europe and not Africa. For European statesmen the focus of power was still Europe. Therefore the reasons for the scramble for Africa must be sought in Europe.

Undoubtedly the most important cause for acquisition of African territory was economic. Prior to the scramble most European governments could see little economic advantage to be gained in Africa, particularly since its greatest export, slaves, had been curtailed. The British, economically dominant throughout the world, had very little money invested in the continent. The argument of the Manchester school was that if any of these areas wished to trade with Europe they would buy primarily British goods and would sell their exports to Britain. The dominant theory of economics in Europe particularly after mid-century was that of free trade. However, by the 1870s the opposing theories of men such as List of Austria were being accepted by many French and German businessmen and traders. Briefly stated, List called for national self-sufficiency. By extension this meant protective tariffs and a return to a mercantilistic empire which would provide for the mother country a steady source of raw material and presumably also guaranteed overseas markets.

French statesmen such as Jules Ferry were among the first to accept the imperatives of the new protectionism. Still fresh from the disastrous defeat in the Franco-Prussian War, they were concerned for the long-term future of France. They came to believe that France would continue as a great power only by acquiring a new empire. At approximately the same time Leopold II, of the small, relatively new state of Belgium, came to similar conclusions concerning his kingdom. He was willing to gamble on the future wealth of the territories of the Congo basin so recently explored by Stanley. In Germany in the early 1880s some businessmen and traders accepted List's conclusions. Many patriotic Germans viewing the economic dominance of Britain came to the erroneous conclusion that its prosperity depended upon the possession of a large territorial empire. For some German imperialists the solution to Germany's problems was simply to acquire an empire.

These more generalized and theoretical approaches to the economic advantages which could be gained from an African empire were reinforced by the experience of a few entrepreneurs actively engaged in trade with Africa. European firms anxious to secure more access to inland markets were active in pressing their governments for more direct support. In the Senegambia, the Gold Coast, and along the Niger coast the merchants had maintained the European presence throughout the early part of the century with little official encouragement from their governments. In the last quarter of the century they added their support to the expansionists. In Egypt, a territory crucial for the scramble, European investors created the conditions which led to the British occupation. In other instances business leaders, impatient for their governments to adopt more forward policies, agreed to their companies assuming government functions. Such was the case in the revival by Britain of the chartered company. Goldie's Royal Niger Company, MacKinnon's East Africa Company, and Rhodes' South African Company were designed as much to hold African territories for Britain as to make a profit.

There are many other factors which acted to create a favorable atmosphere for the "new imperialism." One was the acquisition of more knowledge of the African continent and the inevitable romanticizing of this Dark Continent whenever the explorers wrote of their adventures. West Africa was the first area to be considered by the geographic societies of Europe and particularly by the British African Association. During the thirty-five year period between Mungo Park's first expedition and Richard Lander's discovery of the mouth of the Niger, intrepid adventurers had cleared away much of the ignorance and myth concerning West Africa. This urge to explore was transferred to Central and East Africa in the 1850s with the same results. Livingstone, Burton, Speke, Stanley, and many others suffered terrible hardships to provide for their European audiences data concerning the human and physical geography of the continent. While there was much territory yet to be explored, the main outlines of Central and East Africa had been exposed by 1880.

Most of the explorers were British or were in the employ of a British agency. They therefore reflected the predominant feelings of Evangelicalism and the self-assurance that European culture, particularly British, was best. The European observer was appalled at many aspects of African societies. Human sacrifice, killing of twins, and various religious practices convinced Europeans that what portions of Africa required was the firm, just control of a Western state. The cruel and dehumanizing slave trade was recorded by every traveler whether in West or in East Africa. So deeply ingrained in African society were these practices that individual Europeans felt powerless to end this evil and they, therefore, called for more direct action from their governments. In West Africa this greater involvement took the form of the West African Naval Patrol and a growing interference with the internal affairs of coastal states. In East Africa the British government sought at first to end the trade by convincing the sultan of Zanzibar to act against the trade. It became obvious in the 1870s that such pronouncements by titular rulers of an area could, at best, only divert the trade.

Christian missionaries who were at work in significant numbers in Africa by the 1840s were influential far beyond what their numbers would indicate. Western Europe and particularly Britain was committed to advancing the cause of Christianity in all the "pagan" areas of the world. Explorers, traders, humanitarians, and government servants all considered the implantation of Christianity one of their major tasks. In Nigeria the missionaries at Badagry, Abeokuta, and Ibadan played a crucial role in the more direct intervention of Britain in the Yoruba wars. Missionaries who responded to Livingstone's message and example in Central Africa soon became convinced that peace, order, and an end to "barbarism" would come only with British annexation and they joined the chorus of those who demanded a more expansionist policy. Similar actions by the missionaries can be noted in other African territories. The missionary commitment was crucial in later determining British annexation of the areas near Lake Malawi, Bechuanaland, and Uganda.

Strategic considerations also played a small role in the scramble. Britain more than any other state was affected by this reasoning. Almost immediately after its opening in 1869 the Suez Canal became a major factor in British diplomacy. British occupation of Egypt in 1882 was largely conditioned by concern that France, a potentially hostile power, would become dominant there and be in a position to threaten the canal. Later fears of another state controlling any portion of the middle and upper Nile helped the Salisbury government decide to occupy the Sudan and Uganda. However, throughout most of Africa the military or strategic importance of certain areas had little effect upon the decision of European states to control the territory.

The last general factor to consider is the almost indefinable term "national pride." The French had been humbled by Prussia in 1870. The conservative forces of the state had been temporarily discredited. One key to the foreign policy of the new German empire led by Bismarck was their desire to isolate France diplomatically. Thus in the two decades following the creation of the Third Republic, French statesmen were not able to exercise power in the manner of their counterparts in the second empire. However, they discovered that their ambitions to create an overseas empire met with the general approval of Bismarck. Thus the French could gain in Africa not only a new mercantilistic empire, but could also regain a measure of their lost prestige. To a lesser extent national pride affected Germany. Bismarck did not wish an overseas empire. However, many Germans in the full flower of their dominance of Europe looked jealously toward Britain and erroneously concluded that British power depended upon its empire. Some important Germans, therefore, lent their influence to the formation of colonization societies. Rather than gain the enmity of these factions, Bismarck in the early 1880s supported their desires for African territory. British national pride from the mid-1880s onward forced reluctant governments to adopt a more active role in the race for territory. After 1895 the openly imperialistic sentiment of the "jingoes" had become the attitude of the government. Portuguese reaction to the scramble in areas which Portugal claimed because of historic connections were determined in large measure by a sense of proprietary pride.

With these general principles in mind one can turn to the African scene and attempt to detail the most important events connected with the scramble in each geographic segment. It is necessary to point out that events relating to European imperialism in Africa during this period are so intertwined that it is always necessary to look beyond these arbitrary geographic divisions and to attempt to consider the total picture of expansion.

West Africa

As detailed in an earlier chapter, European interest in West Africa, although small by comparison with the commitments of those states elsewhere, nevertheless grew considerably in the period after mid-century. The British, despite disclaiming officially any desire to acquire a territorial empire, had interfered directly in the domestic affairs of many African states. They had acquired Lagos in 1861 and slightly over a decade later the Dutch forts on the Gold Coast. This latter development involved them in a major war with Ashanti. The French government, ostensibly echoing British nonexpansionist policy, had extended its territory in the Senegambia and allowed its merchants to establish quasi-governmental stations on the Ivory Coast. French merchants in the late 1860s and early 1870s were also responsible for committing their government to protecting their spheres of influence on the Mellacourie River adjacent to Sierra Leone and at Cotonou and Porto Novo in Dahomey.

The French government in the decade after 1875 concentrated its minor expansionist efforts on the coastal areas of West Africa and its immediate hinterland. They extended their influence over Whydah by means of a blockade and in 1878 were firmly established at Cotonou. Four years later the French declared a protectorate over Porto Novo. By 1885 the French coastal sphere in Dahomey extended as far west as Anecho in Togoland. In 1878 French claims to the Mellacourie River territory were expanded and Matacong Island was occupied. The British administration at Freetown reluctantly accepted this larger French sphere. After 1881 the French area near Grand Bassam on the Ivory Coast was slowly but systematically extended.

This coastal occupation was in part military and was done primarily to assure French merchants a dominant position in trade. However much both protagonists might deny the accusation, Britain and France were engaged in a protectionist war in Africa. Customs houses were opened soon after the declaration of a French protectorate and British merchants found themselves at a trading disadvantage. Some British administrators such as Sir Samuel Rowe wanted to react to such tactics with an immediate show of force. However, they were restrained from any hasty action by the Colonial Office. The nonexpansion dictum of the 1860s remained in effect. Britain did not covet territories beyond that which was already controlled. Colonial Office opinion held that most of Africa was economically worthless and, therefore, its occupation would be a liability. Between 1875 and 1882 British officials attempted to arrange a line of demarcation between the spheres of influence of the two nations. To this end they were willing to concede Bathurst and the Gambia river possessions.

Proposals for an exchange of the Gambia were kept alive until the Convention of 1889, but no suitable line was ever agreed upon. In the 1880s the British were content to allow French expansion in areas not considered vital. Those territories defined as important were the hinterlands of Freetown, the Gold Coast, Lagos, and the Oil Rivers.

The situation in West Africa was further complicated by the entrance of Germany into the imperial race. Germans had been active along the Togo coast since 1847 when the *Norddeutsche Missionsgesellschaft* opened its first station. Later merchants had followed and by the early 1880s they controlled the bulk of the Togo palm oil trade. In the Camerouns a number of German firms based at Hamburg and Bremen operated very profitably even though British missionaries and traders there outnumbered them. The British government refused, in 1881, the offer of some powerful Douala chiefs to take their territories under British protection. In early 1884, Chancellor Bismarck ceased to oppose the desires of his more territorially minded countrymen and in May authorized the extension of protectorates over those areas where German traders were threatened by encroachment from foreign competitors. Areas specifically mentioned by Bismarck in his instructions to Consul Nachtigal were Angra Pequeña in Southwest Africa and the territory east of the Niger delta. The consul was instructed to avoid any friction with France. Acting partially on his own discretion on July 5, Nachtigal proclaimed a protectorate over Togo and one week later declared the Cameroun under German protection.

The rapid acceleration of French and German activities along the Niger coast caused a swift reaction from the British. Edward Hewett, British consul to Calabar, although unable to ward off Nachtigal's protectorate over the Cameroun, did conclude a series of agreements with rulers of the coastal areas west of the German protectorate. These formed the basis for the British Oil Rivers protectorate proclaimed later in 1884. The major factor forestalling German and French penetration into British spheres in Nigeria was not the British government but George Goldie Taubman (later Sir George Goldie). Coming to Nigeria first in 1877, he was instrumental in creating the United African Company by merging together the four largest British trading firms. By the time the company's name was changed to the National African Company in 1882, it had more than one hundred trading stations on the Niger and Benue rivers and exercised a near monopoly of riverine trade. Goldie and other officials of the National African Company who were avowed imperialists were alarmed by the forward activities of the French and Germans. To block any counterclaims to territory dominated by the company its agents entered into a number of treaties with African rulers. These were accepted by the conferees at the Congress of Berlin as primary evidence of British paramountcy in southern Nigeria. In June 1885, Joseph Thomson further extended the company's sphere by signing treaties of cession with the sultan of Sokoto and the emir of Gwandu.

In the context of West Africa the scramble was already far advanced before the Congress of Berlin in 1884–1885. However, the congress, because of the rationale for its decisions, speeded up the imperial process. It established rough rules by which European states could be secure from claims by its competitors. The congress thus seemed to be encouraging the rapid partitioning of the continent. The decade following the break-up of the congress was the most aggressive period during the scramble.

The most dramatic example of this increased European imperialism was the French military occupation of the interior. By early 1885 French officials had decided to resume their advance into the Western Sudan which had been temporarily halted after Gallieni had reached Bamako. In early 1885 they were operating a gunboat on the upper Niger and in the following year French forces defeated the followers of Mahmadou Lamine, a leading marabout of the upper Gambia. Gallieni signed a treaty of protection with Aguibou of Dinguiray in 1886 and two years later the Alimamies of Futa Jallon placed their territories under French protection. The explorer Captain Binger carried out a thorough two-year exploration of the Mossi areas which showed that the "Mountains of Kung" were no barriers to trade between the Ivory Coast and the Western Sudan.

In 1886 the French began a long series of campaigns against Samory Touré who after 1866 had built a major empire from his small Mande state in upper Guinea. After being defeated by the French in one campaign he sued for peace and presumably accepted French protection in 1886. However, his followers returned to harassing the French within two years of the treaty. In 1889 he was again beaten and promised once more not to oppose the French, but the war was soon renewed and in 1891 a military column under Colonel Louis Archinard occupied Kankan. Thereafter Samory continued a war of mobility against the invaders which did not end until his capture in the Ivory Coast in 1898.

Long before Samory's kingdom had been completely occupied French armies were attacking the western borders of the Tucolor empire. In 1890 the French occupied Dinguiray and then Segu. Ahmadu, the son of al Haji Umar, fled eastward to continue the struggle. French armies then moved slowly into the heart of his kingdom taking Djenne and Macina in 1893 and Timbuktu the following year. From their dominating position in the Western Sudan, French forces turned southeastward and occupied the bulk of the Mossi territories in 1896 even though they would not be completely masters of the area until 1902.

While pursuing their aggressive policies in the interior, the French did not ignore the coast. By a convention with Britain in 1889 they received recognition of their claims to territory in the Senegambia, Ivory Coast, and Dahomean territory. In Dahomey the French had turned the coastal vassals against their Fon ruler. King Behanzin who came to the throne in 1889 insisted upon dominating the coast, particularly Cotonou. This made conflict inevitable. In 1892 war began between the well-armed, powerful African kingdom and the French. Despite bitter fighting the French occupied the capital, Abomey, in November 1892, deposed Behanzin, and in the following year declared Dahomey a French protectorate.

British official attitudes toward expansion slowly changed in the decade of the 1880s. This was partially the result of administrators such as Rowe, Carter, and Johnston who, whenever possible, pursued an activist policy. More pertinent, however, was the necessity to react against the French and Germans whenever territory considered vital was threatened. This reactive process was applied even to the Gambia which the Colonial Office was still hoping to trade for more meaningful territory elsewhere. There the French were openly negotiating with some of the war chiefs on the north bank of the river and had sent troops to intervene in the later stages of the internecine wars. It appeared that, Britain might lose its favorable position on the river and have little left with which to bargain later. The Foreign Office finally arranged a high-level conference with the French to settle the Gambian question as well as boundary disputes elsewhere in West Africa. When the British delegation to Paris in April 1889 discovered that the French were not amenable to territorial exchange they pressed for unequivocal control of the Gambia River. The French, expecting that eventually they would gain control of the river, did not question British hegemony. However, both sides viewed this as a temporary arrangement. The British administrator, Gilbert Carter, was nevertheless instructed to enter into treaties of protection with the Gambian chiefs and to begin the design of a protectorate system of government. Boundary teams between 1891 and 1904 traced the snakelike borders. With the ending of the scramble and a return to friendly relations between Britain and France, a suitable exchange was never decided upon. The temporary boundaries became permanent, monuments to the arbitrary way European states divided the African continent.

The British position regarding the hinterland of Freetown was clearer than in other areas of West Africa. The Creole population of the colony had been viewed as a special charge since freed slaves had first been landed there. Even the parliamentary report of 1865 which had recommended a nonexpansion policy had recognized the unique position of Freetown. Therefore French activities in Guinea were watched carefully. The agreement with France over the Mellacourie secured the northwest boundary of the Freetown hinterland. The Convention of 1889 extended the agreed upon boundary between French and British spheres along the coast into the interior as far as the 13° longitude. Despite some worry over French aims, the Colonial Office was not called upon to react to direct French threats in the decade of the 1880s. The success of the war against Samory, however, brought the French dangerously close to the Temne and Mende country adjacent to the colony. Thus threatened, the British in 1896 responded by declaring a protectorate over these areas. There had been little if any British consultation with the major interior chiefs prior to the annexation. When the newly appointed district commissioners attempted to collect a Hut Tax in 1898 some chiefs refused to pay. One of these, Bai Bureh (a Temne chief), gave his name to the revolt which followed. Troops were sent into the protectorate and taxes were forcibly collected. The Poro secret society of the Mende was particularly important in resisting British authority. Creole traders and missionaries in the interior were considered agents of the British and hundreds were killed before the revolt was crushed. After the hanging of over thirty chiefs for their part in the actions, the new protectorate area was finally considered by the British to be pacified. Following the rebellion a distinct division between the coast and the interior continued to exist for over fifty years with the coastal Creole minority dominating the country.

The development of the dominant British presence on the Gold Coast has already been discussed through the Ashanti War of 1874. Technically that war had caused little change in the relationship between the British and the Ashanti. After assessing an indemnity and receiving pledges from the Ashanti for future good behavior and the abolition of "barbaric" practices, British troops were withdrawn from Ashantiland. The asantahene, Kofi Karikari, was destooled by his people and a new ruler, Mensa Bonsu, was chosen. His policy was to avoid, whenever possible, conflict with the British. Therefore the Ashanti presence in coastal politics was minimal. Mensa Bonsu's cautious attitude was denounced by many important Ashanti leaders as servile capitulation to British power and in 1883 Mensa Bonsu was destooled. There followed a five-year period of near anarchy in Ashantiland. Finally in 1888 the Ashanti asked the British to help them unravel the complexities of the succession to the throne. On the advice of a British commission, sixteen-year-old Prempeh was chosen asantahene.

Britain's relatively dominant position which carried no correlate political responsibility was threatened in the late 1880s by French and German success elsewhere along the coast and in the interior. The first example of British recognition of this change came in the treaty of protection proposed to the Ashanti in 1890. Prempeh and his advisers rejected the treaty and in the following years the asantahene began to utilize his considerable military power to reimpose Ashanti rule over disaffected areas. French activities in the Mossi areas north of Ashanti led to the two-year treaty-making expedition of George Ferguson in 1892. Ferguson was able to gain treaties from most of the Mossi states, but the French refused to recognize the validity of such treaties, insisting instead on effective occupation. The British then realized that, if the French were to be forestalled in the Upper Volta region, Britain had to assume a more active political role in Ashantiland which now blocked the way to their occupation of any of the Mossi areas. The first example of this more aggressive British policy toward the Ashanti was the demand that Prempeh reject the use of force in his foreign policy. They further demanded that he accept a British resident since residents had been used elsewhere by the British to control policy making by native rulers. Prempeh refused, and by the end of 1895 the more imperialistic Conservative government decided to use force on the Ashanti.

In January 1896, 2,000 British troops invaded Ashantiland. Prempeh decided to offer no resistance to the invaders and Kumasi was occupied without fighting. Prempeh was ordered to pay an indemnity of 50,000 ounces of gold. Upon his statement that the sum was too great for him to pay, he, the queen mother, and a number of influential Ashanti were taken to the coast and finally sent into exile. The British authorities then proceeded to break up the Ashanti Union by entering into separate treaties with individual rulers. There was no new asantahene appointed to replace Prempeh. Pushing beyond Ashantiland, the British conquered Bole and Wa and occupied Dagomba and Mamprussi. Subsequently border agreements were concluded with France and Germany, and the British created the administrative unit called Northern Territories.

The humiliation inherent in the British treatment of the asantahene combined with the activities of the authorities in enforcing rules against slavery and the slave trade had, by 1900, driven the Ashanti to the point of rebellion. Governor Sir Frederic Hodgson had decided to tax the Ashanti and assured them that the measures against slavery would continue and the asantahene would never return. On a visit to Kumasi he completely outraged the Ashanti by demanding: "Where is the Golden Stool? Why am I not sitting on the Golden Stool at this moment?" This unfortunate statement indicating the governor's wish to sit on the collective souls of the Ashanti precipitated a full-scale war. The governor and 700 British troops were besieged at Kumasi for over two months. British units from throughout West Africa were diverted to the Gold Coast and they eventually were successful in defeating the Ashanti and relieving Kumasi. Following the uprising Britain annexed Ashanti as a crown colony.

By the mid-1880s the scramble had effectively separated the British possessions on the Gold Coast and in Nigeria. At the time this did not perturb the decision makers in London. Despite the actions of men such as Johnston and Goldie, the British were content to maintain trading control in specific areas with a minimum of expenditure. In the decade of the 1890s British expansion in Nigeria was accelerated because the French were increasingly in a stronger position to threaten the previously secure hinterland.

In Yorubaland the British administration at Lagos in 1886 acted to bring about a truce in the half-century Yoruba civil wars. Two years later an agreement was reached with the alafin of Oyo whereby a paper protectorate was proclaimed over his kingdom. Nevertheless, hostility between various Yoruba states continued. The Ijebu were responsible for a number of incidents construed by the British as disrespectful to their officials. Sir Gilbert Carter, the administrator of Lagos, reacting to this and also feeling the potential French threat from the west, sent a military column into Ijebu country in 1892. The following year on something of a "grand tour," Carter entered into treaties with Oyo, Abeokuta, and Ibadan whereby British judicial authority was extended into those areas. By 1896, of the Yoruba states, only Ilorin remained independent from British rule. Except for the Ijebu campaign and a small expedition to Oyo in 1895, the northward extension of the Lagos protectorate was peaceful.

The Lagos government, disturbed by the interference of Ilorin in the affairs of Yorubaland and its support of the slave trade, wanted to conquer the town. However, Sir George Goldie claimed that Ilorin was within his and the Royal Niger Company's sphere of influence. Previously in 1894 Goldie had sent Captain Frederick Lugard to Nikki in Borgu to forestall French designs on that area. Despite Lugard's presence, the French continued as a threat to Borgu and Ilorin. Finally the colonial secretary, Joseph Chamberlain, ordered Goldie to conquer Ilorin, and company troops subjugated Ilorin and neighboring Nupe in 1897.

The company, however, was under attack from the press and from government officials. Its trade policy, notwithstanding official prohibition of the practice, was monopolistic. In the eastern areas this led to the choking off of trade for independent coastal cities such as Brass as well as diverting trade from merchants operating in the Niger coast protectorate. By 1895 the more expansionist-minded British were unhappy with the inability of the company to confront the French on equal terms. Thus in 1897 the company police were replaced by an imperial armed force commanded by Lugard. In 1898 a convention between Britain and France fixed the western and northern boundaries of Nigeria. The eastern line of demarcation with Germany had been established in 1893. In this new British imperialistic atmosphere there were few reasons to continue the company. Negotiations were begun in 1898 to purchase the company's political and territorial claims in Nigeria. An agreement was finally reached and on January 1, 1900, Britain assumed control of company territories and Lugard became high commissioner of the new protectorate of Northern Nigeria.

Britain had by 1900 resolved its international differences over Nigeria and the boundaries were theoretically fixed. There were vast areas within these limits where no European had ever been. This was particularly true of the hinterland of the Niger coast protectorate. British functional control extended only a few miles into the interior. In 1899 Sir Ralph Moor planned and finally three years later executed the military occupation of Ibo territory. British authorities expected major opposition from the Aro who controlled the great oracle Aro-Chukwu and who were suspected of holding the Ibo in subjection. However, little resistance was offered to the British military and by 1906 most of the Ibo territory had been absorbed by the British. In 1906 the Yoruba and Ibo hinterlands were amalgamated into one government entity called the Protectorate of Southern Nigeria.

In the northern areas Lugard moved to make effective the protectorate proclaimed in 1900. The first series of campaigns were directed against the slave-trading emir of Kontagora. Lugard then gained effective control over many smaller kingdoms which welcomed the British as a counter force to the Fulani. A military expedition to the Lake Chad area secured a large portion of Bornu for Britain. Lugard played upon the Fulani emirs' fear of the French and promised them minimal changes in their system. He encountered only a small degree of resistance mainly from the sultan of Sokoto. In areas which had submitted to Britain, Lugard confirmed the local rulers in their rights and privileges. This system, later called indirect rule, became the general pattern for the north and played a large role in the peaceful occupation of the area.

By the early twentieth century European rule was firmly established in all West African areas. A bewildering number of meetings, conventions, and verbal agreements had resulted in the division of the vast areas among the competitive powers. Once these divisions had become effective European states ceased to vie with each other in acquisition and turned to the far more difficult task of establishing governmental systems to make effective their rule in the conquered territory.

The Congo

European traders had been in contact with the coastal portions of the Congo basin since the late fifteenth century. At one time the Portuguese appeared to be on the verge of converting the Bakongo to Christianity. However, the slave trade and the growing impotence of the Portuguese crown meant an end to any such philanthropic experiments. Portuguese interests receded southward to the immediate hinterland of Luanda and with the passing of time even their Angolan possessions became moribund. Until the early nineteenth century other European states were concerned with the territory near the Congo River only as a fruitful area for the collection of slaves. As in West Africa, this did not imply territorial acquisition. In the 1830s some chiefs near the mouth of the Gabon River ceded a small amount of territory to the French for use by their anti-slavery naval squadrons. In 1849 the French released a cargo of slaves from a captured vessel on the Gabon coast. These slaves formed the nucleus of the town of Libreville. In the years following, the territory near Libreville was increased slightly, but the French showed no desire until 1875 to explore the interior or to increase substantially their small enclave. In that year a naturalized Frenchman, Pierre Savorgnan de Brazza, began to explore the interior adjacent to the Ogowe River.

In 1877 Henry Morton Stanley reached the mouth of the Congo at the conclusion of his long, arduous, three-year exploration of East and Central Africa. The knowledge of his discoveries and optimism concerning the future of the Congo basin preceded him to Europe. One very interested observer of Stanley's exploits was King Leopold II of Belgium who was the guiding spirit behind the ostensibly philanthropic African International Association. This association was composed of separate national committees in European countries and the United States. In 1877 at the only plenary session of the association ever held, its major funciton was defined as suppressing the slave trade in Central and East Africa. Its announced intention was the establishment of a series of posts linking the Great Lakes with the Indian Ocean coast. The Belgian committee of the association approached Stanley soon after his return to Europe and in time convinced him to return to the Congo as its chief agent for furthering

Christianity and civilization there. With Stanley's return to the Congo in 1880, the focus of the international association was irrevocably shifted from East Africa to the Congo. By 1885 Leopold II had bought out the other stockholders in the Belgian committee and thus had practically separated it from the other national groups. The previous Committee for the Study of the Upper Congo was reconstituted the International Congo Association.

Before Stanley reached the Congo a second time, de Brazza had explored further up the Ogowe River, established the post of Franceville, and later crossed from the Ogowe to the Congo. There he obtained from local rulers the cession of a small amount of territory and established the post of Brazzaville before returning to the coast and Libreville. Stanley, who arrived in the Congo in 1880, began immediately to establish the association's claim to the left bank of the Congo from Stanley Pool to the sea, to gain the grant of territory between these points from African chiefs, and to improve communications in those areas. Stanley's major bases on the Congo were Matadi and upriver a new town called Leopoldville located across the river from Brazzaville. Stanley was too late to secure the right bank because of de Brazza's earlier activities. De Brazza returned to the region in 1883 as a commissioner for France with troops and financial support from the Third Republic. There ensued in the following year a race between Stanley and de Brazza to secure the cession to their governments of as much African territory as possible.

These activities by the agents of France and Leopold caused the Portuguese government to become active and it laid claims to the lower Congo based upon its long history of contact with the area. In 1884 Portugal was assured of a short-lived triumph when Britain agreed formally to support these historic claims. The Anglo-Portuguese treaty which ignored the claims of both France and the association focused the attention of the chancellor of Germany, Otto von Bismarck, upon the Congo arena. Acting in his assumed capacity of the "honest broker" seeking to avoid international problems, he summoned all interested European parties to convene in Berlin to solve the Congo dilemma. In answer to Bismarck's invitation, representatives of fourteen European nations and the United States met in Berlin in November 1884. For thirteen weeks the delegates confronted not only the Congo problem, but a full range of questions relating to the entire African continent. Britain soon ceased its support of Portugal and gradually veered toward the acceptance of Leopold's claims. Leopold's agents came to the conference with full support from the United States. More important was Leopold's modus vivendi arranged with France. Not having the backing of Britain or Germany and believing that Leopold would not have the funds to carry out his aims in the Congo, France agreed to support his claims to the left bank of the lower Congo. In return Leopold recognized French rights to the area claimed by de Brazza and promised to support French claims to the entire basin if in the future the association proved inadequate to the task.

At the close of their deliberations the conferees had defined the "conventional basin" of the Congo and had recognized the association's primacy to the left bank of the river below Stanley Pool. They also confirmed French claims to the Gabon and to the right bank of the Congo River. The conference declared that navigation on all rivers of the Congo basin as well as the Niger River and all future roads and railroads of the Congo would be open to traders of all nations. Of more importance for the future of European activities in Africa was the stress placed by the congress on the necessity for European states to prove "effective occupation" when claiming African coastal territory. French opposition to the application of this doctrine in the interior regions was sufficient to assure its defeat. In sum, the most important decisions of the congress related to the various agreements concerning the Congo basin. Contrary to the popular view, the Congress of Berlin did not begin the scramble nor did its concepts of effective occupation have much influence on the future development of European imperialism in Africa. However, because the congress had met and reached some decisions on Africa, the scramble was given legitimacy. All important Western states were represented and there were few delegates who defended the rights of the African to be left alone. Although in time most of the doctrines agreed to in Berlin were ignored by European imperialists, all agreed that there was a moral as well as economic imperative to divide the continent.

After the Berlin decisions de Brazza moved rapidly to extend French control over the Gabon and middle Congo regions. His lieutenants explored the hinterland far beyond any established post. Paul Crampel investigated the Sangha River area obtaining treaties from African rulers which bound them to France. Another aide, Albert Dolisie, explored the Sangha and Ubangi territory and established the post of Bangui on the Ubangi River. In the 1890s French explorers moved northward from the Congo area toward Adamoua and Lake Chad, attempting to link up with the southward-moving French columns from the Sudan.

Leopold II wasted no time in assuming the premier position on the lower Congo assigned the association by the conference. He received permission from the Belgian parliament to declare himself sovereign of the association's territories. He then proclaimed, without consulting other members of the association, the existence of the Congo Independent State. In the five years after the congress, Leopold spent a large portion of his fortune in constructing bases on the lower Congo and in creating an administration for the area flexible enough so that it could later be expanded to include other larger areas of the Congo basin. In doing all this he attracted other European entrepreneurs, particularly Belgian investors. Although the Independent State was theoretically free from Belgian control, it actually was tied closely to the fortunes of that state.

The creation of towns, roads, and an administrative structure, as well as the cost of the military campaigns in the deep hinterland, cost more than Leopold had imagined. In 1889 at the Brussels conference, he received the right to charge a ten percent ad valorum duty on all goods brought to the Congo. However, this did not begin to meet the expense of the construction of the railway being built from Matadi to Leopoldville or the telegraph line or regular steamer service from the Congo. Such unexpected expenditures meant that all possible means of extracting revenue had to be pursued. Leopold was instrumental in organizing concession companies which were given monopolies to work certain areas of the Congo basin. Government agents were instructed to expedite the collection and transportation of raw rubber to Matadi. These two factors changed irrevocably the nature of the government of the Congo. Free trade in the Congo ceased to be the practicing ideal of the government. The harsh, cruel treatment of Africans by Leopold's agents while collecting rubber made a mockery of the humanitarian theories on which the state was theoretically based. By 1900 Leopold, Belgian financial interests, and some great companies ruled a greatly expanded Congo in an autocratic fashion never imagined by the signatories of the Berlin conference.

One of the first hinterland territories acquired by the expansive Independent State was Katanga. There Msiri, a crafty king, kept a great variety of different peoples pacified by means of his superior intelligence and firearms. Rumors of great mineral wealth in the Katanga grew as more European missionaries entered the area after 1885. Msiri's kingdom became an eminently desirable area for the Portuguese who were eager to link up their possessions on the east and west coasts. However, their dreams of such a solid bloc of territory was thwarted by the joint labors of the British prime minister Salisbury and the capitalist prime minister of Cape Colony, Cecil Rhodes. Rhodes, the driving force behind the British movement into the interior from Cape Colony, had learned of the potential of the Katanga soon after the pioneer column of his British South Africa Company moved into Rhodesia. He commissioned the explorer Joseph Thomson to visit Msiri and secure the Katanga for the company. Thomson never reached the Katanga because on the way he encountered a smallpox epidemic. However, later in 1890, Alfred Sharpe, the British vice-consul in Nyasaland, arrived there. Msiri made it clear that he had no intention of signing away his country to the British. His attitude, however, changed radically the following year due to a series of rebellions of his subjects which he believed were fomented by the Congo Independent State government and the newly formed Katanga Company. Three separate Independent State expeditions were sent to Msiri's court in 1891. The king decided to invite Sharpe back to discuss a protectorate and had written him a letter to that effect. The letter fell into the hands of one of Leopold's agents, Captain Stairs, who decided to act swiftly to forestall the British. After a meeting with the king, Stairs quarreled with Msiri and in the scuffle which followed, shot the king. Stairs immediately declared the territory annexed to the Independent State.

Meanwhile upriver from Stanley Pool there was open warfare between the armies of the Independent State and the Arab slavers who had turned the eastern Congo region into a huge slaving ground. By the early

1890s the presence of the great slave trader, Tippu Tib, for whatever unity it might earlier have brought, was no longer felt in the territory west of Lake Tanganyika. Initially the wars went in favor of the Arabs. By the close of 1892 they had forced the Independent State to abandon all its posts above Stanley Pool. The tide was turned the following year with the success of Baron Francis Dhanis and his Zanzibari troops operating in the Kasai region. Slowly the Arabs were pushed out of their favored slaving grounds. Warfare continued between the two groups until 1900 but, by 1895, the Independent State was dominant in the eastern Congo.

Explorers and leaders of military columns in the latter 1890s penetrated into the area along the Luapula River, in the high Katanga, and up the Kasai and Kwango rivers. Independent State troops even occupied briefly a part of the Bahr-al-Ghazal until a high level agreement with France forced them to retire in late 1894. By the beginning of the new century Leopold's agents had established a rudimentary form of government throughout most of the territory claimed by the association. The limits of the Independent State was also established by conquest and boundary agreements with other European states. Britain declared a protectorate over the area from the Kafue River to Lake Nyasa in 1894 and Germany claimed Ruanda and Burundi after the Heligoland Treaty in 1890. A series of agreements with Portugal between 1891 and 1914 established the southern boundary with Angola.

The vicissitudes of Leopold's administration of the Congo in the 1890s were the results of two conflicting objectives. As stated at the Congress of Berlin, his motives were to end the slave trade, maintain free trade, and spread Christianity and Western civilization throughout the basin. These theoretical goals foundered upon the harsh realities of the need for money to maintain the state and to extend its influence. Until the opening of the twentieth century the administration of Leopold's empire was a curious blend of efficiency, idealism, and cruelty. Reports from missionaries of the exploitation of Africans in the collection and transportation of rubber was confirmed in 1902 by the report of the British consul, Roger Casement. From that date onward pressure from British and Belgian liberals and the British government forced Leopold to institute reforms and eventually to negotiate the transfer of the Independent State to Belgium in November 1908.

Angola

Although his effect on Angola was only temporary, Sousa Coutinho, governor in the 1760s, was the first modern administrator of the Portuguese empire. He wanted to halt the trade in slaves and secure the systematic occupation of the interior by Portuguese immigrants. He was responsible for beginning the colonizing of the Bié highlands. By 1800 there were over 250 Portuguese and 15,000 Africans in the vicinity of the fortress of Caconda. As with so many of Coutinho's ideas, this colonizing effort was not effectively supported by his successors and by

the mid-nineteenth century there were few evidences of Portuguese settlement. Coutinho also wanted to make Luanda a city based upon a viable
agricultural hinterland, supported by trade and commerce other than
slaves. This, too, failed and Luanda for all its exterior appearance of
wealth and beauty continued throughout the nineteenth century to be
only the chief city of a listless and growingly decadent colony. The major
source of income in Angola was the relatively stable trade in slaves to
Brazil.

The disturbances associated with the Napoleonic Wars and their
aftermath were deeply felt in Angola. Brazil became independent from
Portugal in 1822. The revolutionary ardor reached Luanda where the
garrison troops mutinied. A junta ruled for a short time in Luanda and
the merchants and leaders of Benguela briefly toyed with the idea of
joining Brazil. Portugal was wracked by conflicts between absolutists and
liberals for over a decade. Only with the triumph of the liberals in 1834
did stability return to the Portuguese empire. They proceeded to develop
an idealistic program which would eventually lead to Portuguese citizenship for the population of their overseas territories. Most of these plans
foundered because of the resistance of entrenched interests and lack
of funds to carry out the proposals. This can be clearly seen in the attempts of the Marques Sá da Bandiera to end the slave trade. A decree
of 1836 made it illegal to trade in slaves. Angolans ignored the provisions
of the decree and there was no perceptible decrease in the traffic until
the British West African Squadron began to seize Portuguese ships suspected of engaging in it. After 1845 one can see a definite decrease with
the actions of the more aggressive governor Cunha. By mid-century the
trade from Angola had been perceptibly lessened.

In 1858 a compromise decree was issued which was to end domestic
slavery in twenty years. No person could become a slave during this
period and after 1869 the slaves became *libertos*. As in Mozambique,
there was resistance to this law both openly and covertly. The vagrancy
provisions of the decrees allowed government agents to assign Africans
who were not employed to work for either the government or private
employers. The system of contract labor to São Thomé and Principe
which caused such a scandal in the early twentieth century was begun
at this time. The abolition of both traffic and slavery itself was closely
tied to the difficulty of creating an alternative source of capital. All attempts to get Portuguese to colonize areas such as the Bié highlands failed
because of the counter lure of Brazil. Only after the revolt of 1848 at
Pernambuco in Brazil was it possible to get significant numbers of Portuguese to migrate to Angola. The ports of Benguela and Luanda prospered
in the latter part of the century after they were opened to ships of all
nations. Slowly traders such as Silva Porto penetrated into the territory
adjacent to the Bié highlands to exchange goods with the Ovimbundu
people. Trade with different African groups in the territory inland from
Luanda became more important in the same period.

Despite the slowly developing prosperity of Luanda there was little
contact with Africans in the more remote interior. One observer of Angola

commented that the Portuguese knew more of the inland kingdoms in the seventeenth century than they knew in the nineteenth. Before the spate of explorations in Africa just prior to the scramble there seemed little reason to the Portuguese to expend funds on territories already proven to be uneconomic. There were a few major expeditions undertaken by the Portuguese in the first part of the century. The nine-year adventure of Pedro Baptista and Amaro José in crossing the continent began in Angola. Silva Porto traveled throughout the Bié highlands in the 1840s and attempted a journey across Africa in 1852. In the 1850s the government sponsored Friedrich Welwitsch in making a botanical survey of Angola. Hermenigildo Capelo and Roberto Ivens in the late 1870s made a thorough survey of Kasanje. However, these few efforts were not given much publicity and they were not followed by missionary or trading ventures. When the other European powers became interested in African territory, Portugal could claim historic rights to certain areas but could show little activity in Central Africa after the eighteenth century. Some Portuguese administrators in the last two decades of the nineteenth century attempted to counter these deficiencies by sponsoring expeditions by Pinto, Cordoso, Carvallo, Ivens, and others. The goal of Foreign Minister de Barros Gomes in the 1880s was to assure for Portugal the bulk of the interior between the twelfth and eighteenth parallels. In 1884 the Anglo-Portuguese treaty recognized Portugal's claims to the Congo basin. However, the Berlin conference which assigned the greater part of the area of the Congo to Leopold II destroyed this hope. Between 1885 and 1891 Portugal was forced to abandon its claims to the Katanga, Barotseland, and the Nyasa territory.

Although denied the opportunity to link its Atlantic and Indian Ocean possessions, the area assigned to Portugal in Angola was far greater than they had ever governed before. In the two decades after the settlement of the majority of the boundary questions, Portugal made effective its control over most of Angola. Utilizing metropolitan and African troops and many convicts, the Humbe region of the Cuanhama was pacified by 1910. The last major Ovimbundu revolt on the Bié plateau in 1902 was put down with a huge loss of African lives. Between 1907 and 1910 Dembos territory was entirely brought under Portuguese control. The last serious reaction against Portuguese rule was the Bakongo uprising of 1913. After this the major problem faced by Portuguese officials at Luanda and Lisbon concerned the creation of viable governmental structures which would enable Portugal to rule the vast area of Angola. By the close of World War I these institutions based upon historic philosophical concepts were in effect in Angola. They remained relatively unchanged until the massive African uprising in northern Angola in 1960.

Mozambique

Portugal, as late as the mid-nineteenth century, held only nominal control of the areas immediately behind the coastal towns of Ibo, Mozambique,

Portuguese Central Africa

Sofala, and Lourenço Marques. Some idea of the importance of those towns can be seen in the population of the largest—Mozambique. There were approximately 5,000 Africans and 800 Portuguese, Goan, and mixed residents on the island. Christianity which had been such a dominant force in the initial Portuguese expansion clung only to the towns. It has been estimated that in 1825 there were only ten priests in the Zambesi hinterland. Seven of these were Goan. The governor-general and lesser Portuguese officials had no power to enforce on interior peoples their decrees or those decided upon in Lisbon. The Portuguese armed forces were composed largely of African levies or convicts. Later in the century when the government attempted to negate the prazeros' (described below) influence, the governors discovered how poor the Mozambique armed forces were. The farthest practical inland extension of Portuguese authority throughout most of the century was the town of Tete on the Zambesi River.

The inland areas of the Zambesi were held by powerful, feudal-like landlords called prazeros. These estates or prazos were begun first in the sixteenth century as a way by which Portugal could control and make profitable the lands adjacent to the Zambesi River. With the waning of Portuguese influence in the Indian Ocean area and the limitation of support to the governors, the prazeros became a law unto themselves. The size of the prazos varied from three-square leagues to over eighty-square leagues. It was possible to cultivate only a small portion of these areas and thus the masters lived by taxes, some legitimate trade, and the traffic in slaves. They were complete masters of their lands and people and maintained their own standing armies. Throughout the nineteenth century they obeyed Portuguese decrees only when it was to their advantage to do so. Originally Portuguese, the prazeros had by intermarriage with Africans and Indians lost much of their European racial and cultural characteristics. Men such as Joaquim da Cruz ruled their empires more as African chiefs than as European administrators. The Lisbon government recognizing the nature of the prazo system, outlawed it in 1832 and re-enunciated this in 1836, 1841, and 1854. These legislative actions had no practical effect upon the continuance of the prazo system.

African peoples in the hinterland were relatively undisturbed by the Portuguese presence on the coast. Even in the seventeenth century, when the Portuguese were more active, they had exerted little influence on African polities. The exception to this had been the empire of the Monomotapas which had been destroyed partially because of Portuguese interference. However, by the nineteenth century, African groups were deeply affected by the upsurge in demand for slaves in the coastal areas. Chief among African slavers were the Makua, Yao, and especially the Nguni people. One of the most dramatic events in interior history concerned the migrations of the Nguni caused by the mfecane in South Africa after 1820. One group of Nguni under Zwangendaba invaded the Delagoa Bay area and joined briefly with other Nguni led by Soshangane. After threatening Lourenço Marques and absorbing many of the peoples of its interior, the Nguni under Zwangendaba moved north into the Shona area of the Changamire. After crushing this empire they crossed the Zambesi in 1835 and disrupted the Nsenga and Cewa near Lake Nyasa. One group of Nguni migrated even further north to the Nyamwezi areas before circling back through Bemba and Bisa lands and settling in northern Rhodesia. Another segment of the Nguni moved eastward into the lower Rufiji River territory. Meanwhile the Nguni under Soshangane had consolidated their control in the extreme south. By the 1840s his men were threatening the prazos as far north as Sena and many of the prazeros were paying tribute to these Nguni. After mid-century the bulk of the Nguni had ceased their migrations and became less of a threat to the prazos and the Portuguese.

The slave trade was the one major problem in Mozambique which had international significance. In the three decades before mid-century the coastal slave trade had been in a gradual decline. The opening up of new lands in Cuba and the needs of French planters on the Indian Ocean islands of Nossi Be, Mayotte, and Reunion reversed this trend. In order to circumvent the government decree against the slave trade the French utilized the guise of the émigré system where they claimed that African workers were colonists entering the island of their own will. The Portuguese minister of overseas, the Marques Sá da Bandeira, prohibited the use of the émigré system as a pretext for continuing the trade. This had little effect in Mozambique. Even the decree by the French emperor, Napoleon III, abolishing this system in 1864 did not keep the sugar planters from continuing to import Africans. By 1875 it was estimated that the Mozambique area was absorbing 7,000 Africans a year under the name of émigrés. Livingstone reported in the mid-1860s the continuing slave raiding activities of the prazeros and the open selling of these Africans at Quelimane. He accused the Portuguese officials of complicity although he recognized that they had little power to end it. The slave trade continued throughout the last quarter of the century in a much modified form. Pressure from Britain and renewed Portuguese interest in Africa was partially responsible for its demise. However, the major reason was the drying up of the markets for either slaves or émigrés.

Closely allied to the slave trade was the question of slavery in Mozambique. In 1869 the institution was abolished in all Portuguese territories. However, the slaves did not become free automatically. They were declared *libertos* but still subject to punitive action. In 1875 and finally in 1878 the position of the *libertos* was further defined. They became free persons but were required to be employed. The vagrancy clause of the edict of 1878 gave the government the power to assign unemployed *libertos* to labor for the government or private employers for a maximum of two years. Throughout the rest of the century there was much underhanded dealing by private labor contractors in utilizing the services of *libertos*.

The onset of the scramble for Africa forced Portugal into a more active role in both the Mozambique and Angolan areas. Livingstone opened up the interior of Africa in a way that no previous Portuguese explorers had done. By the 1870s it was obvious to many Portuguese officials that they would have to expend more effort and funds if they hoped to maintain claims to their historic empire. Prior to this period there had been, in the nineteenth century, few explorations sponsored by the Portuguese. In 1798 Francisco Lacerdo had explored the Luapula Valley and made contact with the Kazembe empire. Pedro Baptista and Amaro José were the first to cross the continent. They left the Kasanje district of Angola in 1802 and were detained for over four years by the Kazembes before reaching Tete in 1811. In 1831–1832 a government expedition led by José Monteiro and António Gamitto reached the headwaters of the Zambesi. None of these expeditions had major commercial or political significance since the discoveries were not followed up by traders or government agents.

The renewed interest of Portugal in the hinterland was symbolized by the creation in 1875 of the Geographical Society of Lisbon. It sponsored Hermenigildo Capelo and Roberto Ivens in 1877 to survey thoroughly the Kasanje and Malange areas. Alexandre de Serpa Pinto explored the Zambesi area while traveling from Angola to Durban. Capello and Ivens, in 1884, established potential basic trade routes between Angola and Mozambique while Augusto Cardosa reached the Katanga and obtained the signature of Mutianvua, chief of the Katanga Lunda, to a treaty of protection. Pinto explored further the Shire areas adjacent to Mozambique. However, much of this renewed activity was for nothing since Britain, France, and Leopold II had become interested in the same interior areas. The Berlin conference of 1884–1885 dealt a major blow to Portuguese aspirations in the Congo basin. By 1894 final agreement on borders had been reached with the Congo Independent State. The activities of Rhodes' British South Africa Company in Central Africa and Harry Johnston's expeditions in the Nyasa area denied finally the Portuguese hope to link their Atlantic possessions with Mozambique. The treaty of June 1891 solved most of the major border problems with the British. Although Lisbon was blocked from achieving its most grandiose schemes, it obtained recognition of its primacy over a huge interior area where few Portuguese had ever been.

The first task of the Lisbon government, if it was to extend its influence over the areas assigned to it by agreements with other European powers, was to negate the power of the prazeros. The Mozambique government during the 1880s concentrated its major efforts against the huge Massangano prazo of the da Cruz family. This prazo located forty miles below Tete was in a position to block downriver communications to Sena. Mozambique had attempted in the 1850s and 1860s to crush the da Cruz power but with no success. Five major expeditions were sent against the prazero Bonga in the two-year period after 1867. Each one was either cut to pieces by Bonga's troops or the expedition was decimated by disease. The conflict between Portugal and the Massangano prazo began again after 1885. Augusto du Castillo, the governor of Mozambique, an excellent soldier with a major force of trained soldiers, took the Massangano fortress in September 1887. A further campaign the following year pitted the

Portuguese against the da Cruz—supported by the African population of the mountain area. The ferocity of the fighting can be seen in the casualties. Approximately 6,000 were killed before Massangano was conquered.

The Portuguese had also moved against the other prazeros and had by the 1890s brought them under control. The last of the great prazeros to be tamed was Manuel Antonio da Sousa. His prazo was located near Barué inland from Sofala. He had become chief of the Macombe in the 1880s and later served the Mozambique Company. Da Sousa was killed in 1892 and his interior empire fell apart. With his death the prazero resistance against Portuguese authority came to an end.

Elsewhere in Mozambique, Portuguese military columns were active against African rulers. Lourenço Marques was attacked in the mid-1890s by Africans, but this was a desperation move. Within a year the immediate hinterland was pacified. The paramount chief of Gaza was captured in 1895 and sent into exile. The Barué area south of the Zambesi continued to resist the Portuguese until a major campaign in 1902 pacified the territory. The hinterland behind Mozambique Island was occupied by the military between 1906 and 1910. The Yao of the Niassa district were systematically brought under Portuguese control by 1912. While this pacification went on, men such as António Enes, Freire de Andrade, and Mousinho de Albuquerque were evolving the new mechanisms of control which replaced the older structures of government that were totally inadequate for the large areas then dominated by Portugal.

East Africa

European interest during the last quarter of the nineteenth century in East Africa came from three different directions. Baker and Gordon in the 1870s in their operations in Equatoria had as one of their objectives the annexation of the interlacustrine areas to the empire of the Egyptian khedive Ismail. In the decade of the 1890s these same kingdoms were briefly threatened by the forces of Leopold II moving from the eastern sections of the Congo. However, most European activity, and thus the greatest threat to the continued independence of East African states, came from the sultan of Zanzibar's possessions along the coast of the Indian Ocean. As has been noted previously, the sultan's East African empire was primarily a commercial one. Although his influence was felt deep into the hinterland, he did not attempt to conquer the Bantu or Nilotic people of the interior or to subvert native polities. Due largely to the plantation system established along the coast and on Zanzibar which provided greater commercial opportunities, the slave trade increased enormously in the fifty years after Sultan Said established his hegemony on the coast. This increase in the slave traffic brought the area to the attention of the British government. Long before Burton, Livingstone, and Speke wrote of the horrors of the trade some British officials had attempted to limit it by entering into agreements with the sultan. By the terms of the Hamerton Treaty signed in 1845 Said agreed to prohibit transportation of slaves from his

African to his Asian possessions. In 1873 the near ultimatum of the British government delivered by Consul Sir John Kirk led Sultan Barghash to abolish the trade throughout his territorie$. In return for the sultan's official aid in controlling the traffic, British officials in London and Bombay assumed the role of protector of the sultan's territories from the ambitions of other European states. In the late 1870s Kirk was not only the British representative on Zanzibar but also the sultan's most trusted advisor.

European interest in and knowledge of eastern Africa was greatly enhanced by the work of the explorers of the 1870s. Most of these adventurers commented that only European occupation would halt the trade in slaves. Official pronouncements notwithstanding, Arab slavers from the coast and from the southern Sudan continued to ravage the interior. Thus the imperative for European direct intervention in hinterland affairs was present before the scramble. The British who were in the best position to take advantage of this situation had no intention of underwriting any costly military or political venture despite their concern with the trade. This attitude was clearly indicated by the official attitude toward the so-called MacKinnon Concession. Sir William MacKinnon, the founder of the British India Steam Navigation Company which operated a number of ships in the Indian Ocean area, was a confirmed expansionist. In 1877 Sultan Barghash offered to turn over the administration of all his mainland territories to MacKinnon and his associates for a share of the customs revenue. MacKinnon was willing to assume this responsibility if the British government would recognize such an arrangement and promise to support it. This, London refused to do and the entire scheme fell through. Consul Kirk was also convinced that Britain should do much more to support the sultan in consolidation of his hinterland possessions. He particularly wanted the sultan, with British aid, to establish a series of posts stretching as far into the interior as Ugogo. Prime Minister Gladstone's liberal government in 1880 refused to cooperate in this scheme.

The activities in 1884 of a twenty-eight year old German adventurer and nationalist, Carl Peters, fundamentally altered power relationships in East Africa. Peters who had spent some time in Britain was convinced that its greatness lay in its empire and therefore Germany, if it wished to challenge Britain for supremacy, would have to acquire overseas territory. In pursuance of this goal, Peters and a number of other young activists had formed the Society for German Colonization. Despite warnings of non-support from Chancellor Bismarck, Peters, Karl Juhlke, and August Otto traveled in the autumn of 1884 to Zanzibar. Crossing to the mainland, they had by December secured over 120 "treaties" with chiefs and headmen in the immediate interior from Bagamoyo. Peters claimed that each of these men was a free agent and not in any way a subject of the sultan. Hurrying back to Germany, Peters used these treaties to gain a *Schützbrief* or charter for his company from a still reluctant Bismarck. This *Schützbrief* granted the company the right to administer a large undefined area between the sultan's territories and Lake Tanganyika. Armed with this recognition, Peters returned to Africa and renewed his treaty making with new fervor.

Sultan Barghash protested Peters' activities directly to the German emperor. Sir John Kirk also recommended that the British government intervene to halt Peters. The British vice-consul to Zanzibar while in Britain urged MacKinnon and others to form a chartered company to secure a protectorate over the rich territory in the vicinity of Mt. Kilimanjaro. Reports from Harry Johnston and the explorer, Joseph Thomson, had been enthusiastic about the area. Nevertheless, the British government refused to support such a scheme and within a few months the Germans had extended their theoretical control over Kilimanjaro and the territory of Witu. The German government, now more openly imperialistic, dispatched gunboats to Zanzibar in August 1885 to show the sultan that it was prepared to back Peters' claim to Witu by force if necessary. The Gladstone and, later, Salisbury governments, far from seeking a confrontation with Germany to protect the territory of their friend, the sultan, welcomed German intervention. They believed Germany would bring order to the territory, stamp out the slave trade, and introduce Western ideals. For a period of approximately two years British statesmen supported German expansion since it would achieve certain desired ends without costing the British taxpayer a shilling.

In 1886 a mixed commission was appointed to study the conflicting German, British, and Zanzibari claims. The members of the commission agreed to a convention which recognized the sultan's control only over a ten-mile deep strip between the Rovuma and Tana rivers. This convention represented the almost complete British abandonment of the sultan since the hinterland, which Barghash claimed, was divided into two spheres of influence. The Germans gained recognition of their premier position in the southern part and in 1888 they forced the sultan to lease to them all his mainland possessions in their sphere.

Peters and his associates continued to expand the territory controlled by the company. For over a year after 1888, German occupation of the coastal towns was resisted by Abushiri ibn Salim and his followers. African troops, askaris, trained and led by Germans, ultimately defeated Abushiri and hanged him. Afterward there was sporadic coastal resistance but the towns were soon overawed by German power and the willingness of men like Peters to use it. In 1890 Emin Pasha, by then in the service of Germany, led an expedition into the interior and hoisted the imperial flag over the major trading center of Tabora.

Peters' attempt to utilize the disturbances in Buganda to extend German influence was eminently successful. The treaty of protection obtained from Kabaka Mwanga was nullified only by his own government which, by the Heligoland Treaty, recognized Britain's supremacy there. The company was not able to meet its financial responsibilities, and in 1891 the German government assumed the direct administration of its East African possessions and Hermann von Wissmann was sent out to become the first commissioner of the territory. Between this date and 1894 the Germans pushed into Hehe country despite the hard-fought resistance of some of their chiefs. The most inflexible of the Hehe leaders was Mkwana who continued to fight the Germans long after most of the Hehe area had been conquered. Hehe resistance came to an end only with Mkwana's capture in 1898. Meanwhile Peters and other German leaders had subdued the Gogo in central Tanganyika; and the Chaga in the region of Mt. Kilimanjaro were brought more firmly under German control. Von Wissmann as early as 1895 led expeditions into the deep interior and also campaigned against the Yao in the extreme south. By 1898 the Germans had asserted their authority over the native peoples in most of the areas in German East Africa. Between 1898 and 1900 the Germans, in the face of opposition from Leopold II's troops, occupied the small heavily populated areas of first Ruanda and then Burundi.

While the Germans were skillfully utilizing diplomacy mixed with open force to consolidate their sphere of influence, the British to the north were much more halting in their interior expansion. In 1887 MacKinnon's British East Africa Association received from the sultan full political control over his northern mainland territories. The situation in Egypt and Buganda had changed substantially since the British government had refused to support MacKinnon and Johnston's ideas of expansion. By 1888 the British began to fear active encroachment by a foreign power on the headwaters of the Nile. Salisbury's government was not yet prepared to sanction the unlimited use of government funds to secure African terrritory. However, Salisbury agreed to grant a royal charter to MacKinnon's company. The Imperial British East Africa Company, unlike the other chartered companies operating in Africa, was undercapitalized from the beginning. The lack of operating capital combined with the relative poorness of the immediate interior restricted what the company could attempt. Most of the company's interests in the late 1880s was concentrated near the coast. They attempted to establish a few customs posts and forts in the interior, but the company had very little influence on the people east of Lake Victoria until the decision was made to construct a railroad in the late 1890s. Far more important to the company and the British government was the kingdom of Buganda.

European influence on Buganda began with the arrival of the first missionaries in 1877. These Church Missionary Society workers had responded to Stanley's plea that Christianity be brought to the kabaka and his people. Two years later White Fathers, a French based Catholic group, reached Buganda. It appears that Buganda was one area particularly receptive to the Christian message because within a very short period there were a significant number of converts. Unfortunately the missionaries and their growing following proved to be a divisive and not a unifying force. The Church Missionary Society group were Protestant and English while the White Fathers were Catholic and French. Each of the missionaries, although they denied it, tended to reflect the nationalistic aims of their respective European states. Very soon there were two Christian factions at the kabaka's court—the Ingleza and the Fransa. The numerically superior non-Christian element in the country and at court resented the influence wielded by the Christians. They, therefore, plotted to rid the country of the Christians.

A further important faction in Buganda were the Arab slave traders. Deeply suspicious of the Christians and the attitudes they held toward slavery, they also opposed the missionaries. At first this opposition was verbal. It later became physical because the slavers, although few in number, commanded large contingents of well-armed troops.

Kabaka Mutesa managed to placate these hostile elements, but Mwanga who succeeded him in 1884 was younger, weaker, and less experienced. Faced with great potential for civil war and watching the encroachment of Carl Peters in East Africa, he decided to act to clear Buganda of the threat of European intervention. Overjoyed at their success in eastern Africa, the Church Missionary Society appointed James Hannington as Bishop of Equatorial Africa and he left for Buganda in 1885. Because of disturbed conditions along the usual route, Hannington and his companions decided to use the way through the highlands which had just been discovered by Joseph Thomson. Mwanga, already apprehensive of the activities of Peters and the Germans, read this as a further threat to his security. He therefore ordered Hannington and his party killed in Busoga, and followed this by killing many Ingleza converts. In 1886 the Church Missionary Society was reduced to only one missionary in Buganda and the Catholics had only three. However, the missionary societies, far from being willing to abandon their projects; immediately sent more missionaries.

By mid-1888 Mwanga felt himself more threatened than ever and decided to kill all foreigners and their supporters. Before this could be done the Christian factions in Buganda joined briefly with the Arabs in support of Mwanga's brother, Kiwewa. Mwanga was forced to flee Buganda in September 1888. The coalition between Christians and Arabs was short-lived and the Arabs seized power, drove out the missionaries and their supporters, and burned the mission stations. When Kiwewa showed signs of independence of the Arabs, he was starved to death and his brother Kalema became the kabaka recognized by the Arabs. The bulk of the Christians took refuge in Ankole and there they eventually made peace with Mwanga. Supported by many of the traditional elements in Buganda society and both Christian factions, Mwanga's forces were strong enough to invade Buganda in late 1889. In four major battles the majority of the Arabs were driven from the country and Mwanga was restored to power. He then granted religious liberty to his subjects.

Before his final victory, Mwanga, soon after invading his kingdom, wrote a series of letters pleading for help from the British East Africa Company. One official of the company, Frederick Jackson, was at that time near Buganda. His party was too small and weak to intervene on behalf of Mwanga and Jackson proceeded northward without becoming involved. Some of Mwanga's letters for help fell into Carl Peters' hands and he decided that Germany could profit by the difficulties in Mwanga's kingdom.

Peters, therefore, traveled immediately to Kampala. Mwanga, whose fortunes by this time had been restored, was nevertheless prone to accept
Peters' offers of German protection. With the reluctant approval of the
Church Missionary Society, Mwanga signed the proffered treaty. Peters
left Buganda immediately for the coast to register his triumph only to
discover that his government had signed the Heligoland Treaty which
renounced all German claims to Buganda.

In August 1890, the British East Africa Company sent Captain
Frederick Lugard to Buganda to secure a definitive agreement of protection from Mwanga. Lugard's small command included fifty Sudanese
soldiers and 270 porters. Arriving in early December, Lugard entrenched
his force in a fort overlooking the kabaka's capital. Despite his weak
military position, he secured the necessary agreement from Mwanga
which gave legality to the company's claims over the area. In the following
months he intervened continually in the domestic affairs of Buganda.
One of his greatest problems was trying to maintain a balance between
the Protestant and Catholic factions, each of which wanted his support.
The agreement signed by the kabaka in December provided that the great
offices of the state would be shared between the two groups. Despite his
efforts at impartiality, Lugard was continually criticized by the Catholic
faction for favoring the Protestants.

Lugard, in conjunction with Mwanga's troops, cleared the western
areas of the country of the Muslim threat. He made contact with Selim
Bey's Sudanese troops near the southwest corner of Lake Albert and
induced them to take service with the company. Ostensibly, in order to
protect Buganda from threats from Kabarega, the ruler of Bunyoro, he
supported the young chief Kasagama in Toro and secured in August 1891
a treaty which placed Toro under company protection. He also entered
into a similar agreement with the Mugabe of Ankole. All of his fragile
successes, however, were threatened by the imminent bankruptcy of
the company. The extra cost of the Buganda venture proved too much
for its finances and in December 1891 he was ordered to retire from
Buganda. Since such a withdrawal would spell probable disaster to their
proselytizing endeavors, the Church Missionary Society in the following
month agreed to meet the company's expenses for an additional year.

The crucial area for decision making in 1892 was London where Lord
Rosebery, the liberal foreign secretary, was attempting to gain enough
popular and parliamentary support to have the government assume the
company's responsibilities. He was able, despite the opposition of most
of his colleagues in Gladstone's ministry, to have the company's expenses
guaranteed until March 1893. Lugard arrived in Britain in October 1892
and, through a series of lectures, committee meetings, informal discussions, and letters he added his support to the Church Missionary Society's
arguments for retention of Buganda. In November the government authorized that a special commissioner be sent to Buganda to determine the
situation there. Sir Gerald Portal was selected as commissioner and left
for the interior on New Year's Day 1893. He reached Kampala on March 17

and spent a total of ten weeks there. On April 1, he declared Buganda, Busoga, and Kavirondo to be under the protection of the British crown. By extension, this temporary state of affairs also applied to Toro and Ankole. In May Portal signed a new agreement with Mwanga which confirmed the premier position of the British government in Buganda rather than the company. Commissioner Portal left for the coast soon after the treaty was signed and reached Britain in early 1894.

Portal's report which supported the imperialists' position was presented to parliament in April 1894. It is doubtful whether the report did much more than change the attitudes of a few. Portal's importance lies in the time it took for him to proceed to Buganda and return with his observations. Rosebery and his supporters used that year to build solid support for the assumption of the company's position in East Africa. Rosebery became prime minister in March 1894 and by that time direct British action in Buganda was a foregone conclusion. Parliament approved the government's plan to declare a protectorate only over Buganda, and following the declaration of the protectorate, the government paid the shareholders of the Imperial British Africa Company £250,000 for their rights. MacKinnon and his associates who had acted to hold East Africa for the crown when the government was reluctant to act lost money since the government refused to pay for debts of approximately £190,000 incurred by the company.

On July 1, 1895, Britain declared the East Africa Protectorate over the hinterland territories lying between the coastal strip of the Zanzibar Protectorate and that of Buganda. On Zanzibar itself British authority had rapidly relegated the sultan to a position of impotence. In 1896 Seyyid Ali, who had held office for six years, died unexpectedly and the office of sultan was occupied by Seyyid Khalid, a son of Barghash. Khalid ordered the British consul to leave and made it clear that he expected to rule, without British help, what little was left of his dominions. However, the appearance of a British naval squadron and its bombardment of the palace forced Khalid to flee to Dar es Salaam. His elderly, placid cousin, Hamed bin Muhammad, was chosen by the British to be sultan.

While the British government was debating what action it should take in regard to Buganda, the situation there continued unsettled. Lugard before leaving for London had been confronted with potential civil war again in January 1892. Fighting between Protestants and Catholics broke out in Kampala and Lugard sided with the Protestant party. He gave arms and ammunition to the Protestants and lent the support of his machine gun to their cause. Mwanga who was the titular head of the Catholic group fled the city and was not reconciled to Lugard until March 30 when he returned to Kampala. Lugard thereupon renegotiated the treaty of 1890. In this Lugard reserved the fertile area of Buddu for Catholic activity but retained five-sevenths of the country for Protestant proselytizing. Lugard's departure later that year left a vacuum in European leadership in Buganda until Sir Gerald Portal arrived. After Portal left Kampala, he appointed Major J. R. L. MacDonald as the British representative with instructions not to interfere in Buganda politics. The instructions were almost immediately shown to be shortsighted. Captain W. F. Owen was dispatched to Toro to withdraw the British Sudanese troops from there. Later MacDonald discovered that his Sudanese garrison at Kampala had been approached by the Buganda Muslims. He disarmed the garrison just in time to prevent it from joining the revolt. The precarious nature of the British occupation convinced MacDonald to end any pretense at neutrality and to end finally the Muslim menace and also check Kabarega's designs on Toro. In December 1893, a joint force of Buganda and Sudanese troops invaded Bunyoro and in less than a year drove Kabarega north of the Nile. There followed a five-year lapse in African rule of Bunyoro until the British recognized Kabarega's twelve-year-old son as the ruler of the state. Even then all major decisions were made by a British subcommissioner while the ruler was a minor.

In 1897 Mwanga, who had never really accepted the realities of British paramountcy, left Kampala and began a final revolt against the Europeans. Although the kabaka raised a considerable force, British authority was so firmly established by then that the bulk of the people did not support their kabaka. Mwanga was deposed and his one-year-old son was declared the kabaka. Mwanga escaped northward and joined his old enemy, Kabarega, in exile north of the Nile. In April 1899, both ex-rulers were captured by the British and subsequently exiled.

Also in 1897 a large portion of the Sudanese military force in Uganda rebelled against the British. Major MacDonald, leading a force of Sudanese northward to counter what was believed to be French designs on the upper Nile, was presented with a series of demands by the Sudanese. They were generally unhappy because their salaries had not been paid and they had been prevented from bringing their women with them. The mutineers retreated to Busoga and joined other Sudanese there. The Baganda who could have taken advantage of the crucial military situation instead supported the government and helped drive the mutineers from Busoga northward beyond the Nile. Their threats to the northern border was not ended until 1901 when the British sent another military expedition against them.

In 1895 the Conservative government of Lord Salisbury, obviously impressed by Portal's description of the difficulties of carrying supplies into the interior, decided to build a railway linking the coast with Buganda. In June 1896, an initial appropriation of £3,000,000 was made. The railway builders were confronted with the full range of technical difficulties in constructing a meter gauge railroad nearly 600 miles over an escarpment over 9,000 feet high. The builders were also hampered by the opposition of the Nandi. In 1896 an expedition to Nandi country failed to defeat these warlike pastoralists. In response to continuing cattle raids and attacks on mail and other convoys, a second expedition was sent against them by the protectorate government in 1900. The troops aided by some Masai spent a number of frustrating weeks chasing the Nandi without any decisive results. The railroad eventually was built through their country only because of an agreement between the Nandi and W. W. Hobley, a subcommissioner for Kavirondo. The Nandi resumed their warlike activities in mid-1905 and it was not until the following year that the British, using Somali troops and Masai warriors, finally subdued the.i.

The Kikuyu and Kamba, as with the Luo, put up no resistance against the imposition of the British protectorate or the railway builders. This was partly because many of the Kikuyu, plagued by drought and rinderpest, had temporarily moved northward before the arrival of the Europeans. The lack of a heavy Kikuyu population later became an important factor in the alienation of Kikuyu lands in what came to be known as the '"white high-lands." The lack of a central organization also prevented the Kikuyu from taking effective joint action against the invaders.

The warlike Masai who could have caused the British considerable trouble instead became supporters of the protectorate regime and British administrators many times used Masai warriors in punitive expeditions. The British, however, encountered great difficulty incorporating the Somali of Jubaland in the protectorate. A series of costly campaigns were necessary after 1898 before they finally capitulated.

Construction of the railway did not interest many Africans and as a result the bulk of the labor force was recruited in India. At one point over 15,000 men were working on the railroad. The Indian workers were given the option of returning to India or staying in East Africa after the expiration of their contracts. Some elected to remain and the additional complicating factor of a substantial Indian population was added to the East Africa scene. The builders of the railroad encountered a series of unusual problems ranging from jiggers to lions since in 1898 work was brought to a complete stop in the Tsavo district by the depredations of two man-eating lions. Despite the difficulties, the road reached Nairobi, a former Masai kraal chosen as one of the major rail camps, in June 1899. The final inspection of the completed railroad was in October 1903, eight years after the initial decision had been made and after the expenditure of almost £8,000,000.

The last act in the assumption of British control over their East African protectorates occurred in the early twentieth century. In 1899 Sir Harry Johnston was sent to Uganda as a special commissioner to report on the future government for the area. By an agreement of 1900 Johnston settled the land question according to Indian models. The complex agreement further recognized the peculiar nature of the institutions of Buganda and the supreme authority of the kabaka, subject to British control, in the definite geographic area called Buganda. Later, in 1900, a simplified version of this type of agreement was extended to Toro and in the following year a similar treaty was made with the Mugabe of Ankole. Thus by the time of the promulgation of the Uganda Order in Council of 1902 there were three specific types of relationships between the peoples of Uganda and the British government. Bunyoro was conquered territory, the ruler of Ankole and Toro had a special position due to the treaties made with Johnston, and Buganda was, in theory, a semiautonomous state.

By the year 1900 Britain and Germany had effectively occupied most of the areas within their respective spheres of influence. There developed in the twentieth century many differences with African subjects which necessitated the use of force. However, with the exception of the Maji-Maji Rebellion in 1905 against the Germans, any disaffection of the conquered people did not develop into major revolts. Therefore, the first few years of the new century were devoted to creating structures of government which would enable the colonial power to dominate their territories as effectively and as cheaply as possible.

The Sudan

The fall of Khartoum and the death of Gordon in January 1885 ended briefly Egyptian hegemony over the Sudan and ushered in thirteen years of rule by the Mahdists. British prime minister Gladstone, using the excuse of renewed trouble in Afghanistan, immediately removed Wolseley's relief force from the Sudan. Within a year after Gordon's death there was only a skeleton force of British troops left in Egypt. The small Egyptian garrisons at Kassala and Sennar had been quickly overrun by the Mahdists, and Muhammad Ahmed's chief lieutenant in the northeast, Osman Digna, began to occupy the Red Sea littoral. Only one port, the small enclave of Suakin, was held by a combination of British and Egyptian troops.

Muhammad Ahmed survived Gordon by only five months, dying in June 1885. He had chosen the khalifa Abdullah as his successor before the fall of Khartoum. Despite this recognition, Abdullah was forced to spend the first months of his reign consolidating his position. He transferred potential rivals such as Wad el Nejumi, the victor of El Obeid, to the frontiers and reduced the Mahdi's relatives to minor positions within the government. Abdullah was a member of the small, fierce, nomadic Baggara tribe and he elevated members of that group to almost all the important positions in the state. He used them openly and skillfully to gradually negate potential opponents. Abdullah put down two minor uprisings headed by men claiming to be the true khalifa. A rebellion in Darfur in 1887 was smashed with such ferocity that many towns were burned and whole areas depopulated.

Abdullah used the memory of the departed Mahdi to further secure his control of the Sudan. He constructed a great tomb with an eighty-foot dome at Omdurman. A large rectangular area approximately one-half mile by three-fourths mile was cleared and roofed over near the tomb. This was the mosque where the khalifa prayed and instructed the people in his hopes for continuing the Mahdi's work. Abdullah, in adding to the myth of Muhammad Ahmed's invincibility, assured that much of the Mahdi's grandeur would reflect upon him. Omdurman became the chief city of the Sudan largely because of Abdullah's desire to concentrate the bulk of his armed forces there and keep its leaders under surveillance. Khartoum, by order of the khalifa, was razed in 1886 and the population forced to move to the new city. Omdurman by 1890 had an estimated population of over 150,000 persons.

The khalifa's rule was harsh, and in many cases brutal, although not as much so as was pictured in European journalistic accounts. During the khalifa's rule there was no mass exodus from the Sudan and the leaders remained loyal to Abdullah even when his theocracy was threatened by an Anglo-Egyptian invasion. The success of Abdullah's policy can be measured by the length and relative stability of his rule. However, the stories of the khalifa's cruelty which circulated throughout Britain supported the new imperialist mood of the nation and caused pressure to mount on the British government to reconquer the Sudan and avenge Gordon.

By 1888, secure in his control of the state, Abdullah began a more aggressive frontier policy. Wad el Nejumi with over 10,000 men invaded Egypt near Wadi Halfa. A large segment of the khalifa's army began to penetrate the exposed western frontiers of Ethiopia. In mid-1888, Abdullah dispatched a large force of 4,000 men and three steamers to the upper Nile to destroy the last Egyptian forces in the Sudan. There at Lado, Emin Pasha (Edward Schnitzer), the governor of Equatoria Province, with over 10,000 Egyptian men, women, and children, still resisted the Mahdists. All the other European governors who had served the khedive had seen their territory overrun and they had been taken prisoner. Henry Lupton, the Egyptian administrator of Bahr-al-Ghazal, died in captivity at Omdurman. Rudolph Slatin, governor of Darfur, survived captivity because he amused the khalifa and he also became a Muslim before his escape in 1895. Emin Pasha's situation in Equatoria was exaggerated in European accounts and Henry M. Stanley was commissioned to lead a large, well-financed expedition to rescue him. Stanley's venture, marred by dissension and hampered by disease, accident, and unexpected hardship, took almost three years of marching from the Congo to the upper Nile and eventually to Bagamoyo. Stanley finally arrived on the east coast with a reluctant Emin in December 1889. The departure of Emin and his followers from the Dufilé area of the upper Nile in February 1889 left the territory to the khalifa's forces.

The succession of almost uninterrupted success of the Mahdists was halted in 1889. Three major defeats placed the khalifa's armies on the defensive and further isolated the Sudan from the outside world. In August Wad el Nejumi's troops were destroyed by British-led Egyptian forces at Toski, sixty miles inside Egypt. This engagement ended the threat of a Sudanese invasion and gave the British time to construct in Egypt a large, well-trained army. Earlier in the year Emperor Johannes of Ethiopia had inflicted a major defeat on the khalifa's forces at Metemma. The third setback occurred when a British offensive launched from Suakin cleared a large area of the adjacent coast of Osman Digna's forces. To this list of defeats in 1889 was added increasingly serious internal problems in the khalifa's state. Diseases such as smallpox were endemic and these in combination with continual warfare had depopulated vast areas of the Sudan. Demands by the khalifa for a large army and the concentration of population at Omdurman meant that much of the arable land of the Sudan had not been under cultivation for years. Food supplies had already become critical when the locusts descended upon the Sudan in 1889. Untold thousands died in the aftermath of this catastrophe. Although the khalifa's theocracy managed to survive these blows, his economic and military situation worsened with each passing year.

In the decade following Gordon's death the shattered Egyptian economy was restored. Under the direction of Sir Evelyn Baring, the British consul, the administrative structure of Egypt was radically altered. British officials held most of the important posts in key agencies such as tax collecting and customs. Even before 1890 there was a budget surplus which could be devoted not only to paying off the foreign debts, but for major development projects in Egypt. Despite the strenuous opposition of the French members of the Caisse de la Dette, some of this surplus was devoted to the reconstruction of the Egyptian army. That army, under the direction first of Sir Evelyn Wood and after 1892 Herbert Kitchener, slowly began to develop into a modern, well-equipped, Westernized striking force. Kitchener was the perfect commander for the new army. Although British attitudes were shifting toward a more aggressive imperial policy, the British government insisted that the Egyptian government pay the expenses of modernization. Kitchener pared all unnecessary frills from the army and, to save money, arranged for much of his supplies to be manufactured in Egypt. He was a strict disciplinarian and, although he had great personal ambitions, he never openly challenged the decisions of his superiors. Kitchener had served a long period in the Sudan, commanded troops at Suakin, and appreciated the special problems of undertaking a campaign against the khalifa.

The transitional period in British imperial policy had ended by 1895. The Conservative government of Lord Salisbury after that date was prepared to follow an aggressive policy of territorial imperialism throughout Africa. The major question relating to the Sudan had ceased to be whether a reconquest should be attempted but when it should begin. The memory of Gordon which had never ceased to be a factor in British politics was now invoked to give legitimacy to this changed attitude. The collapse of the intricate British foreign policy in the Horn of Africa following the Italian defeat at Adowa meant to the active British imperialists that the invasion of the Sudan could not be postponed. Rumors of a French expedition whose objective was to claim a portion of the upper Nile were also a spur to the British government. Thus in March 1896, Kitchener was given permission to begin an open campaign against the khalifa.

Kitchener, fully appreciating the difficulty of the coming war, worried about advancing his career, and operating within a restricted budget, decided to secure his supply route by building railroads in the north before attempting to penetrate deeply into the Sudan. One rail line was planned to follow the course of the Nile to Kerma. When this was almost completed, Kitchener in September 1896 captured the major town of Dongola. In January 1897, a new line across the desert from Wadi Halfa to Abu Hamed was begun. Kitchener's strategy in 1897 was the same as the previous year. As soon as the desert line had advanced far enough, Kitchener launched an attack which secured Abu Hamed on August 7 and Berber on August 31, 1897. The railhead reached Berber in July 1898, two years after the con-

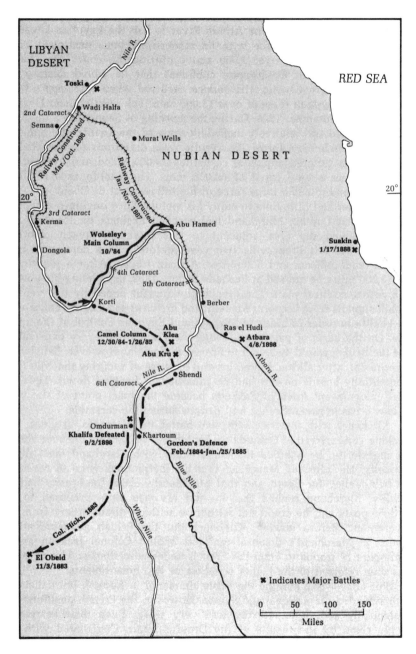

LIBYAN DESERT

Nile R.

Toski ✖

2nd Cataract

Wadi Halfa

Semna

Railway Constructed Mar./Oct. 1896

Murat Wells

Railway Constructed Jan./Nov. 1897

NUBIAN DESERT

RED SEA

20°

20°

3rd Cataract

Kerma

Wolseley's Main Column 10/'84

Abu Hamed

Dongola

4th Cataract

5th Cataract

Korti

Berber

Suakin ● 1/17/1888 ✖

Camel Column 12/30/84-1/26/85

Abu Klea ✖

Ras el Hudi

✖ **Atbara 4/8/1898**

Abu Kru ✖

Nile R.

6th Cataract

Shendi

Atbara R.

Omdurman ✖ ● Khalifa Defeated 9/2/1898

● Khartoum

Gordon's Defence Feb./1884-Jan./25/1885

Blue Nile

Col. Hicks, 1883

White Nile

✖ **El Obeid 11/3/1883**

✖ Indicates Major Battles

0   50   100   150

Miles

Campaigns in the Sudan, 1883–1898

quest had begun. The khalifa's forces, concentrated at Omdurman, had seriously challenged the Egyptian army only once. In April 1898, Emir Mahmoud advanced down the Atbara River to halt the Egyptian advance. Kitchener's disciplined force with its modern weapons destroyed Mahmoud's attempt, killing over 2,000 and capturing the emir. The khalifa continued to wait at Omdurman, confident that he would destroy his enemies in one great battle. His chance occurred when Kitchener's well-rested Anglo-Egyptian force of over 15,000 men took position near Omdurman in early September 1898. During the morning of September 2 the huge but ill-equipped and relatively inefficient army of the khalifa attempted to overwhelm Kitchener's force. The results were disastrous for the khalifa. The Mahdists suffered appalling casualties—9,000 killed and over 10,000 wounded from a total force of 60,000 men. The khalifa escaped from Omdurman and joined a large force of his followers at El Obeid.

Kitchener had little time to enjoy his victory since intelligence reports indicated that Captain Marchand had reached Fashoda on the Nile and had proclaimed the area adjacent to this town as French territory. Marchand had left Brazzaville two years before with a contingent of a dozen French officers and a hundred African troops. After a journey of over 3,000 miles he arrived at Fashoda in July 1898, completing his portion of a daring political plan. The French government hoped by this venture to gain support from Emperor Menelik and arrive at some compromise with the khalifa in order to block the British and Egyptian control of the upper Nile. On the basis of past negotiations the French had every expectation that the British would succumb to French diplomacy. However, Salisbury's government, after all the difficulties and expense of securing the Nile from a potentially hostile power, had no intention of backing down. Thus the small insignificant town of Fashoda became the focal point of the most serious crisis between France and Britain during the scramble.

Kitchener with five steamers, two battalions of troops, artillery, and machine guns arrived at Fashoda on September 18. Despite his overwhelming superiority, he handled the conferences with Marchand most diplomatically. He informed Marchand that his instructions were to reoccupy the Nile Valley for Egypt and that Marchand's claim for France had no validity. Marchand replied that he and his men were prepared to die at their posts and he could not withdraw without direct orders from his government. Before leaving, Kitchener put the British communications system at Marchand's disposal and left behind Colonel Jackson and a contingent of troops to keep the French under surveillance. The question was then referred to the higher echelons of two governments.

For almost two months the crisis simmered in Europe. Journalists on both sides fed the nationalistic flames. However, the French position both strategically and diplomatically was very weak. Even their army was deeply riven by the results of the Dreyfus affair. Confronted with the united, unmoving position of Britain, the French government capitulated in early November. On December 11 the French flag was lowered at Fashoda, their troops evacuated northward, and the crisis was ended. In March of the following year an agreement was signed between the two powers which reserved the valley of the Nile to Britain and Egypt. In the same month Britain and Egypt agreed to rule the Sudan with a condominium form of government and Kitchener was appointed the first governor-general.

During the entire period of the Fashoda crisis the khalifa was still operating in Kordofan with a considerable force. Finally, in October 1899, Kitchener learned that Abdullah with his major advisers were in Baggara country at Jebel Gedir, 400 miles south of Khartoum. Sir Reginald Wingate and 8,000 troops were immediately sent in pursuit. On November 24 the Egyptian forces, having surrounded the khalifa, rushed the camp. The Mahdist losses again were very heavy. After the battle the bodies of the khalifa and his chief lieutenants were found in one place where, after their retreat was cut off, they waited to be killed. Although punitive expeditions continued, the death of the khalifa spelled the end to the Mahdist dream of dominance in northeastern Africa. Finally, in January 1900, the last of the major Mahdist leaders, Osman Digna, was captured.

The 1899 agreement with Egypt did not establish a true equality between Egypt and Britain in the governing of the Sudan. The supreme authority there was a British governor-general nominated by the British. He was the executive authority, could legislate by proclamation, and was until the death of Sir Lee Stack in 1924 the sirdar or commander in chief of the Egyptian army.

The Sudan was divided into provinces each under a British governor and these were subdivided into districts with at first an Egyptian officer in control. In time British inspectors came to be the actual administrators of the districts with the Egyptians shoved into the background. Not until after World War I were many Sudanese recruited into government service.

In the beginning most of the administrative personnel were of the military. Very soon it became necessary to establish a more regular formal procedure for recruitment. The Sudan civil service was developed which operated in a manner comparable to the Colonial Office and India Office. The Sudan government staff was chosen annually in London by a board from hopefuls who had finished their university education. The Sudan service was small with much scope for individual initiative and, since most officers spent their entire careers in the Sudan, they gained considerable expertise in their areas and took great pride in their work.

Sir Reginald Wingate became governor-general when Kitchener was ordered to South Africa in 1899. Wingate was responsible for laying the groundwork for civil government and the establishment of a law system based on Indian models. His administration completed the rail network begun during the 1896–1898 war and began the experiments in irrigation which later resulted in the very profitable cotton-producing area of the Gezira.

The coming of World War I had profound effects upon the Sudan. In the winter of 1914 the khedive of Egypt, Abbas II, was deposed and Britain proclaimed a protectorate over Egypt. This action exposed the shallowness of condominium rule since Britain now directly controlled both Egypt and the Sudan. The war also gave Wingate the excuse to conquer the autonomous sultanate of Darfur. After the defeat of the khalifa, Sultan Ali Dinar had ruled Darfur without interference from the British. But his alleged pro-Turkish views were considered a threat to the Sudan so Wingate sent 2,000 troops into Darfur. El Fasher was taken in May 1916, and Ali Dinar was killed in November. (Final boundary agreements with the French territory of Chad were made in 1919.)

The southern areas of the Sudan had been almost cut off from control by Khartoum during the Mahdia. Imposition of condominium rule in the south was followed by years of ferreting out of the small-scale slave trade. Slavery was not directly attacked since the British hoped that with improved economic conditions it would fade away. One precaution against it was the virtual exclusion from the south of northern Sudanese. This factor added to differences in race, religion, and historical development further estranged the northern segment of the Sudan from the south.

Following World War I nationalist disturbances wracked Egypt and these culminated in British recognition of its independence. Some of the nationalist feelings found supporters in the educated minority of the Sudanese. The first political movement reflecting such ideas was the United Tribes Society led by Abd al Latif. He later formed the White Flag League which hoped eventually to form a united Nile state of Egypt and the Sudan. This league was secretly supported by Egyptians. There were disturbances at Omdurman and in Khartoum in June 1924, and an Egyptian battalion mutinied at the same time.

Sudanese nationalists were dealt a severe blow by the assassination of Sir Lee Stack, the governor-general and sirdar of the Egyptian army, in November 1924. Field Marshal Edmund Allenby, the British high commissioner, ordered all Egyptian troops out of the Sudan and thus Egyptian participation in the practical affairs of the condominium were almost ended and a radical element in Sudanese nationalism was removed. Subsequent British actions showed a deep mistrust of the Western-educated Sudanese. Education on all levels was not adequately supported and military training of Sudanese lagged as British administrators began to depend for support much more on traditional rulers.

The fifteen-year period after the conclusion of the Anglo-Egyptian Treaty is a complex melange of forces. Egypt sought to maintain its special theoretical position in the Sudan and resist what it considered any British attempt to sever these historical ties. Britain, concerned for many years with the many problems in Europe prior to World War II, considered the Sudan merely an adjunct to other more pressing Middle Eastern questions. The Sudanese middle classes associated themselves with one of two major parties which evolved in the 1940s. These parties were the result of a split in an older organization, the Graduate General Congress. Ismail al Azhari in 1943 formed the first genuine Sudanese political party, the Ashiqqa, which stood for cooperation with Egypt looking toward the creation of a new larger Nile Valley state. The other party, the Umma, was more moderate and was prepared to cooperate with the

British toward the goal of Sudanese independence. Each party, to give the British evidence of mass support, associated itself with a major Islamic brotherhood. The Ashiqqa was supported by the Khatmiyya, the most important sect in the Sudan before the mahdi's triumph. The Umma received the sanctions of the mahdi's posthumous son, Abd al Rahman, and the Mahdists. These connections between political parties and religious brotherhoods meant a widening rift between the nothern Sudanese political groups.

In May 1944, the British administration created an advisory council composed of twenty-eight Sudanese members, eighteen of whom were elected. Most of those on the advisory council were Umma party members, but they did not take over the role of the governor-general's council which continued to be, as it had since 1910, the major legislative body. The Ashiqqa was not satisfied with the advisory council and remained suspicious of Britain's plans for the future of the southern Sudan and the Sudan's relationship with Egypt.

In 1946 British Foreign Secretary Ernest Bevin issued a "draft Sudan protocol" which called for ultimate Sudanese self-government but under the "common crown of Egypt." This attempt to please both Sudanese groups failed since it alienated the Umma without placating the Ashiqqa politicians. Despite the growing British-Egyptian difficulties the liberalization of the Sudanese government continued rapidly before 1950. In 1948 the British unilaterally authorized the establishment of a Legislative Assembly which would represent the entire Sudan. Fifty-two members represented the northern areas and thirteen were either directly or indirectly elected to represent the south. An Executive Council, half of whom were Sudanese, replaced that of the old governor-general's. Negotiations between Britain and Egypt over the future of the Sudan produced nothing. Britain's position by 1950 was the same as the Umma-dominated assembly while Egypt and the Ashiqqa wanted a larger Egyptian dominated Nile polity.

Somaliland

The opening of the Suez Canal in 1869 brought hundreds of ships every year into the Red Sea. European states and trading companies became concerned with establishing ports near the Straits of Bab-el-Mendeb and on the western flank of the Indian Ocean. The French secured Obock and later Djibouti. British interests were maintained at Aden while the Italians were engaged with the Eritrean coastline. It was an extension of European attitudes toward the Far Eastern trade which brought Europeans to the hitherto inhospitable Somali coastline. There were few towns of importance along the entirety of the coast stretching from Djibouti to Mogadishu. The vast interior, made up largely of bush land and semi-desert, was inhabited by many postoral Somali clans who wandered with their animal herds as far inland as the Haud and Ogaden areas. The hinterland Somalis, converts to Islam, relatively small in number and fierce warriors, had never evolved large viable state structures. Only along the coast was there a pretense of centralized control. Near the Horn of Africa the sultan of Mijertein maintained a tenuous rule over an undefined interior area. In the 1880s the ruler of Obbia declared himself independent of the sultan of Mijertein and in the ensuing years tried to extend his influence northward.

In order to strengthen themselves in the Bab-el-Mendeb area, the British occupied the major coast towns from Zeila to Berbera and declared this territory. a British protectorate in 1884. They were not interested in the hinterland territories and maintained only casual contact with the Somali clans there. The Italians were at first interested in the Benadir region of the extreme south. A chartered company first secured rights to the coastline near Mogadishu. In 1884 an agent of the company convinced both the sultan of Obbia and the sultan of Mijertein to place themselves under Italian protection. As with the British, this did not imply anything more than theoretical sovereignty. The sultans were interested in obtaining guns and ammunition from the Italians which they could possibly use against one another. They received a cash subsidy from the Italians. The Italian resident at Mogadishu made an annual tour to the north to visit each ruler to pay the subsidy. This was the limit of Italian power until the opening years of the twentieth century despite the proclamation of a protectorate over southern Somalia in 1889. Hostility between the two sultanates became serious in the years after 1897 when adherents of the northern ruler began to raid deep into Obbia. Finally in 1901 the Italians lent military support to the sultan of Obbia and thus the balance between the two areas was restored.

A new factor was introduced in 1895 into this politically confused area. Muhammad Abdullah Hassan, later given the pejorative title the "Mad Mullah" by the British, returned to British Somaliland. He had been born in the Nogal Valley in the 1860s but had migrated first to Aden where he studied Islamic law. Later, after trips to Mecca, he fell under the influence of a famous teacher of the Ahmadiyah sect, Muhammad Salih. Later Muhammad Abdullah became one of the main organizers and instructors in the even more puritanical belief begun by his mentor which was called the Salihiyah. He had already gained considerable fame before he appeared in Somaliland attempting to convince the worldly Qadariyah Somalis to abandon their ways. Muhammad Abdullah's initial success in converting coastal Somali was only minimal and he moved into the interior. As a mullah or judge he soon gained a wide reputation and a considerable following among the Darod Somali. He was strong enough by 1899 to have his forces occupy certain strategic interior watering places and declare a jihad against the unbelievers. He at first directed his war against those who professed Islam but resisted his teaching. However, the British at Berbera believed that he was attempting to establish political hegemony over British Somaliland and the Ogaden areas of Ethiopia and reacted accordingly. Muhammad Abdullah obtained for his followers rifles and ammunition at greatly inflated prices from Sultan Osman Mahmud of Mijertein. By the end of 1900 the mullah's followers had

Northeastern Africa

almost halted trade in British Somaliland and had raided deep into the Ogaden for camels and rifles. A combined British and Ethiopian force of 17,000 men penetrated deeply into Somalia to end these attacks. This invasion was the first of a series of failures in the long campaign against Muhammad Abdullah. In 1903 the British with Italian consent used Obbia as the point of departure for another expedition. This too failed to capture the mullah or to end the activities of his followers. The only concrete result of these campaigns was to cause Muhammad Abdullah to occupy briefly the Nogal Valley. However, in 1904 another British expedition drove him into Mijertein.

The Italians had not participated actively in any of these punitive expeditions. In 1905 the mullah made an agreement with the Italians whereby he agreed to accept Italian protection in return for their promise to recognize him as the ruler of Nogal. For three years there was a minimum amount of conflict between Muhammad Abdullah and the Europeans. From his secure base he sent out converts into all Somali areas and these acted as agents of potential revolt. This three-year period witnessed continual quarrels between the two sultans and increasing exercise of authority by Italy. In 1909 an Italian resident was established in Obbia and at Alula. Disputes within the Salihiyah movement weakened the mullah's position. He was even denounced by Muhammad Salih. Despite this he rejected the proposals brought by Sir Reginald Wingate and Slatin Pasha which would have brought permanent peace to the interior. Perhaps as a belated recognition of the futility of their previous policy, the British abandoned the interior to Muhammad's followers in 1909 and concentrated all their troops in the coastal towns of British Somaliland. Muhammad Abdullah then moved his main base of operations to Taleh, a fortress he constructed in British Somaliland.

During World War I the British and Italians continued to solidify their administrative control over the coast. Increased military force enabled them to intervene successfully in hinterland disputes. At the same time many of the adherents of the mullah began to drift away. His attempt to cement a more definite alliance with Lij Iyasu of Ethiopia was foiled by the overthrow of the young emperor in 1916. At the close of World War I the mullah's direct influence was confined to southeastern British Somaliland. In 1920 the British decided to end the continued threat of raids and warfare posed by Muhammad Abdullah. In January of that year, over 1,500 tribesmen and a cadre of British troops opened the campaign. A new factor was introduced by the British who used aircraft for scouting and bombing. In February Taleh fell to the British, but the mullah and a few of his followers escaped to the Ogaden. The mullah's waning popularity is shown by his inability to gain support for his cause in Ethiopia. British native troops with Ethiopian permission crossed the border and forced the mullah to flee again. The close of the long career of Muhammad Abdullah came in January 1921 when he died of pneumonia. Unlike the mahdi in the Sudan, he had not built a stable state structure nor did he leave behind a competent successor. With his death the political and military overtones of his movement came to an end. The death of the mullah removed the last major obstacle to British and Italian control of the interior. Each European state established a type of indirect rule over the nomads of interior Somali. Boundaries between both British and Italian areas and Ethiopia remained indefinite. This factor later provided Mussolini with the excuse necessary to begin his war of conquest against Ethiopia. In that war General Graziani with one division operated from Somaliland against the southern flank of Haile Selassie's forces. On June 1, 1936, Italian Somaliland became a partner with Eritrea and Ethiopia in a new government structure called Italian East Africa. After Italy's entrance into World War II, Somaliland was an active theater of operations and British Empire forces completed the conquest of Italian Somaliland in early 1941 prior to their main invasion of Ethiopia.

SIX
Consolidation of British power in Southern Africa, 1872–1910

General economic and political developments

The domestic political history of Cape Colony after 1872 is a story of important but generally unexciting decisions made by competent, if not flamboyant, personalities. Sir John Molteno was the dominant figure in Cape politics until his resignation as prime minister in 1878. He quarreled with the governor, Sir Bartle Frere, on the use of colonial troops in the war against Kreli, the Xosa leader. He was succeeded by Sir Gordon Sprigg whose government tended to represent the eastern Cape settlers against the more populous and prosperous western area. Sprigg's ministry was cut short by the adverse reaction to his attempts to disarm the Basuto. Sir Thomas Scanlon, backed by the moderate Boers, became prime minister only to be succeeded by Sprigg once again. Specific domestic issues rather than major philosophical differences determined the composition of Cape political parties. Of far more significance to the history of southern Africa than the actions of any of these political leaders was the influence of two men—Cecil Rhodes and J. H. Hofmeyer.

Rhodes had become by 1884 a political figure with considerable power. His mission to Goshen and Stellaland and his subsequent activities in Bechuanaland indicated how far he was willing to go to further his dreams of imperial expansion from the Cape. His success in finance and politics can be attributed, in large measure, to his understanding of events and men. His idea that anyone could be "squared," meant that all men were amenable to reason and all had their price. To achieve one's goal it was necessary to find out the price, offer to meet it, and then be patient. This concept, however cynical, enabled him to create De Beers Company, the British South Africa Company, Consolidated Goldfields, and finally in 1890 to become prime minister of Cape Colony.

J. H. Hofmeyer in many ways operated similarly to Rhodes.

He believed in reason, compromise, and was content to work behind the scenes. In 1883 he gained control of the Afrikander Bond, a heretofore anti-British organization. He converted it from its narrow adherence to the dream of Boer nationalism to an organization devoted to partnership between Boer and Briton. He envisioned, for the future, a united South Africa wherein each national unit had a meaningful, constructive role. Hofmeyer and the Bond cooperated with Rhodes, supporting him for prime minister twice. Hofmeyer utilized his talents and prestige to help create friendly relations between the British and the Boer republics, particularly with the Orange Free State. The cooperation between Rhodes and Hofmeyer and between moderate Boers and Britons was shattered by the disastrous Jameson raid of 1895.

Political activities in all the states of southern Africa were conducted in the last quarter of the century against a background of rapid economic development. White population in all areas increased dramatically during this period. Cape Colony's white population was almost one-half million by 1899, an increase of almost one hundred percent over the figure in 1872. Natal's European population rose from 20,000 to approximately 90,000 in the same period while the Orange Free State recorded a rise from 27,000 to almost 100,000. The South African Republic showed the greatest increase in its white population from 40,000 in 1873 to 250,000 by the beginning of the Boer War.

These increases in population were closely related to economic developments. Total railroad mileage in 1872 in all of southern Africa was only sixty-three miles. By 1899 it had grown to almost 3,600 miles. Correlate developments could be noted in harbor, telegraph, and road facilities. The railway opened up lands, heretofore unprofitable, for agriculture, particularly cereal crops. Diamonds provided an annual export from the Cape in the five years before the Boer War valued at over $20 million while the average annual export of gold was valued at over $55 million. The export of diamonds alone exceeded the total value of annual exports from the Cape in 1870. The development of sugar and tea plantations in Natal raised its exports from approximately $2.5 million in 1872 to almost $10 million by 1895.

The area under direct European administration grew tremendously in this same period. Cape Colony assumed jurisdiction from Britain over Griqualand West in 1880 and British Bechuanaland in 1895. Continuing problems related to the uprising of the Xosa led by Kreli culminated in the absorption of the Transkei by the Cape; and Natal acquired Tongaland and Zululand in 1897. The expansionist dreams of the South African Republic were largely blocked by the northward thrust of Cecil Rhodes' British South Africa Company, but in 1885 Kruger managed to gain temporary control over Swaziland. Matabeleland, Mashonaland, and much of the area across the Zambesi were secured for Britain before 1895 by the actions of the British South Africa Company.

Two opposing native policies developed in southern Africa. In Cape Colony, while recognizing the uniqueness of African institutions, legislation was aimed at integrating the Bantu into the state. This was but a continuation of a historical trend dating to the passage of the Fiftieth Ordinance in 1828. A special native penal code for the Transkei was established, the peculiar position of chiefs recognized, and the machinery for basic legislation by the governor created. In 1894 the first of the district councils for Xosa in both the Ciskei and Transkei regions was formed. In Natal, native policy continued to follow the general outlines formulated by Theophilus Shepstone during his long tenure as chief native commissioner. This had envisioned the creation of separate native reserves with traditional rulers controlled indirectly by Europeans. Natal formulated a code of Bantu law in 1878 to be supplanted by a more comprehensive code in 1891. On the economic level the Cape's concern with ultimate integration led to the introduction to the Bantu areas of European methods of industry and agriculture. In Natal, except for the intervention of European political officers, the Bantu were left to themselves on their reserves.

The Zulu War and the Transvaal question

Events in southern Africa in the late 1870s were contingent upon two main interconnected themes. One, already noted, was the continuing desire of some British administrators, notably the governor and high commissioner, Sir Bartle Frere, to extend the influence of the crown over the Boer republics. The other concerned the revived martial spirit of the Zulu and the distinct possibility that their impis would spill across the frontier in an orgy of killing. The man most responsible for keeping alive this fear was Theophilus Shepstone, the long-time chief native commissioner in Natal. He was, to the inexperienced Bartle Frere, the recognized expert on the Zulu. He was also trusted by the Zulu who believed he would present their case to the governor with truth and understanding. Shepstone, instead, aligned himself with the alarmists after 1876 and used the Zulu "menace" to excuse the British occupation of the South African Republic.

The Zulu ruler was Cetewayo who had officially succeeded his ineffectual father, Panda, in 1872. Cetewayo, however, had been the actual ruler of Zululand after 1856. In that year Cetewayo's warriors defeated and killed his younger brother, Umbulazi, and the majority of his enemies in a bloody battle on the Tugela River. Centralization of authority returned to Zululand under Cetewayo. The military regiments assumed an importance not seen since the time of Dingane. Cetewayo could not be manipulated easily either by the British in Natal or by the Boers in the north. Although his impis raided to the north and west, Cetewayo was scrupulous to avoid any massive intrusion into British territory. The Zulu also respected the farms of the Boers of the tiny republic of Utrecht.

In 1868 Utrecht was absorbed into the larger South African Republic and almost immediately there arose difficulties concerning the boundary between the Republic and the Zulu. Cetewayo maintained that much of the territory of Utrecht belonged to the Zulu who had allowed the Boers simply to use the land. The South African Republic was a study in contrasts. Their officials were bombastic and at the same time afraid. By the time that Frere arrived in South Africa it was generally feared that Cetewayo was ready to send his 10,000 celibate warriors north against the Boers who continued to press their claims for the land adjacent to the Zulu. Eventually a commission was appointed to investigate the counter claims of the Boer and Zulu to the land. Although no Zulu was represented on the commission, Cetewayo agreed to accept its findings.

Sir Bartle Frere had arrived as governor of Cape Colony and high commissioner in March 1877. He had previously distinguished himself as an administrator in India, but had no African experience. He was an ardent champion of Lord Carnarvon's ideas concerning confederation of all southern Africa united under the crown. Furtherance of this was always foremost in his thoughts. He depended for advice upon African experts, particularly Theophilus Shepstone. Frere and Shepstone both saw in the Boer fears and Zulu resurgence a chance to extend British control northward and also end the potential menace of the Zulu.

The South African Republic was bankrupt. Its prodigal land policy, aggressive attitudes toward neighboring Bantu, lax taxation system, and no important exports combined in 1876 to render the territory economically impotent. An ill-timed war with Sekukuni, chief of the Bapedi, was the final act in the developing insolvency of the republic. In the face of the mounting Zulu threat, President T. F. Burgers invited British aid. Shepstone rode northward to Pretoria with only twenty-four soldiers in December 1876. After discussions with members of the volksraad and against a strong minority feeling exemplified by Paul Kruger, Shepstone on April 12, 1877, raised the Union Jack and declared the state annexed to the crown. Such were the fears of the Zulu menace that few Boers protested this action. One link toward the confederation scheme which had so recently failed had been forged. The next step was to negate the Zulu menace.

A lesser chief of the Zulu in July 1878 crossed into Natal after two of his unfaithful wives, seized them, and took them back to be executed. This incident together with the continued "barbarous" practices of the Zulu and the use of their impis against neighboring peoples served as the ostensible reason for direct military action against them. Frere's schemes were almost upset by the announcement of the land commission that most of the Zulu claims to the disputed northern lands were justified. Frere, instead of using this as a basis for rapprochement with Cetewayo, attempted to mask the decision, and delivered instead an ultimatum to Cetewayo. If the Zulu chief had accepted the demands in the ultimatum, particularly those relating to Zulu military organization, and receiving a British president, Zululand would have ceased to be independent. It would have become a de facto dependency of Britain. Cetewayo was given twenty days to comply. He announced his reservations to the ultimatum and the date (December 31, 1878) for compliance passed. Thereupon Frere ordered General Thesiger (later Lord Chelmsford) to occupy Zululand.

Thesiger who had been alerted to his task some months before was

British Operations in Zululand, 1879

INDIAN OCEAN

NGOME MTS.

Approximate
High Hill Line

Black Umfolozi R.

White Umfolozi R.

ZULU

INHLAZATYE MT.

LAND

● Ulundi ✕

● Mtonjameni

Dingaan's Kraal ●

Ft. Marshall ●

Ft. Cambridge ●

● Isandhlwana ✕

Ft. Marshall ●

Fugitive's ✕ ISIPEZ HILL
Drift

Blood R.

Landman's Drift

Rorke's Drift ✕

● Helpmakaar

Umhlotuzi R.

● Eshowe ✕
✕ Gingindhlova

Tugela R.

Middle Drift

Ft. Buckingham ●

Ft. Cherry ●

● Ft. Durnford

● Ft. Napolean

● Ft. Chelmsford

● Nondkasuka

Ft. Pearson ● Lower Drift

Miles

0   10   20   30

✕ Indicates Major Battles

⇵ 1st Invasion—Jan. 1879

⇵ 2nd Invasion—June 1879

167

not eager for a campaign in the hilly, stream-crossed country adjacent to Natal. He asked for reinforcements of men and material, most of which were refused him. Nevertheless, on January 11, 1879, he invaded Zululand, dividing his 12,000 man army composed of some regulars, Natal and Cape militia, and native troops, into three columns. The plan was for these three to converge on the Zulu capital of Ulundi. Commanding the middle column of 1,600 Europeans and 2,500 natives, he advanced from Rorke's Drift to Isandhlwana. On the morning of January 22, Thesiger took a small force to reconnoiter ahead. The remaining force, occupying an extremely defensible position, was attacked by approximately 10,000 Zulu. There is evidence that the Zulu did not plan to fight at Isandhlwana, but simply chanced on the British force. Nevertheless, the Zulu commanders reacted intelligently to their opportunity. British leadership was never worse. A tragic parade of errors negated the bravery of the individual soldier. Before the day was finished 806 Europeans and 471 African troops had been killed, Thesiger's army was shattered, and except for the heroic defense of Rorke's Drift, Natal itself would have felt the wrath of the Zulu. The defense by less than 200 men, mainly Welsh Borderers under the command of Lieutenants Chard and Bromhead, saved one of the main crossings over the Tugela River for the British.

After Isandhlwana, Thesiger received the support in men and equipment which he had earlier requested. Regrouping his forces, he reinvaded Zululand in May. Armed with field guns, rocket tubes, and gatling guns, his forces defeated the Zulu at Dingane's old capital of Umgungundhlovo. The Zulu lost 1,200 men in this engagement while the British lost two. The campaign continued for almost three months until the final Zulu defeat at their burning capital of Ulundi on July 4. Thesiger had been officially replaced in command by Sir Garnet Wolseley, but Wolseley had not yet arrived in southern Africa. Thus Thesiger avenged Isandhlwana and was responsible for the capture of Cetewayo.

Cetewayo was sent into exile, lived a part of this time in London, and eventually was allowed to return to his country where he died in 1884. But Zulu power was broken. Britain did not annex the territory; it was divided into eleven chieftaincies. Soon these chiefs were quarreling with each other. The royal house was almost destroyed by these disputes. A Boer, Lukas Meyer, and his followers proclaimed one of Cetewayo's sons, Dinizulu, a puppet king of the Boer New Republic in 1884. After British protests over this action that section of Zululand was incorporated into the South African Republic as the Vryheid area. Finally in 1897 Britain, concerned with the possible eastward expansion of Kruger's South African Republic, formally joined Zululand with Natal.

The defeat of Cetewayo removed the major threat to the security of the Boers of the high veld. The high-handed attitudes of Sir Garnet Wolseley, who had been appointed high commissioner for Southeastern Africa and administrator of the former South African Republic, alienated many of the Boer supporters of British rule. Thus within a year after Ulundi the majority of Boers north of the Vaal supported Paul Kruger in demanding an end to British control. In Britain Lord Carnarvon's successor as colonial secretary, Sir Michael Hicks-Beach, was not a confirmed advocate of confederation. The cost in lives and money of the Zulu War had discredited Bartle Frere. Therefore there was no high British official who was willing to defend the previous policy of expansion. In the parliamentary campaign of 1880 William E. Gladstone denounced the imperialism of Disraeli and the Conservatives and promised if elected he would remove the British presence from beyond the Vaal. Gladstone and his Liberal party won the elections. However, other problems occupied his attention and nothing was done to implement his promise concerning South Africa.

In December 1880, abandoning peaceful means, the Boers reconvened their volksraad and proclaimed the restoration of the republic. Paul Kruger, Marthinius Pretorius, and General Joubert were appointed a triumverate to guard the interests of the new state. The first shots of the renewed conflict with Britain were fired on December 16 at Potchefstroom. The British had only 3,500 men in all of South Africa to oppose the uprising. The small British garrisons in the republic were beleaguered and a larger force at Bokhurst Spruit was defeated by Boer marksmen. The lieutenant-governor of Natal, General George Colley, attempted twice to force entrance into the republic but was forced to turn back. In late February, Colley took up a new position in northern Natal on Amajuba, "Hill of Doves," rising over 2,000 feet above the plain. On February 26 Commandant-General Joubert's troops stormed the hill, killing eighty-five regulars and General Colley. Kruger received the British armistice proposals the day after the Majuba action and he immediately accepted them. By the Pretoria Convention signed later in the year the Transvaal received its independence subject to acknowledgment of British suzerainty. This meant that Britain continued to control the foreign and native policies of the new state. In 1883 the rule of the triumverate over the Transvaal came to an end and Kruger was elected president. By the London Convention of the following year the republic was allowed to make its own treaties and Britain gave up the right to veto native legislation. After seven years for all practical, if not legal, purposes, the South African Republic was once again independent.

British activities north of the Limpopo

Imperialism in southern Africa more than any other area of the continent depended upon decisions made by Europeans resident in Africa rather than on officials at home. The man who was the driving force behind British expansion northward from Cape Colony was Cecil John Rhodes. A sickly boy of sixteen when he arrived in Africa in 1870, he had made a fortune in diamonds before he was thirty. From his early twenties Rhodes had been convinced that British culture represented man's highest development. The later popular phrase "white man's burden" was an imperative to action from him. Thus he was prepared to expend his own personal fortune to secure the future of the British empire in Africa. In the period of transition before 1895, Rhodes' willingness to finance imperial schemes enabled him to receive permission to proceed from the home government whereas imperialists with little wealth such as Sir Harry Johnston or Sir Samuel Rowe would be denied such permission. Rhodes, active in all areas of Cape finance, became in the late 1880s deeply involved in the exploitation of gold on the Rand. As head of Consolidated Goldfields, he became the most powerful voice demanding that Kruger ameliorate conditions for the Uitlanders. He combined financial power with political influence, becoming prime minister of Cape Colony in 1890.

In 1881 Rhodes was first elected to the Cape parliament from a predominantly Boer district. Almost immediately he assumed a major role in the debates and actions concerning Bechuanaland. Boers from the South African Republic had established two ostensibly independent governments, Stellaland and Goshen, in the lands of the Tswana people. This, combined with German annexation of Angra Pequeña, aroused fears in Rhodes and other imperialists that the road for British expansion to the north would be blocked. Rhodes played an important role in convincing the British government to send Sir Charles Warren into Bechuanaland in 1885. Subsequently the southern portion of that territory was annexed as a crown colony while a protectorate was declared as far north as the Zambesi. There was little trouble with the Africans since the major Tswana chiefs such as Khama had already requested that the British protect them from the South African Republic. For Rhodes, although he disagreed with the methods used, Warren's actions assured that the narrow strip of fertile land between the South African Republic and the Kalahari Desert would remain in British hands. Thus he could continue to plan on an all "red" map of east and southern Africa so necessary for his later concept of a Cape to Cairo railway.

SOUTHERN RHODESIA

The pursuance of his imperial ambitions led Cecil Rhodes to look beyond the Limpopo to the lands controlled by the Matabele ruler, Lo Bengula. Discovery of gold on the Rand in 1886 lured many gold prospectors and entrepreneurs north into Matabeleland in the hope of duplicating this rich gold find. In 1887 Piet Grobler, an official of the South African government, entered into a treaty with Lo Bengula which would have given Kruger's government the preeminent position in Matabeleland. However, John Moffat, a former missionary and the assistant commissioner in Bechuanaland, secured a repudiation of this treaty in February 1888. This reopened his territory to many concession hunters who came to Lo Bengula's kraal at Bulawayo during 1888. Among them were representatives of a number of powerful German and British concerns. Lo Bengula resisted the advice of his more practical-minded advisers and refused to kill the Europeans. He did not grant any major concessions until October 1888. With advice from Sir Sydney Shippard, the commissioner for Bechuanaland, the Bishop of Bloemfontein, and the missionary Charles Helm, the king finally decided to give Rhodes' representatives, Charles Rudd, Rochefort Macguire, and

Francis Thompson, the sole right to look for gold in his country.

Armed with the so-called "Rudd Concession," Rhodes went to London, formed a company, and eventually in October 1889 secured a royal charter. Rhodes' new venture, the British South Africa Company, was ostensibly designed to search for gold, but to Rhodes it was the necessary vehicle to carry the flag northward to the Zambesi. After securing the charter, he and his close associate, Leander Starr Jameson, went north in early 1890 and secured from an alarmed Lo Bengula the assurance that the pioneers "could have the road." In June the pioneers accompanied by 400 mounted men, the nucleus of the company police, entered Matabeleland. Despite the assurance given Jameson by Lo Bengula, there was great danger that the war party at Bulawayo would gain the upperhand and force Lo Bengula to launch his 18,000 warriors against the pioneers. However, there were no incidents and Jameson proceeded to establish Fort Victoria, Fort Charter, and Salisbury and began to parcel out town and farm sites to the volunteers.

The company had hardly been established north of the Limpopo when the question of Portuguese claims to Manicaland became very important. In September 1890, Jameson traveled to Manicaland and entered into a treaty with one of the great chiefs, Mtasa, which gave the company a preeminent position in his country. However, the Anglo-Portuguese agreement of August 1890 undermined the company's position. Fortunately for Rhodes, the Portuguese Cortes, in a flurry of patriotic indignation, rejected the treaty. The Portuguese dispatched Manuel de Souza, with a small armed force, to occupy Mtasa's village. The Portuguese had hardly settled in when British South African Company troops stormed the village, arrested the Portuguese, and raised the "Union Jack." Thus Manicaland was secured for the company. However, Rhodes' ambitions toward Gazaland were blocked by the Anglo-Portuguese agreement of June 1891 which assigned that area to the Portuguese.

Lo Bengula's initial suspicion of European motives had become a certainty. Although the pioneers had skirted Matabeleland and had settled in Shona territory, this had not eased the king's mind. Why had they settled down and begun to farm and why did more arrive every month? He had only given permission to dig for gold; he had not alienated his control over Shona territory. To the British government there was no doubt that the Foreign Jurisdiction Act applied to Mashonaland. In May 1891, an Order in Council declared all the company territories to be under the protection of the crown. Thus the high commissioner or the administrator could declare, when they so desired, that the Shona were under British protection. The Matebele considered Mashonaland to be theirs—a place to send their regiments to steal the Mashona cattle. This jurisdictional dispute over the Shona led Lo Bengula to discard his caution; and he decided to use his army against the Shona who felt secure in their new-found British protection near Fort Victoria.

A minor incident in June 1893 led to full-scale war. The company administration had confiscated cattle from some Shona, and Lo Bengula claimed the cattle as his. The king at first sent approximately 1,000 men to the area to show the Shona who held the real power. Shona workers were killed on European farmsteads. Thoroughly frightened, many Europeans took refuge at Fort Victoria. Jameson decided not to compromise but to attempt finally to destroy Matabele power in the trans-Limpopo territory. The reasons for Jameson's decision had little to do with the threat of the moment. The presumed rich gold reefs of Mashonaland had proved an illusion. The price of the company stock had fallen to less than one-third of its previous value on the London exchange. If Lo Bengula were defeated, the promise of potential riches in his country would give the company a much-needed financial boost.

By October 1893, Jameson had gathered a force of 600 men near Fort Victoria. He promised them land and cattle in the new territory whenever the Matabele power was broken. Crossing into Matabeleland, Jameson's mounted irregulars fought two major engagements with Lo Bengula's regiments. Repeating rifles and machine guns proved as effective against the Matabele as they had against the Zulu fifteen years before. Lo Bengula burned the royal kraal and fled northward with some of his cattle and the remnants of his army. He died before reaching the Zambesi and within a short while most of the Matabale returned to their homes. Jameson made Bulawayo the administrative center of the area and allocated farms and town sites to his victorious followers. In 1894 the company received permission from the crown to administer Matabeleland. The fortunes of the company had improved so much that in the following year a railroad was begun from Mafeking north to Bulawayo.

Although most of the Matabele had returned to their home areas, their warlike spirit was not completely broken. They were prepared to take orders from the white man as long as they believed them just and as long as the Europeans had superior coercive power. In the eighteen months following Lo Bengula's defeat there were a number of decisions which alienated the Matabele from their governors. The newly formed police force was drawn largely from the Shona, many of whom used their positions to revenge themselves on their former oppressors. European officials who knew little of the Matabele law of property made a number of mistakes in allocation of the nearly one-quarter million head of royal cattle. The policy of forced labor which could be ordered by district commissioners was resented. Finally a serious rinderpest epidemic hit the cattle herds in 1895. Chiefs and religious leaders became convinced that prosperity would return to the Matabele only when the white man was driven out. Their opportunity for this direct action against the Europeans came early in 1896.

Jameson in October 1895 had withdrawn all but forty of the company police from both Mashonaland and Matabeleland in preparation for the hoped rising of the Uitlanders in Johannesburg. The abortive Jameson Raid not only damaged Britain's position vis-à-vis the South African Republic but also offered the Matabele their chance to be rid of the Europeans. By the end of March the Matabele were everywhere in arms. In the early stages of this second Matabele war over one hundred Europeans, mostly traders or farmers in isolated districts, were killed. The settlers flocked to Bulawayo which became the major European defensive bastion in the territory. A small force under Colonel Plummer arrived from Bechuanaland in early May. These troops together with volunteers fought a series of small violent actions against the Matabele. Rhodes was informed by the military that total pacification would depend upon the completion of the railroad and the deployment of several thousand troops. The financial condition of the company did not allow for such a prolonged campaign. Rhodes decided to attempt a quick peaceful solution by direct negotiations with the Matabele chiefs. After five weeks trying to make contact, Rhodes and three companions finally met with the Matabele leaders. He listened to them and agreed to rectify most of the abuses they complained about. On that basis the war in Matabeleland ended. Rhodes later shipped huge amounts of grain at company expense northward to ward off starvation among the Matabele. It is, therefore, understandable that the Matabele in 1902 stood along the route from Bulawayo to Matapos in silent respect for the funeral train of the "great man" who had taken away their freedom.

The uprising in Matabeleland was duplicated by a similar series of events in Mashonaland beginning in June 1896. Handicapped by lack of police and the fact that many of the men were campaigning against the Matabele, the Europeans flocked to Salisbury and other townsites. The fighting against the Shona was in many ways more difficult than against the Matabele. They had no chiefs of large districts so, therefore, all actions fought were small-scale and ultimately peace came not by one general agreement, but by several with individual chiefs. By October 1896, however, the company had restored order in Mashonaland and the Europeans were dominant once again.

Rhodes, in desperate trouble after the failure of the Jameson Raid, nevertheless managed to keep the company intact. He had to accept more direct intervention from the crown in the form of a resident commissioner after 1898. In the last years of his life he devoted most of his time to Rhodesian affairs. In these formative years the pattern of economic development for Southern Rhodesia was set, as well as relationships between the minority white farmers and the once dominant Matabele and Shona people.

NORTHERN RHODESIA

British expansion in the far northern segment of Rhodesia was largely the result of the activities of Cecil Rhodes and his agents. However, the area was so large and the initial contacts so diffuse that it is convenient to consider separately the northeast and northwestern portions of Rhodesia. Although the company agents were active in the northwestern region earlier, this region was not effectively occupied and administered until after the northeast. Until 1894 the northeastern section was considered to be a part of the sphere of imperial influence controlled by Harry Johnston from Nyasaland. In that year an agreement between the British government and the British South Africa Company reserved for the company rights of administration in the northeast. In 1894 a veteran of the pioneer column's march to Salisbury, Major Forbes, became the company's administrator in the territories north of the Zambesi. With his headquarters at Zomba, he was theoretically in charge of the whole north. However, his actual administrative influence never expanded to Lewanika's territory. There after 1897 the resident, Robert Coryndon, although a subordinate of Forbes, was constrained to act on his own.

Company administration from Zomba was, at first, very weak since the powerful Nguni, Bemba, and Lunda chiefs had not asked for British protection and did not recognize British authority. All of the Nguni territory of Chief Mpezeni had been assigned to Britain by the June 1891 agreement with Portugal, although the Nguni ruler never agreed to accept a subordinate position. Major Forbes' situation was made more difficult by the arrival in Nguni country of a number of prospectors who hoped to discover a new gold strike. Their presence as well as Forbes' governmental activities created a genuine fear among the Nguni which in January 1898 resulted in an attempt to drive all Europeans from Nguni country. The company's position was saved by the arrival of 650 men of the Central African Rifles from Nyasaland. Within a short time these troops had defeated the Nguni in a series of small but costly battles. Mpezeni's men were even less able to stand up to modern rifles than had been the Zulu or Matabele. The legal position of the British regarding the Nguni who had never agreed to their overlordship was extremely questionable. Nevertheless, British authorities captured Mpezeni's son, the most important Nguni military leader, and publically executed him for the crimes of murder and instigation to murder. Over one-third of all the tribal herds of the Nguni were then confiscated as indemnity for the "rebellion."

In Bemba country Europeans were in no position to exert much authority until after 1897. "Arab" slavers driven out of their forts near Lake Nyasa had taken refuge among the Bemba and had built a number of stockaded places. European administrators used the divided state of the Bemba to gain ascendancy over them. In 1897 a company force broke the slavers' power over the Senga and in the following year they were driven out of the territory between the Luapula Valley and Lake Mweru. The final campaign against them was conducted by Sharpe in October 1899, directed against those in the Kazembe Lunda area. With its conclusion company authority was dominant in the northeast.

Most of the northwestern area was ruled by Lewanika, the Lozi chief. However, the actual limits of his territory was undefined and this later caused serious international complications. In the 1880s Lewanika, who had been consistently bothered by Matabele raids, first became interested in placing his country under British protection. He inquired of Khama, the Bamangwato chief, regarding his opinion of the British. After Khama had reported favorably, Lewanika formally requested protection. In the same year Lewanika granted rights to look for minerals outside of Barotseland proper to Harry Ware, a prospector. This concession was ultimately purchased in October 1889 by Rhodes for the British South Africa Company. In March of the following year Rhodes sent F. E. Lochner to Lewanika's village. This visit resulted in a treaty whereby the Lozi would receive the company's protection, represented by a British resident at Lewanika's court. For any loss of status Lewanika was to receive a salary of £2,000 annually from the company. In return the company received proprietary rights to minerals in his country and also, by implication, it became the dominant political force in Barotseland.

Despite the central position of the resident in this agreement of 1890, none was sent until 1897. The explanation for the delay must be sought in the list of priorities established by Rhodes. Barotseland was far away and relatively secure. The South African Republic, Matabeleland, Mashonaland, and the Nyasa territories were all more important. Finally, in 1897, Robert Coryndon arrived among the Lozi to become the first resident. In the following June a detailed, well-prepared, final agreement between the Lozi and the company was signed. In 1900 the Northwest Rhodesia Barotseland Order in Council confirmed the area as a British protectorate under the administration of the company. It included the area between the Kafue River and the Katanga which later proved immensely valuable because of the minerals discovered there.

The remaining major problem which was left unresolved after 1900 was the boundary line of Portuguese Angola. The 1891 agreement had stated that the line should follow the western boundary of Barotseland. Unfortunately no one knew where this was and the territory of the Lovale was disputed by Lewanika and the Portuguese. Finally in 1903 an arbitration committee headed by the king of Italy drew the present boundary along conventional geographic lines which separated groups of the Lovale from one another. The question of the possession of the northwest, although never violently contested, was at last settled.

NYASALAND

Long before Cecil Rhodes' company became concerned with expansion north of the Limpopo there were British missionaries living among the Maravi people near Lake Malawi. The peoples of the Lake Malawi area provided a large portion of the slaves for the East African trade in the 1870s and 1880s. The missionaries noted with disgust and a sense of futility the slave trade since they were powerless to halt the raidings of Nguni, Yao, and "Arab" traders. From the date when Livingstone first investigated the lake area, missionary groups had appealed to the British government to intervene. As has been noted previously, the policy of all British governments prior to the early 1880s was hostile to expansion. However, in 1883, as a token of support for the missionaries, they appointed a consul to the "territories of African Kings and Chiefs in the Districts adjacent to Lake Nyasa." The consul had no police and, therefore, little authority. His presence solved none of the pressing problems for the missionaries. Attempting to teach the Africans that profits could be made in legitimate trade, the missionaries aided in the formation of the African

Lakes Company. The company in the 1880s made no headway against the slave trade and was in continual financial difficulties.

Company agents in late 1887 became involved in hostilities with Mlozi, an Arab half-caste who terrorized the Nkonde district. Early the following year the skirmishing between Mlozi and the Europeans was resumed. After June the Europeans were joined by an officer on leave from the British army whose later African exploits became legendary. Captain Frederick D. Lugard's first African experiences were far from successful. Despite considerable bravery, the Europeans and their allies found that they could not take Mlozi's main stronghold of Kota Kota and Lugard was seriously wounded. A situation of armed neutrality prevailed until after Harry Johnston, the new British consul to Mozambique, arrived in the interior in October 1889.

Johnston's name must rank very high in the pantheon of empire builders in Africa. Although only thirty-one years old when he arrived in Mozambique, he was already experienced in African affairs. He had toured the Congo in 1883, and had been greatly influenced by Stanley. Johnston later traveled extensively in East Africa in 1885. His recommendations to the Foreign Office concerning annexation of the area adjacent to Mt. Kilimanjaro came close to being accepted at that time. Johnston was known in London as an exponent of imperial expansion and was important in the ultimate formation of the British Imperial East Africa Company. After his work in East Africa, he had been appointed vice-consul to the Oil Rivers Protectorate where he had been responsible for instituting the forward policy which had overthrown King Jaja of Opobo. It is obvious that the Foreign Office by appointing Johnston was not in a mood to concede hinterland Nyasaland to the Portuguese.

The Portuguese in the late 1880s laid claim to a vast but undefined section of Central Africa which would have linked their Atlantic and Indian Ocean possessions. The bases for their claims were historic connections and some very early interior expeditions. In the Shire River area the most important of these explorations was that of Lacerda in 1798. However, the Congress of Berlin had destroyed the validity of such historic claims. The Portuguese after the conference were forced into a belated effort to secure sovereignty over the Nyasa area. One way of showing their power over the hinterland was to block needed supplies to the missionaries. Another way was to interfere with missionary attempts to control the slave trade. Such activity was facilitated by Portuguese control over the Quelimane mouth of the Zambesi River. This favored position was partially neutralized by the discovery in 1889 of the Chinde mouth. In the same year the Portuguese sent a large expedition under the command of Major Serpa Pinto up the Shire River to establish a modern-day claim to the highlands. However, Johnston intercepted Pinto's column near the confluence of the Shire and Riro rivers and warned him that any further penetration of the territory would be a direct flaunting of British claims. Pinto then found it expedient to withdraw from the highlands. Early in 1890 Lord Salisbury, the British prime minister, removed the potential Portuguese threat to the Nyasa area by a warning to send gunboats to Mozambique if Portugal did not withdraw from the territory adjacent to the Shire River.

Even without Portuguese rivalry, Johnston still faced a near impossible task. In October 1889, he arranged a truce with the slavers near Karonga and then spent the rest of the year traveling northwest of the lake making treaties wherever possible with African leaders. Johnston was later very fortunate in convincing Alfred Sharpe, a big game hunter, to accept the position of temporary vice-consul. In 1890 Sharpe made two important treaty-making journeys. The first, undertaken in March, in the Nguni country ruled by Chief Mpezeni was not productive since the chief refused to consider a treaty of protection. Sharpe was more successful in Nsenga and Cewa territory. Still another trip in July took him to Karonga and thence northwest through the Luapula Valley and finally to the Katanga Kazembes. African chiefs in the Luapula Valley accepted British protection. However, Msiri of the Katanga would not consider any diminution of his influence. In the following year Msiri was killed by an agent of Leopold II and the Katanga was declared to be under Independent State control. Despite the loss of the Katanga, the treaties gained by Johnston and Sharpe bolstered Lord Salisbury's position in negotiations with Germany and Portugal. In July 1890, by the Heligoland Treaty, Germany recognized Britain's claims to the territory between Lakes Malawi and Tanganyika, and the Anglo-Portuguese treaties of 1890 and 1891 confirmed Britain's hold on the Shire highlands.

Johnston's tasks after the treaties with Germany and Portugal ceased to have international implications, but he was still confronted with the problem of ruling a large territory controlled mainly by "Arab" slavers and their African allies such as the Nguni and Yao. Johnston had little money and fewer troops to implement his decisions. His activities were furthered by Cecil Rhodes who in 1890 came to the rescue of the African Lakes Company by granting it an annual subsidy of £9,000. In February 1891, this subsidy agreement was renegotiated with the imperial government as the recipient. In return for grants of mineral and commercial rights to the British South Africa Company, Rhodes promised to provide £10,000 per year to maintain a police force in Nyasaland. In May 1891, the imperial government declared a protectorate over the Nyasaland district and the area which later became northeastern Rhodesia was separated from Nyasaland and given over to the administration of Rhodes' chartered company. The old African Lakes Company was phased out by 1893.

After 1891 Johnston had a police force of over 200 men of whom seventy were Sikhs from India and in 1892 he received two gunboats for use on the lake. He utilized this force first to overawe the people in those areas where the chiefs had submitted. Then, if necessary, he used force to break the slavers' hold on certain districts. By the end of 1895 most of the Nguni and Yao chiefs had submitted to British authority. The last major campaign in the Nyasa area was fought in late 1895 against the "Arab" slavers in the northern territory. With the taking of Karonga, Johnston effectively ended slaving activities in the protectorate. He soon returned to England ill and exhausted by his seven-year campaign, leaving behind the rudiments of an administrative system and the certain knowledge that British power was recognized by all Africans in Nyasaland.

The Rand gold strike and its consequences

There is evidence that the Boers were aware of the presence of gold in the hilly, eroded region near Johannesburg as early as the 1850s. Thus the discovery by the Struben brothers of the huge Witwatersrand deposits in 1884 was not a complete surprise. The Witwatersrand gold was found in microscopic quantities along with pyrites in the intrusive conglomerate rocks of the reef. This was not the type of alluvial deposit which had earlier lured thousands to the gold fields of California and Australia. Fifty years before it would have been impossible to extract the gold profitably from the quartz rocks. Science and technology had provided the methodology and there was sufficient capital in Cape Colony and Britain to underwrite the expensive, complex machinery necessary to mine the gold. Within a few months of the announcement of the discoveries in 1886, companies were already paying high dividends to their investors. However, the more complex the procedures for mining became, the more it was apparent that larger, more viable companies were needed. Thus such giants as Cecil Rhodes' Consolidated Goldfields dominated the mining scene by the early 1890s.

The continual problem of all the Boer republics had been lack of funds. Always impoverished, they had been at the mercy of the more affluent Cape Colony. The South African Republic had never been able to work out a satisfactory rebate system for imports with Cape Colony. In 1885 Paul Kruger had decided that he could not obtain enough capital to construct his own railway to the sea through Mozambique. He had reluctantly agreed to a continuation of the Kimberley railroad line into the republic. The discovery of gold changed all this. Kruger's government which was hardly solvent in 1884 had later a yearly revenue of over $7,000,000. Land transfers, customs payments, license fees, and stamp duties provided Kruger with funds beyond his most fantastic dreams of a few years before. He now had the economic power to secure the political and economic independence of his country from Britain.

Kruger, after the gold strike, began the construction of a railway that would make him independent of the Cape. The line from the border of the republic to Delagoa Bay was finished in 1889 and was connected to Pretoria in 1894. Meanwhile, a railway line from Natal had reached the border in 1891 and one from Port Elizabeth the following year. The Cape line was extended to the Rand in 1892 while the Natal line was not completed until 1895. All rail shipping through the republic was controlled by the Netherlands South African Railway Company which juggled rates and priorities to its own advantage. When the Cape line in 1894 cut the freight rates in the section across Cape Colony, the Netherlands Company increased them threefold in the republic. In the following year the Rand mining companies attempted to bypass the Transvaal section of the Cape line by off-loading their goods to ox wagons for the trip through the republic. A major crisis arose in 1895 when President Kruger closed the fords across the Vaal River to these shipments. This action showed conclusively that Kruger intended to keep control of the economic mechanisms of his state.

Gold was not an unmixed blessing for the farmers and burghers of the republic. Necessities connected with extracting and refining the gold brought a flood of foreigners to the Transvaal area. With them came the industrial world of the nineteenth century. Men whose entire lives had been bounded by the veld, their farms, families, and their strict religion now confronted a mass intrusion of foreigners. Kruger and his volkraad if they wished the newfound prosperity to continue could not prevent the entry of those necessary to work the mines. However, they could attempt to exercise strict control over them. The two most obvious examples of Kruger's attitude are the rule established for the operation of companies and the government's attitude toward the mass of outsiders or Uitlanders.

The government maintained its control of the mining operators by forcing them to deal with state monopolies for essential goods. Particularly onerous to the operators was the dynamite monopoly. Operators were forced to purchase what they considered poor material at inflated prices for this most necessary product. Railway rates would have been high under any circumstances, but Kruger's policies and the actions of the Netherlands South African Railway Company made them even higher. State control and the distance of the mines from the sea combined to limit the profits of the British and Cape entrepreneurs.

The Uitlander population which by 1895 numbered approximately 175,000 posed a threat to the republic if laws were not passed restricting their participation in political affairs. Until the discovery of gold there were no rigorous tests to determine citizenship. Men could travel freely, do business, and own property in all areas of southern Africa. Three presidents of the South African Republic had been British citizens. After the gold strike the Boers began to emphasize *Het Volk*, the people, and their uniqueness as a nation. Kruger's government systematically raised the citizenship and franchise requirements to the point where after 1895 it was almost impossible for an Uitlander to become a citizen. This disenfranchised class, twice the size of the Boer population, paid nine-tenths of the taxes.

The reaction of Kruger's government toward the mine operators and the Uitlanders created tensions by the mid-1890s which would have to be resolved if the republic were not to be torn apart. The expansion of British influence northward into Central Africa complicated the resolution of the Uitlander problem within the republic. The failure of Kruger to moderate his internal policies combined with increasing British imperialism throughout Africa were the major factors which led to the Boer War.

The Jameson Raid and preliminaries to war

Cecil Rhodes had followed a moderate course of action in wooing the Boers within Cape Colony and in the republics until 1894. Although one of the "Rand lords," he had given scant attention to the complaints of the Uitlanders concerning the franchise and other alleged abuses by the Kruger government. However, by 1895 he had emerged as one of their defenders and had openly assumed a more bellicose attitude toward the Transvaal government. Finally, in late 1895, he abandoned all caution and sanctioned military intervention in the internal affairs ◦of the South African Republic. Why this sudden shift in policy? One answer is obviously the worsening condition of his health. The illness which had brought him to South Africa had never been completely cured and after a serious influenza attack in 1891 he seemed less vigorous. He stated a number of times that he did not expect to live past forty-five. If he were to achieve his aims of a unified South Africa, then he could not afford to wait much longer. Correlated with this was his fear of the growing strength of the South African Republic and the possibility of its alliance with Germany. Perhaps he realized that Kruger could not be "squared"; he wanted nothing which Rhodes could give him.

Rhodes was not the first high British official to think seriously of direct imperial intervention into the Transvaal with an uprising of the Uitlanders. The governor and high commissioner, Sir Henry Loch, after his visit to Pretoria in 1894 became convinced that the Uitlanders were ready to begin a revolt. Loch formulated a plan for intervention by imperial troops in the eventuality of such an uprising. These plans were communicated to the colonial secretary, the Marquis of Ripon, who appears to have restrained the aggressive high commissioner.

In December 1894, Rhodes went to London to lend his support to the selection of Sir Hercules Robinson to replace the retiring Loch as governor. Robinson had previously been governor from 1881 to 1889. He had supported Rhodes over the issue of granting a charter to the British South African Company and was deeply involved in the operations of that company and also that of De Beers. Further, he was over seventy years old and was in poor health. He could obviously be used to further Rhodes' plans. Despite a few minor notes of protest, Robinson was appointed governor and high commissioner.

Rhodes' plans for direct intervention were basically the same as Loch's. The high commissioner was pressured to turn over a strip of British territory connecting the Cape with the Rhodesian frontier to the company. This ostensibly was to further the construction of the railway and was accomplished in October 1895. Rhodes could then strip Matabeleland and Mashonaland of company police and concentrate these at Mafeking under the command of Dr. Leander Starr Jameson. The key to the plan was the actions of the Uitlander leaders in Johannesburg. In 1892 they had formed a National Union to agitate for Uitlander rights. Financed in 1895 by Rhodes and other "Rand lords," they began to organize for an armed uprising. Guns and ammunition were smuggled into the Transvaal. At the signal the Uitlanders were supposed to stage their revolt, seize the armory at Pretoria, and keep Kruger's forces tied down. Jameson, on the pretext of protecting British lives and property, would then invade the western Transvaal. At this juncture Robinson ostensibly acting as a peacemaker would go to Pretoria. Backed by imperial troops, he would then dictate terms to Kruger.

By mid-December 1895, everything was in readiness and the date for the uprising was set for the end of the month. Jameson's force at Pitsani on the border eagerly awaited the signal. Then the leaders in Johannesburg began to quarrel among themselves. In the light of harsh reality they began to see that most Uitlanders, although dissatisfied over some things, were in no mood for armed rebellion. The date for the revolt was postponed until after a general meeting to be held on January 8. Rhodes, fully informed of these events, decided on December 28 to call off the invasion. He sent an ambiguous telegram to Jameson informing him of this. Jameson was also visited by representatives of the Johannesburg committee and told of the developments there. Jameson, nevertheless, on his own initiative decided to precipitate the general revolt and took his armed force across the Transvaal border on the last day of the year.

Kruger, who was aware of the general outlines of the proposed action, kept the Johannesburg area under surveillance. Piet Cronje, hearing of the invasion on Sunday, December 30, called up a commando of some 200 men and later joined a force of approximately 300 under H. P. Malan and F. J. Potgieter. Jameson's force attempted to fight its way through a narrow valley and was later surrounded at Doornkop. Poorly led and attempting to implement an ill-conceived plan, the tired invaders surrendered to Cronje. The column lost fifty-eight men dead and wounded. More important, Jameson's precipitous action all but destroyed any chance of peacefully resolving the differences between Britain and the South African Republic.

The raiders were taken to Johannesburg and tried, most of them escaping with heavy fines. A few were sentenced to death, but these sentences were immediately commuted to prison terms and a fine. Dr. Jameson and his immediate staff were turned over to the British government for trial. By this shrewd move Kruger placed the responsibility for punishment on the British. The leaders were duly convicted and given light terms, and Jameson served only four months. Far more important than these actions was the question of determining who was officially responsible. Rhodes immediately resigned as prime minister of the Cape. Never again would his influence be such that he could expect the British government to accept automatically his solutions to South African problems. A committee of inquiry of the Cape parliament did not assess guilt. A further commission of the House of Commons investigated, condemned the actions of Rhodes and Jameson, but exonerated other high British officials including Robinson and Joseph Chamberlain, the colonial secretary.

Afrikaner leaders such as President Steyn of the Free State and W. P. Schreiner of the Cape who had previously followed a moderate policy moved to support the Transvaal. Kruger's harsh attitudes and suspicions of British motives appeared to be vindicated. The volksraad of the Orange Free State committed their nation to an alliance with the Transvaal. Kruger's government passed new harsh legislation directed at the Uitlanders and their position became even more untenable than before the raid. Kaiser Wilhelm's telegram congratulating the Transvaal on the Jameson action and subsequent German actions disturbed Britain and gave Kruger hope for definite German support in case of future difficulty. Before 1896 there was a large body of Afrikaner opinion which disagreed with Kruger's policies toward the Uitlander. After the raid this opinion was all but silenced. Kruger had little difficulty winning the presidential election of 1898.

In 1897 Sir Alfred Milner replaced the aged Robinson as governor of Cape Colony and high commissioner. A trusted friend and confidant of Chamberlain, he became the key figure in a growingly aggressive British policy in southern Africa. Heretofore the attitude of the London government toward imperialism had been cautious, allowing men such as Rhodes to plan and finance expansion. Chamberlain brought a new aggressiveness to the Colonial Office. This was shown in his willingness to support Rhodes' plan for the raid. Milner transferred this aggressiveness into action as the chief representative of the crown in South Africa. After 1897 he, rather than Cape politicians, made the major policy decisions.

Although convinced from the beginning that conflict was inevitable, Milner proceeded very carefully until after the Transvaal elections of 1898. After that date he began to press the Uitlander case upon the Kruger government. Kruger refused to grant any significant concessions. Milner was aware that the Uitlander issue was only a mask to cover the British decision to control all of southern Africa. A final attempt at compromise was made by moderate elements who brought Milner and Kruger together at Bloemfontein in June 1899. The failure of the conference spurred such advisers to Kruger as the young Jan Christian Smuts to urge the acceptance of major modifications of the franchise laws. By early fall of 1899, the Transvaal had granted Milner the majority of his demands concerning Uitlander rights. However, Milner had shifted his attack to the question of suzerainty. Milner claimed that the Transvaal had been given only conditional independence by the London Convention and that Britain had retained ultimate control over the republic. This contention was too extreme even for Boer opponents of Kruger to accept. In September and October both sides were preparing for the inevitable conflict. The war came when the Transvaal delivered an ultimatum calling for the withdrawal of all British troops from the frontier by October 11. The ultimatum was ignored by Milner and Chamberlain, and the Boer War began.

The Boer War

The onset of the war caught the British totally unprepared. If Milner and his superiors had any intention of carrying out the implications of their planned ultimatum, they were guilty of gross negligence in building up the military. Total British strength in South Africa was 29,000 men of which over 10,000 were volunteers. These forces were scattered from Natal in the east to Mafeking in the west. The bulk of the British forces were in Natal. There Sir George White commanded over 13,000 regulars and 3,000 volunteer troops. Approximately 8,000 of these were concentrated in the town of Ladysmith. Small garrisons were scattered along the northern border. Colonel Robert Baden-Powell commanded 1,250 troops at Mafeking while Colonel R. G. Kekewich deployed not quite a battalion of regulars at Kimberley.

Even before hostilities started, the Transvaal began to call all adult males to serve. Kruger's forces thus at the beginning of the war numbered over 85,000 men. They were supplied with the finest equipment available from European arms manufacturers. Their Mauser rifle was superior to the British Lee-Enfield and the Afrikaner field guns were also better than those of the British. The Afrikaners from both Boer republics were hardy outdoorsmen used to hard work and long hours in the saddle. Boer leaders were very familiar with every section of the country and they were operating on short supply lines. The deficiencies of the Afrikaner armies which became apparent soon after the war began were related to their informal militia organization. There were few regular troops, officers were elected, and none had ever commanded large units before. The major commanders, Joubert and Cronje, were old, conservative, and not prepared to act with the same dispatch as the younger officers, Botha, de Wet, de la Rey, and Smuts.

The Boer offensive in the opening phase of the conflict was designed to keep pressure on the long northern front while Commandant Joubert with 20,000 troops drove through Natal and secured the port of Durban. By mid-October Mafeking and Kimberley were invested and Joubert's forces had met no real resistance in Natal. Sir George White attempted to break out of Ladysmith and fall back to join expected reinforcements from Britain, but the Boers forced him into the city after White's troops had suffered over 1,500 casualties. Joubert failed to follow up his advantage and settled into a siege of Ladysmith.

Sir Redvers Buller arrived in Cape Town on October 31 with the only organized army corps then available to Britain. The situation was so crucial that Buller decided to break up the corps and sent part of it north under the command of Lord Methuen to relieve Kimberley, and another segment under General Gatacre· to Molteno. Buller, with the bulk of the reinforcements, proceeded to Natal where twenty years before he had won a Victoria Cross in the Zulu War. Now, over sixty, conservative, and with years of sedentary duty at Whitehall behind him, he was called upon to accomplish a near miracle.

Methuen's forces on November 25 were briefly halted by Cronje on the Modder River. British casualties in this engagement numbered over 450 men. Regrouping, Methuen pushed north only to lose another battle at Magersfontein on December 11 with twice the number of casualties of the previous battle. Gatacre at Stormberg on the previous day had been defeated by another Boer force. There British casualties amounted to over 700 men. The final blow came when Buller in Natal attempted to cross the Tugela River near Colenso. In two coordinate actions the British lost almost 1,700 men and were forced to retreat. This "Black Week" was to be the height of Boer success and the lowest point of British fortunes. The only good news for Britain was the tenacity with which the defenders of Ladysmith, Kimberley, and Mafeking held out.

Joubert and Cronje, by besieging certain cities, halted the war of movement and gave the British government time to build up their forces. Lord Roberts, the most outstanding British general, was given command of all troops in southern Africa. Sir Herbert Kitchener, fresh from his victory over the Mahdists in the Sudan, was appointed second in command. Reservists were called up and offers of assistance from all parts of the British empire were accepted. In the late months of 1899 troops from all parts of the empire flowed into South Africa. Martial law was proclaimed in Cape Colony largely because of the fear of the large numbers of Boer sympathizers resident there. Kruger, who had expected more direct aid from Germany, was sadly disappointed. All the Transvaal received from the rest of the world were expressions of sympathy.

Roberts and Kitchener reached Cape Town on January 10, 1900, just before Buller attempted another movement into northern Natal. At Spion Kop Buller lost over 600 men and once again was forced to retreat. By the end of the month, however, Roberts had completed his plans for counterattack and deployment of the necessary forces. Since the bulk of the Boer armies was in the east, Roberts decided to force the center, invade the Orange Free State, and then drive directly toward Pretoria. The offensive began on February 11, and despite considerable resistance, broke Cronje's front and relieved Kimberley. The Boer army's retreat was cut off and on February 27 Cronje was forced to surrender with 4,000 men. The following day Buller's army which had finally managed to cross the Tugela River relieved Ladysmith. In one major stroke Roberts had smashed the old Afrikaner army organization. Boer forces retreated in considerable disorder, particularly those operating in the Orange Free State.

On March 13, 1900, Bloemfontein fell and British troops pressed inexorably on toward Pretoria. Mafeking was relieved on May 17 after being under siege for 217 days. Baden-Powell's troops there had lost over 300 men and over 460 civilians had died, but they had pinned down a much larger Boer force. Louis Botha succeeded to commandant-general of the

Afrikaner forces on the death of Joubert on March 25, and began to organize the Boer armies into smaller striking forces. However, he could not prevent the fall of Johannesburg on June 1 and Pretoria three days later. Paul Kruger left the Transvaal for Europe in August, broken in health but still hoping to find European support for his battle. Lord Roberts formally annexed the Transvaal in September. Believing the war to be over, he relinquished his command to Kitchener and returned to England. The British government assumed that all that was left to be done was the formality of a peace treaty.

The Boers under the leadership of ex-President Steyn of the Orange Free State and Botha, however, had no intention of surrendering. Smaller mobile units under brilliant commanders such as de Wet, de la Ray, and Smuts harassed the British. They tore up railway lines, attacked smaller British forces, burned supplies, and their cavalry audaciously moved even into Cape Colony. Operating in friendly country, these guerrilla forces were almost impossible to apprehend. Kitchener, with an army greatly depleted by a government which believed the war to be over, evolved new tactics. He converted a large portion of his forces to mounted infantry to increase their mobility, built blockhouses along the rail lines, burned farmsteads, and instituted the century's first concentration camps. Knowing that he had to deprive Botha's groups of the help of civilians, he cleared whole districts and put them in a number of camps. By mid-1902 there were over 125,000 civilians in these detention areas. Poor sanitation facilities and the inadequacy of medical science to treat many diseases rather than British cruelty combined to kill over 26,000 women and children in these camps before the war ended.

In March 1901, Kitchener met Botha at Middelburg and offered lenient terms to the Boers if they would surrender. However, the terms also dictated a yielding of their independence and this the Boer leaders refused, and the war dragged on for another year. Finally exhausted and convinced of the futility of further resistance, thirty representatives of each republic on May 15, 1902, discussed at length the British terms. After almost two weeks of conferences with Milner and Kitchener the five Boer generals, Botha, Smuts, de Wet, Hertzog, and de la Rey signed the Treaty of Vereeniging on May 31. The Boer War was over.

Reconstruction

The war had caused profound changes not only in southern Africa, but also in Britain. Liberal opposition to the war was at first masked by the initial disasters and the quick counterthrust of Roberts in early 1900. Nevertheless, in the so-called "Khaki" election of 1900 the Conservative party received only fifty-three percent of the votes. As the war dragged on and civilian casualties increased, more Englishmen became openly pro-Boer. The war also showed how dangerously alone Britain was. Only the Dominion areas supported the Conservative action. No major state expressed sympathy with Britain's position. The Anglo-Japanese treaty of

1902, the French Entente of 1904, and a similar agreement with Russia in 1907 flowed directly from Britain's sense of isolation during the Boer War.

In South Africa the war which had first seemed so simple had caused tremendous problems. Loyalties were not clear cut. Men with English names had fought with the Boers while most Cape Boers remained loyal to Britain and many had joined the British forces. By the Treaty of Vereeniging, Milner had become the chief executive officer of two new crown colonies. But these new additions were impoverished. Whole areas had been depopulated, farmsteads burned, and the mines had ceased production. The immediate economic task confronting Milner was to resettle the land, begin mining operations, and restore the railways to working order.

By the treaty the British provided £3,000,000 immediately; and later a £35,000,000 loan with extremely low interest was floated to continue development. With the cooperation of most of the Boer leaders, Milner and his "Kindergarten" began immediately to direct the huge task of reconstruction. This so-called "Kindergarten" was composed of brilliant young men such as John Buchan, Lionel Curtis, and Philip Kerr who were later to forge distinguished careers in government and the law. In the years immediately following the war they provided Milner with a competent, idealistic administrative nucleus for the two defeated areas. By the time Milner left South Africa in 1905 the major task of economic reconstruction was completed. The Transvaal area, with the mines once again producing, was able to assume a major financial role in southern Africa.

Political development which involved reconciliation betwen Boer and Briton was more difficult to achieve. By the Treaty of Vereeniging Britain promised to grant responsible government to the two conquered areas as soon as possible. Martial law was ended and normal civilian government reinstituted in Cape Colony in 1902. Responsible government had continued in Natal during the war. Lord Milner was afraid that the institution of responsible government in the Transvaal and Orange Free State would result in a resurgence of Afrikaner nationalism. In the Orange Free State, Fischer and Steyn had already begun the *Oranje Unie* party and in the Transvaal Botha and Smuts had started the *Het Volk* party. Lord Selborne, who succeeded Milner, favored responsible government and after the Liberal victory in the British elections of 1906 this became a reality. The Transvaal received responsible government in 1906 and the Orange Free State the following year.

One of the purposes of the Boer War had been to provide one government for all of southern Africa. That had only been partially achieved by bringing the ex-republics under the crown. There still existed four different governments administering four differing sets of laws. The old divisive factors of customs and railroads which had contributed so much to disunity in the past were still operative. Each colony also had its own separate policy toward black Africans and Asiatic immigrants. To rationalize some of these problems Governor Selborne issued his famous memorandum on closer unity, and the political leaders of the colonies agreed to meet and discuss a full range of problems relating to cooperation.

The convention to consider common problems met at Durban on October 12, 1908, and later in November moved to Cape Town. Each area was represented by its prime minister, leading figures in the government, and also some members of the opposition. Key figures were Botha and Smuts from the Transvaal, Jameson and Sauer from the Cape, Hertzog and Steyn from the Free State, and Morcom and Smythe from Natal. It soon became obvious that closer economic cooperation would be nearly impossible without a concomitant political reorganization. The convention thus constructed a draft constitution in early 1909 which was then considered by the parliaments of the four areas. After approval it was passed by the British parliament as the South Africa Act of 1909. By its terms on May 31, 1910, just eight years after Vereeniging, the Union of South Africa became a political reality.

The South Africa Act provided for a unitary government system with one parliament and ministry. The parliament consisted of an elected house of assembly and a partially nominated and partially indirectly elected senate. The executive consisted of a governor-general to represent the crown who initially had substantive powers over the defense, trade, and foreign affairs. The ministry, headed by a prime minister, was responsible to the lower house. To protect certain interests of the smaller colonies there was created provincial councils with powers of control over local matters among which was education. A supreme court with appellate and provincial divisions was also established. The high court very soon established the principle of judicial review.

Three questions almost destroyed the functioning of the convention. One concerned the location of the capital. A compromise was reached by which Cape Town became the legislative center, Pretoria the executive capital, and Bloemfontein the seat of the appellate court. Another factor concerned the national language while an even more difficult problem related to franchise qualifications. The problem of national language was solved by designating both Dutch and English as official languages. No workable compromise could be reached for reconciling differing attitudes toward the black African and his potential use of the franchise. The Cape was the only area which allowed the vote to nonwhites, and the Cape delegation refused to abandon this principle. Botha, Smuts, and Hertzog would not accept the granting of the vote to blacks, even in theory. In the South Africa Act, therefore, voting regulations were left as they had been before the act, although it was stipulated that only Europeans could serve in parliament. Language equality and the franchise regulations were guaranteed by the so-called "entrenched clauses" of the act. These stated that to change either stipulation required not a simple majority vote of the Assembly, but a two-thirds vote of both houses sitting togeher. Thus in one crucial area, native affairs, the Union Act left unchanged the four separate attitudes toward Africans and Cape Colored.

SEVEN
European mechanisms
of control in Africa

Political activity in most of the territories of Africa were minimal until after World War II. Egypt, Ethiopia, South Africa, and Liberia were the only independent states. The rest of the vast area was directly controlled by European powers. These European states ruled their dependencies in differing ways. Since African traditional societies had largely been governments of consensus there was little African experience upon which the leaders of African political opinion could draw. Thus the rapid advancement of African areas toward independence was accomplished in a political environment almost totally European. The nationalist leaders had been educated in European schools either in Africa or Europe, worked in European firms, and drew their concepts of the nature of the state from European models and philosophies. Perhaps even more restrictive was the fact that the various concessions leading to independence were granted in sequential modifications to an existing colonial system. The colonial systems of France, Britain, Belgium, and Portugal differed radically in their form and philosophy. Thus African states after independence were various reflections of European educational and political systems present in Africa. Before detailing the development of political movements in African territories, one must look carefully at the different political systems created by the European powers to control their African empires.

British Africa

Before introducing the skeleton of the British form of rule in Africa one must be aware of certain factors implicit within the British system. The most obvious of these is the stress placed on the workability of any administrative unit. The British of the nineteenth century operated on the presumption that their system was best and that they could bring law and order to "lesser breeds without the law." This did not mean that individual administrators understood completely what their system was. They were not ideologists and therefore did not attempt to rationalize their control of a given territory with any preconceived ideology. Their experience in the older portions of their empire had confirmed for them the rightness of their approach. Thus the British could be very flexible in the establishment of their control systems in Africa without feeling it necessary to follow exactly a standardized model.

A second point to stress is the decentralized nature of British institutions. Although theoretically the British parliament retains supremacy of legislative, executive, and judicial functions, in practice this power by the mid-nineteenth century had been shared for over a hundred years with local officials of the shires and the boroughs. Any dependent government system designed by the British would, therefore, leave a large measure of power in the hands of the governor and councils of a given territory. The Colonial Office did have the authority to make crucial decisions without consulting lesser officials. However, in practice it seldom acted this way, preferring to consult directly with the governors of its empire before arriving at any major decision. The Colonial Office came to depend upon this advice and they generally allowed such strong governors as Lord Frederick Lugard or Sir Donald Cameron to exercise almost total practical control over the territories which they administered.

After the scramble, there were three differing systems of control practiced by the British in Africa. The first form of possession was the eighteenth-century colony where large numbers of English persons had actually migrated to the overseas area. Cape Colony, with its large Boer and, later, English population, and Natal, settled largely by the English, conformed.to this type of colony. In both areas advanced forms of representative and, later, responsible government was granted freely to the white population before the so-called scramble for Africa began. With the successful conclusion of the Boer War, the two Boer republics of the Transvaal and the Orange Free State were soon associated with the British areas to form the Union of South Africa. The union from its inception had responsible government with an almost total control of its own domestic affairs. By 1926 the union had gained the right to manage its own foreign affairs; and, as a member of the Commonwealth, it was to all extents an independent state freely associated with Britain.

The second type of British possession was Egypt where Britain did not legally exercise sovereign powers until 1914. Before that date the khedive and Egyptian government agencies were ostensibly in control. The reality was considerably different. The British consul was the real power in Egypt although he worked behind the facade of Egyptian and Turkish legalism. During World War I, Britain was the open, legal protector of Egypt. However, they accepted a large portion of Egyptian governmental practice and institutions, modifying these only when it became necessary. The reconquest of the Sudan had been completed in 1898 based upon Egyptian, not British, claims to the territory. The condominium government which was established for the Sudan was a hybrid system and made of the Sudan, as with Egypt, a special case.

The third type of British possession in Africa was what could be called the dependent empire. These territories had largely been gained in the period from 1880 to 1900 even though British possession of some of the coastal areas predated the scramble. These older enclaves were generally designated colony areas while the much larger hinterland territories were normally called protectorates. In the areas under direct administration the form of rule was a modified crown colony system. This consisted of a governor, secretariat, executive council, and legislative council. In the much larger protectorates, the British early adopted the system of utilizing indigenous rulers to carry out most of the processes of local government. This system, called indirect rule, could be conducted with a minimum of British personnel and at very little expense. Customary law was accepted as was African land tenure. The theory was to upset the life of the people as little as possible. Traditional rulers were supervised and directed by representatives of the central government. A typical British dependent area would be governed thus:

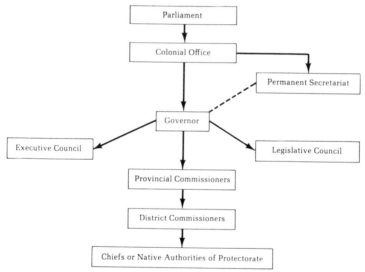

British colonial administration in the dependent empire in Africa until the grant of independence to a territory is a study of unity and diversity. The unity was that of similar structures of government established in all areas of British Africa. These institutions were basically simple and extremely malleable. Thus, while the outline of government of a colony or protectorate was of the same type as imposed elsewhere, its actual function could be quite different. Contrary to the French attempt to create unity, the British were normally pragmatic, attempting to modify the structure to fit a given environment.

This diversity within a common framework can be seen most clearly in the protected areas where there were already established highly structured and efficient African systems such as in Uganda and Northern Nigeria. In such territories the British attempted few administrative changes. Most of the changes instituted were designed to bring the administrative and judicial practices in rough alignment with British policies. District officers in Uganda and Northern Nigeria performed a dual role. Where the central government wished a specific reform enacted, the district officers became in fact the real rulers of their areas. However, in most cases district officers were content to allow the traditional authorities to govern while they assumed advisory roles. In less developed areas the British authorities tried to recreate what they believed to be the traditional system. In some cases the British organized what they thought to be an African system of government indigenous to an area but which was really foreign to the people. In many places the British created their own chiefs who were not totally accepted by the people. With native rulers of such questionable traditional antecedents, provincial and district officers played a more direct role in all areas of local government. They became, in fact, paramount chiefs. Thus, although the facade of indirect rule was maintained, the reality of power rested with the British local officers.

Indirect rule in British Africa was, at first, a pragmatic solution to the problem of governing large territories with a minimum of expenditure. One must remember that of all the imperial powers Britain had possessed a large empire before the scramble. It had already considerable knowledge of governing nonwestern people. Indirect rule of various kinds had already been used throughout the empire, particularly in India. Thus the British system of rule in its African protectorates was not a new creation but rather a modification of an already extant, successful one. Even as British control over African territory progressed, the governors and administrators were applying indirect rule to the conquered or ceded areas. After expansion had ceased, the Colonial Office and governors attempted by a series of modifications in all their protectorates to organize the ad hoc systems into comprehensive, more rational entities. Later Lord Frederick Lugard and other theorists provided the philosophical underpinning for the system and indirect rule came to be regarded by the Colonial Office in the interwar period as an almost sacrosanct institution. It did seem to fit the needs of both the governors and the governed. Its costs were minimal and it apparently did not disturb the Africans' traditional pattern of social, economic, and political life. Indirect rule throughout the British dependencies thus tended to become static and in some cases moribund. Needed improvements in land utilization and conservation, health, communication, and education were often delayed or in many cases never effected because it was feared that these reforms would upset the balance of traditional rule. The practicalities of protectorate rule became contrary to the wishes of such administrators and theorists as Lord Lugard and Sir Donald Cameron. They had envisioned indirect rule as a vehicle for change compatible with African institutions: a system which would preserve the best of African culture while allowing for progress. However, despite the efforts of a few colonial administrators, the protectorate systems remained static and progressively isolated from developments in the colony areas.

Almost all the machinery of the government was concentrated in the colony area. Despite the reluctance of Britain to spend money, these sections were the most developed in British Africa. Streets were paved, modern sewage and drainage systems were built, harbors improved, and the railway and road systems began there. Most of the medical and educational facilities were concentrated in the colony area or in the larger, Westernized cities. All the important firms and banks maintained their main offices near the seat of government.

In time there developed in the colony and urban areas, without direct government encouragement, an African intellectual elite generally composed of the professional middle class. Small in numbers, these lawyers, doctors, and teachers had been educated in Britain and some were steeped in the ideas of European liberty. In the 1920s and 1930s they began to demand that the autocratically appointed government be modified to give the African a voice in his government. By 1939, in the Gold Coast and Nigeria particularly, there had been formed the nucleus of colony-based political parties.

The British administration prior to World War II had in some cases begun to modify the central government apparatus by appointing Africans to positions on the legislative councils and executive councils. Further, the British utilized large numbers of European-trained Africans in the civil service. Most of these held only the lower echelon positions, but their numbers complemented the smaller, more influential group of native traders and professional men. In some areas such as in Northern Rhodesia, African schoolmasters and teachers formed the leadership segment of early political movements. The coalescing of all these groups provided the nucleus of the post-World War II political parties.

It is important to note that all African political parties in British Africa before 1945 were created by a Westernized middle class and had no popular base either in the cities or country areas. The British administration was convinced that the key to the future for their African dependencies lay in modifying the system of indirect rule already established. Thus educated Africans were carefully watched to make certain they did not interfere with the functioning of the protectorate systems. Whenever an organization appeared to be gaining broad popular support, the British authorities would ban it. It was not until the 1950s that the Colonial Office finally abandoned its support of traditional rulers and began to make real concessions to the educated few who controlled the urban political parties.

A factor even more important for the dependent empire than Britain's commitment to indirect rule after World War I was its dedication to frugality. The most sacrosanct rule for governments of British territories was to "live within one's income" and not to expect the British taxpayers to support development schemes, no matter how worthwhile, beyond the financial capability of a territory. Reeling financially from the excessive expense of World War I, Britain could not afford her dependencies. This dictum enunciated by the home government caused all British African administrations to plan their finances in a most conservative manner. Thus a combination of caution and penury damned such poor areas as Sierra Leone and the Gambia to only minimal programs of harbor, road, and city improvements. The backwardness of the educational and health facilities in all British African territories is attributable, to a large degree, to lack of money. As one commentator noted, Britain ran her administration in tropical Africa "on the cheap."

When Britain ruled a multiracial society the forms of dependent government were modified. The actual development of Southern Rhodesia and Kenya will be detailed elsewhere. It is sufficient to note here only a few salient points concerning these territories. Southern Rhodesia, which enjoyed responsible government after 1923, was controlled entirely by the white minority. The government of Northern Rhodesia was also complicated by the presence of a large European population which was either engaged in farming or mining. Kenya, whose politics were complicated by both European and Indian minorities, ostensibly had the typical crown colony protectorate system. Actually the presence of the influential farmers of the white highlands precipitated in 1919–1920 demands for self-government. Although these demands were refused, the white minority was confirmed in its special prerogative in the highlands. They controlled the economic wealth, and white representatives were the first to be nominated to the executive and legislative councils. The presence of a white resident population in all these areas complicated and, in the case of Rhodesia, prevented the devolution of authority to the African majority.

French Africa

French colonial administration until World War II was direct with ultimate control over colonial areas resting with the minister of colonies in Paris. Not surprisingly, it reflected domestic governmental organization and showed the French penchant for detailed organization and centralization. Although there were many changes in the form of government in France in the nineteenth century, there was no change in the concentration of government power in Paris which had been so noticeable after the revolution of 1789. French constitutions, whether monarchical or republican, tended to be complex structures reflecting general theories and goals. It is, therefore, not surprising that where British administration was distinguished by its pragmatism, French government in colonial areas was derived from ideological concepts. With the exception of Senegal, French occupation of West and Central Africa occurred in the brief period from 1880 to 1900 during the early years of the Third Republic. Much of this occupation had been accomplished by the military whose approach to governing these territories was simple and direct. These ad hoc military regimes were soon replaced by relatively complex civilian structures which, however, retained the major decision-making powers for French authorities in Paris.

Important factors which contributed to the decrees which created civil government in much of Africa were the political and cultural goals which France hoped to achieve in her empire. Frankly stated, Frenchmen felt they must not only maintain order and financial stability, but they should also civilize the Africans under their control. This led to a policy of attempting the assimilation of some Africans concurrent with a policy of association with the mass of the population. By establishing the machinery of French culture in Africa, France made it possible for educated Africans to associate themselves directly with France. They could, by renouncing their African heritage, become Frenchmen with all the rights and privileges of citizens of metropolitan France. To be sure, only a small minority of Africans prior to 1944 had made this transition. However, for those who had become assimilated, it was necessary to provide for their inclusion into the political system, even to allowing them to become members of the metropolitan government.

Assimilation was an all inclusive goal and did not apply to only one territory, although Senegal was the prime beneficiary of the policy. The government organization of French Africa was relatively uniform and does not present the diversities which one notices in British Africa. The early decision to create two large federations also facilitated the adoption of a uniform policy for all of the African territories. This uniformity continued until the adoption of the *Loi cadre* in 1956 and the hope for some measure of uniformity existed in France through 1958.

By a decree of 1895 the Ivory Coast, Guinea, and Soudan were placed under the governor-general of Senegal. However, each territory had its own governor and the power of the governor-general was therefore minimal. Dahomey which had recently been conquered was not included, even theoretically, under his control. There were many shifts in attempting to federate these various territories until 1904 when the French West African Federation (AOF) was declared. This was composed of five territories— Senegal, Guinea, Dahomey, the Ivory Coast, and Upper Senegal-Niger. In 1920 Mauritania was declared a colony and added to the AOF, and by shifting boundaries and renaming territories, there emerged three new areas— the Soudan, Niger, and Upper Volta. In 1910 a similar grouping of the four territories of Chad, Ubangi-Shari, Gabon, and the Middle Congo was created. This was the Federation of French Equatorial Africa (AEF). These were entirely administrative entities with no independent rights and powers for the component territories. The chain of command was simple and direct, very similar to a military organization. However, the administrative officers at all levels were advised by councils whose powers were minimal but whose composition was quite complex. Government practices in each of these federations were modified until by 1920 they assumed the form which they retained until World War II.

With the exception of Senegal which will be discussed later, the system of government established in the AÓF and AEF was the following:

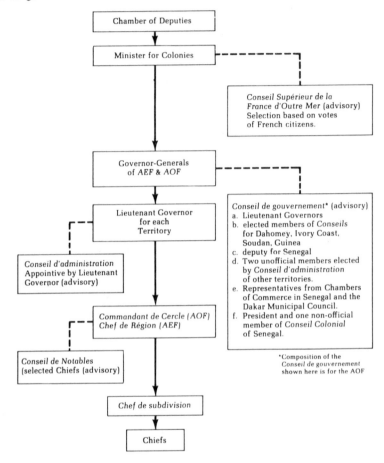

The administrative structure of each federation resembled a pyramid. At the apex was the governor-general, the only official in the federation empowered to deal directly with the colonial ministry in Paris. He was required, in theory, to gain approval for most of his actions from the minister. In actual practice, particularly in the earlier years of the century, the governor-general because of poor communications often acted on his own initiative. This factor combined with his discretionary power in issuing decrees decided upon in Paris into action in the federation enabled the governor-general to offset partially the undue centralization of the system. Each colony within the federation also had a lieutenant-governor and a staff of French civil servants. Under normal circumstances they served to carry out orders passed on to them by the colonial ministry and the governor-general's office.

Within each colony the largest administrative unit in the AOF was called a *cercle* and in the AEF a *région*. These were further divided into smaller units called subdivisions which were in turn composed of cantons, a collection of African villages. Each of the segments of a federation was administered by French officials whose primary responsibilities were to maintain law and order and to see that the decrees from higher authority were carried out by the African rulers.

At the level of local government, direct administrative control by the *Commandants de Cercles* and the *Chefs de subdivision* was more obvious than in most British territories. Although it is true that the British form of indirect rule was more direct than is often believed, the traditional chiefs in British areas were allowed a large measure of autonomy from direct administrative guidance. In French territories the chiefs were maintained and supported but left with little discretionary powers of their own. In time they became paid servants of the administration and as such were expected to carry out orders of their superiors in the hierarchy.

At each successive level of government there existed advisory councils. These councils had no power to act independently of the responsible authority and each executive from the minister for colonies down to the *Commandant de Cercle* could accept or reject the advice of his councils. In 1925 the *conseils d'administrations* of the Ivory Coast, Dahomey, Soudan, and Guinea were increased by having two French citizens elected for the *conseil* by the Chambers of Commerce and Agriculture and by three non-citizens elected by a special African electorate. All other members continued to be appointed. In Mauritania and Niger the members of the *conseils* remained totally nominated until 1945.

Municipal government also was welded into the central administration. There were basically two types of municipalities. The first type had an elected council and an elected mayor with considerable administrative powers. Until 1955 there were only three cities of this type—Dakar, St. Louis, and Rufisque. The reasons for granting these cities more responsibility are to be found in the earlier grant of freedom to the communes of Senegal. The second type of municipal organization was one in which the French administration exercised a large degree of control. There were three different grades of cities in this latter type of system. The first grade had its municipal commission totally nominated by the lieutenant-governors. The second grade had the commission elected by a small portion of the electorate, while the third had its commission elected by universal suffrage. Cities in all three grades of this second type had mayors appointed by the lieutenant-governors and they could also be removed by the same process. Thus except in rare instances the cities in French colonial Africa were controlled by the French central administration.

Senegal differed from all other territories in French Africa because of its long association with metropolitan France. In April 1848, *originaires* of annexed territory were given the right to vote for a representative to the Chamber of Deputies in Paris. In the nineteenth century this area was divided into four communes—St. Louis, Goree, Rufisque, and Dakar. Citizens of these four communes were regarded as French citizens and these divisions were legally confirmed in 1916. In the beginning only Europeans and Creoles were chosen as deputies. The first African deputy, Blaise Diagne, was elected in 1914. To secure this seat and maintain it, Diagne created a powerful political organization which dominated Senegalese political life until the 1930s. Councils headed by an elected mayor were elected within the four communes to deal with municipal affairs. The powers of the elected councils were limited by the central administration. In other communes throughout French Africa there was a form of representation allowed, but the average African could not meet the requirements to vote.

In Senegal there existed from 1879 onward a *Conseil Général* of twenty members elected by the French citizens in the four communes and in the territory under direct French control. All other areas were considered protectorate areas and were not represented on the *Conseil*. Its powers were basically advisory except in budgetary matters. Here they exercised real control. Between 1890 and 1920, during the reconstruction of the government of Senegal and the creation of the federations, the financial and advisory powers of the *Conseil Général* were greatly restricted. In 1920 the protectorate which had been under separate jurisdiction since 1890 was again joined to the direct control areas and the *conseil* became once again the major legislative body. The name was changed in 1920 to the *Conseil Colonial* and was expanded to include twenty chiefs representing the protected areas. Various changes were made in the ratios between the numbers of chiefs and elected members before 1939. In that year a substantial addition of eighteen elected French subjects was made to the *Conseil Colonial*. The *conseil,* although supervised by the administration and checked by the veto power of the governor, played an important role in Senegal. It affected policy making because it could withhold funds necessary for the implementation of new projects. It also served as an important training ground for Africans in the exercise of government on a high level. Taken together with elected deputies to the French legislature, municipal government, and the French type of indirect rule, the *Conseil Colonial* gave the Senegalese a voice in their government prior to 1939 unique in French Africa.

Belgian Africa

In the decade prior to the end of World War I, Belgium had a twofold problem in the Congo. One was the creation of a viable political system to rule the huge area of the Congo basin. The second closely interrelated problem was the repeal of those punitive measures enacted by the regime of King Leopold II. The constitution of the Congo for almost fifty years was the Colonial Charter of 1908. This charter established the basic framework of the reconstructed government with a resident governor-general and governors for each of the four provinces which were later expanded to six. The charter and subsequent legislation curtailed the use of forced labor, labor taxes, and abolished producer monopolies. Land controlled by concessionaire companies was also reduced in size and agents of the companies were prohibited from exercising government functions. The size of the Congo, the lack of staff, and Belgium's deep involvement in World War I delayed the implementation of many of these paper reforms. However, by 1920 the paternalistic Congo government which continued until independence had become a reality. This paternalism was predicated upon a strong centralized form of government with the locus of decision making in Belgium. Although the governor-generals had discretionary powers in administration and legislation, they acted in most cases as agents of policies decided upon by the colonial ministry in Brussels.

Belgian colonial policy was only partially motivated by the desire to exploit efficiently the mineral wealth of the Congo. It was also based on a series of assumptions, most of which were valid through the late 1950s. On the theoretical plane, Belgium assumed a relative equality of the African with the European. Colonial authorities viewed the Congo as a trust, an area where they, as representatives of a more advanced state system, should plan for the present and future well-being of the African. The Congo was by far the most planned for of any dependency of any European power. Belgian paternalism demanded this type of planning to effect ends held to be beneficial for both Africans and Belgians.

Europeans who entered the Congo had to prove that they had future employment and post monetary guarantees for their return to Europe if they should lose their positions. As a result, relatively few whites became permanent Congo residents. Those who did were, normally, government employees, skilled and professional persons, businessmen, or missionaries. In order to develop industry, particularly mining, a proportionately larger number of African workers were utilized in semiskilled positions than in French or British areas. This policy was quite important for thousands of Africans since companies such as Union Minière du Haut Katanga were exploiting systematically the mineral wealth of the Congo in the period after 1920. No European could own land in the Congo. Even the large companies held only long-term leases. This again was fully in accord with Belgian ideas of protecting the African.

Aside from maintaining law and order, the government saw its first responsibility to be the economic welfare of the African. Wage scales for urban and government workers were excellent by comparison to other territories. The government supervised building and attempted to maintain wherever possible reasonable living conditions. Medical facilities, government-run and those operated by missionaries, were among the best in Africa both as to size and quality, particularly in urban areas. In the field of education the Belgian government supported primary, secondary, and technical education through grants to missions and directly by operating its own schools. The Congo by the 1950s could boast a literacy rate of over forty percent while most dependencies of other European powers could show only a rate of between ten and thirty percent. However, little provision was made for advanced education in secondary schools and universities. Few Congolese attended European universities and until 1954, when Lovanium University was opened, the government actively discouraged higher liberal education.

This benevolent paternalistic attitude was carried over into the political organization of the state. European residents had no special rights as existed in other multiracial territories such as Rhodesia. Congolese were associated in large numbers with their government only on the lowest levels. Decision making in the Congo was reserved for Belgian appointive officials. The councils which existed on all levels of government were purely advisory and had no powers even comparable with the French advisory councils. The basic organization of the government of the Congo was as follows:

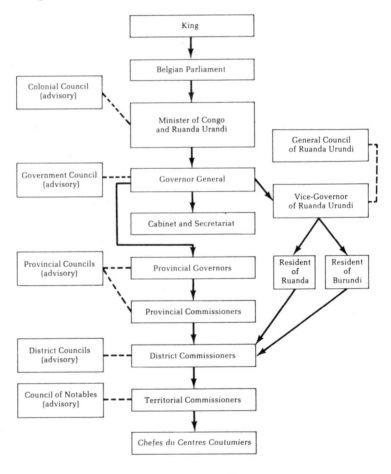

As the chart indicates, the government of the Congo was a European autocratic system with its center of control in Belgium. Only on the lowest levels were the Africans allowed to participate directly in political affairs. Over seventy-five percent of the Congolese population lived under a modified system of traditional rule. Here in these *Centres Coutumiers* traditional authorities were allowed to govern, subject to the control of officers of the central administration. Belgium before World War I followed a policy of supplanting traditional rulers with either European officers or government-appointed chiefs. Although these traditional rulers were later allowed to exercise more jural and executive authority than before, the district and provincial commissioners still retained ultimate power. In the 1950s certain further changes were instituted which created larger administrative units under the direction of appointed paramount chiefs. Also in the 1950s there were changes in the composition of the various councils to include a broader spectrum of representation from other social and economic groups within the African community.

The Belgian system of traditional chiefs met the needs of the majority of the agricultural people of the Congo. However, it was tightly controlled and did not serve as a school for future government leaders. Nor did the system give to the people of the Congo a sense of unity. The territory was so large and the peoples so diverse that the Belgians never considered inculcating in the people a feeling of loyalty to a political entity higher than the tribe. Therefore the ancient hostility between segments of the Bantu people of the Congo continued to thrive. Whatever unity existed in the Congo prior to independence was only that of the Belgian administrations, laws, and police.

A second type of governmental procedure was provided for the Africans who had left their native villages to work for Europeans or in industry or mining. Most of these partially detribalized Africans lived in towns close to urban centers in the large cities. Such areas were called *Centres Extra Coutumiers* by the Belgians. They were administered by native chiefs appointed by the central government and advised by an appointive council under the direction of district officers. The nature of government in these areas differed from the strict traditional rule of the rural districts because of changes occasioned by the detribalization of the· majority of the people living in these *centres*. It was in these *centres* that the Belgians planned to begir a slow process of democratizing the administration of the Congo. Although many high officials in Belgium and the Congo had been considering political reforms for years, prior to 1958 no serious proposals were ever made for extensive grants of power on the central level before implementing changes on the lower levels.

After 1919 Belgium received a League of Nations mandate over Ruanda and Burundi which had been carved from German East Africa. Belgian administration of the two territories was subject, in theory, to control by the League of Nations. In actual practice the League interfered very little in the government of any of its mandates. Belgium linked the administration of Ruanda and Burundi to the Congo and made its chief executive officer, the vice-governor, subordinate to the governor-general. However, because of distance and the special conditions of the mandate, the vice-governor was in many ways independent of his superior. Finance was kept separate from the Congo and the judiciary was also independent. The vice-governor had decree-making powers as well.

Ruanda and Burundi are among the most densely populated areas in Africa. The society of the two territories was highly structured and had hardly been affected by the German occupation. There were three distinct people in each territory, each with a specific place in society and a definite function. Most of the people were Bahutu who were Bantu agriculturists. The second largest group was the dominant Nilotic Watutsi who had invaded the highlands centuries before. They were pastoralists and controlled the wealth and politics of both territories. The third and smallest population was the Pygmy Batwa who acted as servants of both others groups.

All the higher offices in each state were held by the Watutsi and each was ruled by an autocratic king or mwami. Belgium retained the traditional structure, modifying it only by the assignment of a resident to the court of each mwami. The only counterbalance to the autocracy of the mwami and the aristocracy was the power of the vice-governor and his staff, particularly that exercised by the residents. European settlement was prohibited and almost all the land except for two huge parks was reserved for African use. There were no urban areas except those towns which grew up around the Belgian administrative centers. Most of Belgian activity in each area was concentrated upon the improvement of agriculture and animal husbandry. Little attention was paid to education. The authorities were willing to leave elementary education to the missionaries. Therefore there was not developed in either area a nucleus of Western-trained Africans. Belgium was content to do nothing to broaden the base of representation until after 1950 when it was decided to experiment with change in each of the regions.

Portuguese Africa

The Portuguese empire in Africa was not constructed in the same manner as colonial governments of the other European states. Except in rare instances, the British, French, and Belgian territories in Africa were the results of late nineteenth-century imperialism. However different their colonial systems, they were the product of a similar time and similar challenges. Because of the competitive nature of late nineteenth-century expansion, the governing instruments of most African areas were hastily arrived at and were pragmatic to the extent that the governments were a compromise between that of the mother country and existing African forms. The Portuguese empire by contrast had existed in the coastal areas of Angola and Mozambique since the fifteenth century. Time, therefore, hallowed many theories of Portuguese rule in Africa and their application, and even though many of these were out of step with the demands of the modern world, they were clung to tenaciously by the Portuguese.

Except for a brief period in the early sixteenth century, the Portuguese were interested in Africa for the single purpose of its economic value. At that time the Portuguese in dealing with the Bakongo were motivated by the desire to Christianize the African and inculcate him with Portuguese culture. However, the growing demand of her colonies (primarily Brazil) for slaves almost totally negated the cultural aspect of Portuguese occupation. Slaves became the most important product of Africa and the Portuguese from their bases in Angola and Mozambique entered directly into not only the overseas distribution but also the gathering of slaves. For over three centuries the slave trade was the major occupation of the Portuguese in Africa. Their attitudes toward Africans were formed in this period. Of all the European powers, only Portugal retained her large permanent establishments from the mercantilist period to modern times. Britain and France were deeply affected by the economic revolution of the eighteenth and nineteenth centuries and they discarded, at least for a time, mercantilist economic organization. Portugal did not. Although the slave trade is gone, the Portuguese territories in Africa still exist economically for the good of Portugal.

Portuguese desires to dominate a major portion of Central Africa during the scramble were frustrated by the ambitions of more powerful European states. Partially because of European competition, but more because of its weak economic position, Portugal was not able to make good its occupation in many territories assigned to her until just before World War I. The Dembos area and the territory of the Cuanhama people in Angola, and Yao country in Mozambique, were not pacified until the first decade of the twentieth century. The stringencies of such conquests reinforced the Portuguese belief that because of their long contact with Africa they alone knew how to govern the African. Despite such confidence in their ability to rule, the Portuguese did not evolve any coherent colonial system until the 1890s. Central to the new system as enunciated by the Colonial Regulation of 1899 was the emphasis placed upon teaching the African the sanctity of work. Much of the responsibility of lower echelon civil servants in all the colonies was directed toward the recruitment of African workers. This recruitment could take the form of demanding that Africans work on public works in their districts or rounding up eligible males to be exported to work outside the territory as contract laborers. Despite widespread criticism of the system of overseas recruitment, particularly in the period just before World War I, Portugal continued the practice.

Over ninety-eight percent of the population of Portuguese Africa are *indigenas* and they have borne the full weight of the authoritarian Portuguese regime. The *shibalo* system of compulsory labor was particularly harsh since it was based upon the premise that the African should be forced to accept the European concept of work. The system was also necessary for the Portuguese to show a profit from their territories. All natives were required to offer proof that they were employed for at least six months of the year. *Indigenas* were exempt from compulsory labor if they could show a certificate from the agriculture department stating that they worked their own farms or were employed in urban work or in mining. Only a small proportion of the population could qualify for this exemption. The rest could be forcibly compelled to work. In theory, workers so recruited were to be utilized only on government projects. In actual fact large numbers were recruited by the government and presented with mass contracts which enabled the government to assign them to work for European farmers. In addition, by the 1950s over one-quarter of a million Africans a year were provided for work in the mines in South Africa and the Rhodesias. These workers were initially supplied by Mozambique as its part in a commercial agreement signed with the Union of South Africa. By this treaty the Union agreed to employ a maximum of 80,000 workers a year and in return ship a certain portion of their products on Portuguese railroads to the port of Lourenço Marques. Later agreements were reached which helped the Portuguese to build up the ports of Lobito and Beira with foreign capital so the one cost to the government in recruiting was that of gathering the natives while the government profited in three ways—from higher taxes and increased use of its rail facilities and its ports.

Far more onerous and more feared than the *shibalo* and contractual work was the transporting of Africans to work the cocoa plantations on the island of São Thomé. A number of observers have pointed out that the so-called *contractos* did not volunteer for this service. They were generally collected in Angola although some came from Mozambique. Natives who were on such service were totally at the mercy of their employers and a long sea voyage separated them from the mainland. As late as the 1940s former Inspector General Galvão of Mozambique reported that the death rate of these workers was over thirty percent.

In addition to these policies, there were numerous other indignities which the African had to suffer from the Portuguese. He had to carry a pass and in urban areas abide by the curfew. Portuguese prisons and jails were far from being models of modern penology. Although, in theory, African traditional rulers continued to function, they were servants of an authoritarian regime whose local agents in some cases used harsh, brutal methods in carrying out their duties. The practice of beating the palms of the hands, the *palmatorio*, was outlawed by the 1950s, but some observers even at that late date reported its continued use by Portuguese authorities.

The Portuguese empire in Africa constitutes a closed mercantilistic system. Portugal, one of the most economically backward European states, created a structure which welded the colonies to the mother country politically as well as economically. After 1951 the Portuguese territories were officially known as overseas provinces and considered by the government to be an integral part of Portugal. This action merely solidified the long-held belief that there could be no evolution of the African areas separate from Portugal itself.

A complicating feature of the Portuguese empire is the presence of relatively large numbers of Europeans in the colonies. This factor alone would make difficult the devolution of power to Africans even if Portugal had not been so poor that its future prosperity was considered tied to its empire or if its regime were more liberal. The history of other multiracial areas such as Kenya and the Rhodesias in the 1950s illustrates this. By the mid-1950s there were almost 70,000 Europeans in Mozambique and over 100,000 in Angola. Many of these became increasingly dissatisfied with the nature of their authoritarian government after World War II. However, their dissatisfaction with the regime of Prime Minister Salazar never reached the point where they wished to exchange his rule for that of an African majority.

It is a mistake to believe that the authoritarian, centralized, and inflexible colonial system of Portugal was a product of the Salazar dictatorship. It was a creation of the liberal republic and predated Salazar's regime by a generation at least. The system in general resembles those established by France and Belgium in the early twentieth century. However, the government of Salazar which concentrated power in the hands of a few persons in Portugal simply increased the degree of control and made the system less flexible to respond to the sweeping changes occurring elsewhere in Africa. The Portuguese colonial system as it existed in the early 1950s is shown by the chart below:

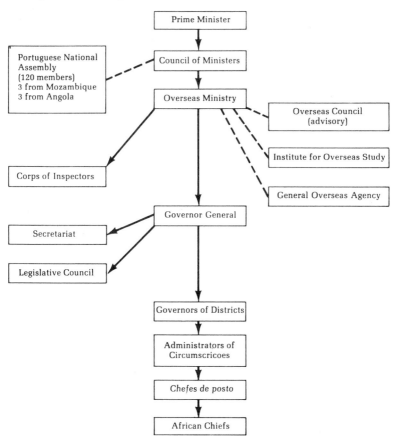

The real authority in the Portuguese government is the council of ministers controlled by the prime minister. This has not been a responsible ministry since the overthrow of the liberal republic in 1926. The council of ministers has the right to legislate as well as to direct the policy of the state. The elected national assembly does not have policy-making powers. Its function since 1932 has been to legislate on matters referred to it by the council of ministers or any individual ministries. The national assembly is composed of 120 elected members. Three members represent Angola and three Mozambique. The influence of elected members from Africa would be negligible even if the government was not as autocratic as it is.

Direction of colonial policy is determined mainly by the overseas ministry. In discharging this responsibility, the ministry is aided by a permanent advisory overseas council and two subsidiary agencies, the Institute for Overseas Study and the General Overseas Agency. The institute exists primarily to train administrators while the agency acts as an information and propaganda center. The chief official resident in a colony is the governor-general appointed for a four-year term of office. He is unchecked in his legislative and executive power by any agency other than the overseas ministry. He is responsible for finances, heads the colonial bureaucracy, directs the native authority system, and sees that the orders of the council of ministers are carried out. The legislative councils in Angola and Mozambique have a majority of elected members, but they have only advisory powers. They do not have the usual right of scrutinizing the budget.

In each district the governors have similar autocratic powers except on a more restricted scale. There have been many regroupings of districts since 1930, but by 1950 there were twelve districts in Angola and nine districts in Mozambique. To ninety-five percent of the Africans in Portuguese territories, the most important European officers are the administrators of the Circumscricoes and the Chefes de Posto, positions roughly comparable to the British provincial and district officers. They act as registry officers, judges, tax collectors, finance officers, and general coordinators. Traditional African rulers are subordinate to the European officers. These chiefs are simply the lowest officials in the government hierarchy with little power to act on their own, and they can be replaced at any time by higher authority. All officials are either appointed by the governor-general or the home officials and they are directly responsible to the governor-general.

Partially obscuring the authoritarian, centralized nature of Portuguese rule has been its stated assimilado policy. Portugal has never had rigid prohibitions against intermarriage between the races. This attitude has resulted in a substantial mixed population. The assimilado system as a natural political extension of this racial attitude has been official Portuguese policy since 1917 and was restated in the Colonial Act of 1930 and the Organic Charter of 1933. Briefly this theory holds that all persons, no matter what their race, will be accorded the same status if they meet certain qualifications. To qualify for this status, an African had to adopt the European mode of life, speak and read Portuguese fluently, be a Christian, complete military service, and have a trade or profession. To many European observers unacquainted with the total picture of Portuguese colonialism, this seems a reasonable, even enlightened policy. The failure of this policy, however, can be measured statistically. In 1956 there were 4,550 *assimilados* in a population of six million in Mozambique and approximately 31,000 in a population of four million in Angola. The major reason for the small numbers of *assimilados* is the difficulty in achieving this station. The Portuguese government does not support education to any extent. Even in Portugal the illiteracy rate is over thirty-three percent. In Africa there are few secondary schools with a total enrollment measured in the hundreds. Elementary education is similarly neglected, most emphasis being given schools specifically designed to impart only rudimentary levels of training. Here the students are taught a few moral principles and basic Portuguese. Such an educational system makes it nearly impossible for a young African, even if he wanted to, to become an *assimilado*.

EIGHT

Colonial Africa: the interwar period

Economic development and social change

The basic impetus which had propelled European powers into Africa had been economic. The economic reasons for any European power's territorial expansion in a given area had been either to dominate assured markets or mineral wealth, or to be in a position to control future discoveries. The latter attitude was the most widespread of the two. French expansion and that of Leopold II had been predicated largely upon the gamble that there were unfound riches in the new territories. They had been spurred on in this belief by the discoveries of gold and diamonds in areas of southern Africa previously considered almost worthless. These factors combined with an uncertain knowledge of the interior and myths of riches were enough to convince many European statesmen and businessmen to support a forward policy in Africa. After the scramble had been completed it became necessary to open up the hinterland of Africa to government and business agents. Prior to World War I there was a considerable investment of private and government capital in all areas of sub-Saharan Africa. This was the period when the bulk of the railway and telegraph lines were constructed. Harbors were improved, docks built, river transport subsidized, and a host of trading companies loosed on Africa.

Railway construction had high priority on the list of economic improvements. There was a twofold reason for this. New government stations in the hinterland demanded a steady supply that, in the very earliest days, could be maintained only by large, expensive, slow-moving caravans. Effective government control in most areas demanded a more efficient system of communications. Northern Nigeria, Buganda, the Rhodesias, and the Congo are good examples of territories where railroads were begun for this purpose long before there were materials or products of known economic value. Later when mineral deposits were discovered in the Katanga, Sierra Leone, and the Rhodesian copper belt, the railways were either extended or spur lines built to facilitate the exploitation of the areas. Correlate with the construction of railway lines was the improvement of the road system which in most African territories, by 1940, linked the major interior towns with the coastline. The imperial powers in the interwar period cut back drastically on major government expenditures in the territories. Nevertheless, where there was sufficient economic justification all would invest money in harbor improvements, better railway rolling stock, or an extension of railway and road lines.

Government and private investment tended to be concentrated on extraction of minerals or trade goods in most areas of Africa, and this, in conjunction with other factors, resulted in a tremendous growth of cities and towns. In order to exploit diamond, manganese, copper, or iron discoveries, it was necessary to concentrate a large number of skilled and unskilled workers in one place. The copper belt of Rhodesia and the Katanga and the full range of mining activities in South Africa are the best examples of this type of industrially induced urbanization. Another reason for the growth of cities and towns was the need to service the new mines or in some cases the developing argicultural sectors. Seaports such as Dakar, Lagos, Abidjan, Luanda, and Lourenço Marques had a phenomenal growth rate in the first fifty years of this century. Similar developments could be seen in the size of cities and towns selected to be the site of national, provincial, or district headquarters. Here were concentrated not only the government services, but major offices for trading or mining companies and banks. One of the most phenomenal examples of developing urbanization is Nairobi which did not even exist when the decision was made in the 1890s to construct the railway through Kenya. By 1940 it was one of the major cities of East Africa with a population in excess of 25,000.

Each step in improving economic or government efficiency in a given territory was accompanied by changes, often subtle, in the traditional African political and economic system. Something as simple as the construction of a railroad or a laterite road near a village facilitated, at the least, the greater mobility of the population. Men who previously had never imagined traveling more than a few miles from their village soon found it easy to visit areas hundreds of miles from their homes. Even traditional markets were affected in the time, locale, and nature of the product sold. In a much more direct way all European-controlled areas soon became converted to a money economy. Young men found it much easier to obtain money by working in the towns, at first for government and then later in a full range of jobs in the civilian sector. Greater mobility combined with greater economic opportunity facilitated the rapid growth of urban centers. In the beginning a man who had worked for government or European firms might be content after a time to return to his village and reassume his place in the traditional order. However, many found that a traditional agricultural existence was stultifying after the excitement of the cities, and many more refused to be constrained within the older political and societal framework. Thus in most African states, although there continued to be migrations between cities and countryside, an ever-increasing number of Africans became urban dwellers.

Urban life wrought many changes upon the African. Familial and tribal ties were loosened and in some cases ceased to be a factor in behavior. Their jobs provided many Africans not only with money and the Western products this would buy, but also introduced them to a new scale of values and gave them the necessary skills to move into more important positions. Some Africans became traders either with European firms or on their own, and with luck and hard work a few could become affluent or even wealthy men. Those Africans in good positions with government, private firms, or who had their own business acted as an incentive to other young village or city Africans. The cities as lodestones did not always fulfill the expectations of Africans. There was only a limited number of jobs and therefore there was an increasingly high unemployment rate which contributed to the feeling of grievance many Africans had against the imperial government. There was little government planning in the organization of these new cities and very soon they were overcrowded with minimal sanitation facilities. Around the centrum of each major city there developed unplanned African communities which in some areas soon deteriorated into slums. In such communities crimes which would have been reprehensible in traditional society became commonplace. Here the normal pattern of life to many became a form which combined the worst elements of both European and African societies.

In many areas where agriculture remained the most important export product, there were significant changes in the economic structures of the country. Cocoa planters in the Ivory Coast, Gold Coast, and Nigeria, coffee growers in Tanganyika and the Ivory Coast, and peanut cultivators throughout West Africa found an ever-increasing demand for their product. Better methods of cultivation, better varieties of plants, and more improved selectivity brought farmers large profits. Where such was the case there evolved a definite agricultural African middle class which in many cases had goals at variance with the traditional structures of authority.

Detribalization became a fact of African life. Urban Africans came to measure success not in traditional terms, but in those of the colonial power. On one level it could be the ownership of European clothes or a bicycle while on a higher level it was to live in the European style, own a car, and educate one's children. Thus while all European governments continued to use the traditional ruler in governing their African possessions, the chiefs' authority even in British territories had been undermined by the new economy and urbanization. Educated Africans, or even those who believed themselves skilled, began to be more vocal in their criticism of a system which excluded them from political power yet rewarded a chief who could not read or write. The policy of European governments and businesses of reserving the upper echelon positions for whites came increasingly under attack by Africans who either were prepared for such responsibility or thought they should have these jobs. Double standards in

employment convinced many Africans to join a variety of pressure organizations seeking better opportunities.

Western education and Christianity began to advance in sub-Saharan
Africa only after the scramble had been completed and urbanization begun.
Christianity had made few converts when the village African could see
little advantage in abandoning his traditional ways. In the twentieth century with the added impetus of economic gain, more detribalized Africans
began to find advantages in at least a partial adherence to Christianity.
Except in the Belgian Congo, the bulk of African education was shifted
by a penurious government to missionary societies. In the new atmosphere
of the towns and cities education for the African was immediately trans-
latable into economic advantage. Prosperous Africans were willing to
invest the necessary money in school fees with the assurance that their
sons would be able to compete in the new world. In some cases whole
villages, as among the Ibo, would subsidize the entire cost of educating
a promising young man. In return the student would bring his village
honor, prestige, and later money. This interest evinced by some Africans
in education should not be construed to mean that there were ever many
schools in Africa. Approaches toward giving a primary education to all
African children had to wait until the latter 1950s. But to the more affluent
Africans, Christianity came to mean education, and education was provided through the secondary levels for an ever-increasing number of
African boys. The more promising could, if financing was available, get
university degrees in Britain or France.

The demand of government for more Africans to staff the lower range
of the civil service also was translated into a form of education. This type
of on-the-job training in public works, agriculture, marine, treasury, and
other departments meant that in time diligent Africans could become reasonably skilled in a variety of European-type occupations. Belgium was
particularly interested in this form of education. In the Congo many positions in industry and the mines normally associated with whites were
filled by Africans. To a lesser extent this was true also in British and
French areas. Clerks and junior storekeepers throughout their areas were
invariably African.

It was then the juxtaposition of a Westernized economy and government structure on Africa which created the need for more educated and
trained Africans. These in turn were much more aware of the political and
economic injustices of colonial rule. African doctors, lawyers, and teachers
who had encountered the fundamental documents of European freedom
and had read widely in liberal or Marxist literature began to question the
dichotomy between European theories and colonial practices. African civil
servants began to wonder why their upward mobility was arbitrarily
blocked and why certain positions were always reserved for Europeans.
Even workers in the mines, on the railroads, and on the docks began to
question why their wage rates were so much lower than European workers.
Once introduced to the competitive wage system, it was a short step for
some Africans, whenever their economic aspirations were thwarted, to
turn to European-inspired trade union activity or political parties.

Until after World War II the colonial administrations pursued administrative policies which might have been adequate a quarter of a century before but which had become out of step with reality. The new reality had been created, sometimes inadvertently, by the demands of government agencies, economic exploitation, and the advance of education. The cities and towns provided the intellectual leadership, the African economic underpinning, and the unsatisfied partially detribalized masses which in combination became the potent anti-imperialist political movements that eventually forced rapid and revolutionary changes throughout Africa. Political parties, themselves a Western idea, had their origins in the centers of the economically new Africa—the urban areas.

Separatist church movements

The activity of dedicated missionaries in the nineteenth century produced differential results throughout the continent. Although the early optimism of many mission societies proved to be unwarranted, there were many areas which proved to be very receptive to Christianity. Most of these, until the twentieth century, were coastal areas. A combination of factors such as poor communications, disease, and the advance forces of a proselytizing Islam tended to minimize the conversions of interior people. In only a few hinterland areas did the missionaries have great success. Uganda and Nyasaland were the best examples of such fertile fields.

By the beginning of the new century there were many Christian Africans in certain areas. Continually expanded mission activities in the fifty years after 1900 made even further inroads on traditional African religions. It should be emphasized that a convert to Christianity was required to deny himself many things which his clan or tribe considered normal and proper. The greatest general effect of Christianity was the stress placed upon the native community and the extended family system. Christianity required a man to limit himself to one wife. If he already possessed more than one, he was forced to divest himself of the others, sending them and their children back to their families. Christian converts were also taught to look upon the society from which they had been emancipated as heathen and to pride themselves on achieving a higher level. In all conversions there was a factor, unconnected with pure theoretical religion, of accommodation of the African to the white man's world. Such emulation also added to the feelings of superiority a Christian African held for his unconverted relatives. Thus there was present, from the very earliest periods, pressures to accommodate Christianity to the cultures and needs of the African. Such syncretistic movements became particularly effective in the twentieth century and they represented one of the earliest forms of African rejection of complete Europeanization.

At the same time as this type of accommodation was proceeding there developed among the better educated, urban African, a different and less subtle type of reaction to the European. Missionary activity, however, varied from one Christian group to another and in differing places, normally had one common factor. It was firmly controlled by Europeans, although Nigeria was one seeming exception. The conversion of so many of the Niger River peoples to Christianity had been due to the activity of black Christians. However, after 1890 the decisions of the Church of England and its associated missionary society relegated Africans in Nigeria to only secondary positions within the church. Everywhere in Christian Africa this pattern was repeated. Europeans were the administrators, preachers, teachers, and doctors; Africans were only their active, willing supporters. Christian missionaries preached egalitarianism and practiced supremacy.

Throughout Africa breakaway or so-called Ethiopian churches developed in response to the twin pressures of the need to accommodate Christianity to the needs of African societies and the reaction against European domination. African churches represented one of the earliest anti-European manifestations by their stress upon the worth and uniqueness of African culture. However different these churches were from one another, they all emphasized the Old Testament. There they could find sanctions for many practices which European missionaries found distasteful in African society. Most of the churches were only covertly anti-European, but some participated directly in early political movements designed to dislodge the European from power. There were a wide variety of these native churches and it is impossible to do more than to mention a few of these organizations.

One area particularly susceptible to African reforming church movements was central and south-central Africa. One of the most receptive areas for a new synthesis was Nyasaland and the catalyst there was an American fundamentalist missionary, Joseph Booth. Arriving in Nyasaland in 1892, he was immediately struck by the divergence between the theory of Christianity and the practices of European Christians. He noted the wide differences between the economic and social position of whites and blacks. Booth later stressed the Christian imperative for egalitarianism in his writing and preaching at the Zambesi Industrial Mission. In 1899 he petitioned the British government for an end to colonial rule since it perpetuated the differences between the races. Such overt actions stamped him as a radical and the government attempted to arrest and deport him in 1899. He was allowed to return the following year and continued his propaganda campaign against the government in favor of African rights until 1902 when he left the area for South Africa. Five years later he planned to return to Nyasaland, but the government refused to allow him to enter the territory.

Booth's teachings and activity had made a deep impress upon a young Yao convert, John Chilembwe. He became Booth's servant in 1892 and learned to read and write while at the mission. Due to Booth's influence he was admitted to a Baptist seminary in the United States where he trained for the ministry. Chilembwe returned to Nyasaland in 1899 as a missionary for the National (Negro) Baptist Convention. He was largely responsible for constructing and directing the Providence Industrial Mission at Mbombwe. At first conservative in dress and manners and reluctant to lend himself to political causes, Chilembwe gradually adopted more radical concepts. By 1914 his position was that European colonial rule was a mockery of Christianity and further that the only way that Africans could free themselves from European control was by force. Thus Chilembwe lent his considerable local prestige and that of his followers to an attempt to overthrow the government of Nyasaland in 1915. This revolt will be treated in more detail later. It is sufficient to note here that Chilembwe's power base was slight. The revolt failed and Chilembwe was killed. His movement is important, despite the failure of its immediate goals, because it was the first nationalistic movement led by an African which had as its goal the idealistic motives of Christianity.

Meanwhile in Barotseland another charismatic African, Willie J. Mokalapa, was organizing his separatist church. Mokalapa, a Suto evangelical, had previously assisted white missionaries working among the Lozi. He obviously had reacted to the inferior treatment of African Christians since, at a later date in South Africa, he joined a church organization, first founded in the United States in 1816, which opposed the color bar within the church. A group of Africans in 1892 disaffiliated themselves from the South African Wesleyan Church and formed their own extension of this group and took the name South African Ethiopian Church.

Mokalapa returned to Barotseland as the presiding elder in Rhodesia. He persuaded the powerful Lozi chief, Lewanika, to offer protection to the new church. Mokalapa gained a large number of converts but challenged British authority only in an indirect fashion. Instead, he concentrated upon the church and on starting a number of African controlled schools. Nevertheless, the authorities viewed him as a threat and attempted to influence Lewanika to order him from the country. This the chief refused to do. However, in 1904, Mokalapa visited South Africa on business, was swindled of the funds entrusted to him, and never returned to Lozi country. Without Mokalapa to guide it, his church rapidly declined in numbers and potential influence.

Another important religious movement in Central Africa was associated with Jehovah's Witnesses. This Christian fundamentalist group taught that all human governments were doomed. All men would soon be judged after the imminent cataclysm at which God would institute a divine rule among men. African adherents to this doctrine such as Elliot Lamwana, founder of the Free Church and another associate of Booth, believed in the peaceful revolution of the masses. In Nyasaland and Rhodesia the believers were referred to as belonging to the Watchtower movement. In the Belgian Congo the movement was called kitwala. During World War I the movement was proscribed in Northern Rhodesia and Nyasaland. After the war it was allowed to continue and soon became quite strong in certain districts. The Watchtower movement was given much of the blame for the minor disturbances on the copper belt in 1935.

Black ministers from the United States were viewed by the imperial powers as carriers of revolutionary social and political beliefs. Reference has already been made to the activities of Booth, Chilembwe, and Mokalapa, and the reactions which they caused in Central Africa. In 1908 Belgian authorities detained missionaries of the African Methodist Episcopal Church when they attempted to enter the Congo. In 1914 the British also prevented missionaries from this church from working in the Gold Coast. Despite such precautions, Ethiopian churches continued to flourish in most African areas. In Nigeria the decision in 1890 to relegate African ministers and laymen to secondary positions resulted in the rapid growth of break-away churches at first in Yoruba and later in Ibo areas. Schismatic movements among educated Nigerians were greatly influenced by the writings of Edward Wilmot Blyden, a West Indian who migrated to Liberia in the mid-nineteenth century. Not only did he approve of the religious motivations behind the Ethiopian churches, but he stressed the anti-imperialistic doctrine of Africa for Africans.

The Watchtower movement or kitwala in the Congo changed considerably in time. Leaders there tended to stress the degradation of the black man under the existing colonial regime. All this would be rectified by the apocalypse when black men would be changed to white. In the early 1920s the movement had a very powerful anti-Belgian base in the eastern Congo. Later in some places, it blended with the Kimbanguiste sect which owed its beginnings to the prophet Simon Kimbangu. Simon who had been baptized a Protestant, began in 1921 to preach, and according to his followers, he performed miracles. Although he stressed the Bible and the next world in his preaching, the Belgians saw in his popularity a threat to the state. He was arrested, charged with disrupting order, and sentenced to death. The sentence was commuted to life imprisonment, and until his death thirty years later, Kimbangu was confined in exile in the Katanga. Kimbangu was deified by his followers and despite the loss of their leader, the movement flourished and spread throughout the western Congo and into Angola. It took the name of The Church of Jesus Christ on Earth by the Prophet Simon Kimbangu. Kimbanguiste churches modified the liturgy, admitting many African details to the worship ceremonies. It also encouraged African dissatisfaction with Belgian rule and took an active part in Congolese politics in the 1950s. In August 1969, the church began by Kimbangu, having grown to over three million members, was admitted to the World Council of Churches.

In Kenya in the 1920s Henry Thuku led the first organized Kikuyu political agitation against British authority. This blended into the reaction of the Kikuyu to missionary endeavors to end female circumcision. As a result a series of separatist churches were created. Some segments of this reaction became fanatically anti-Western. One example of such a group was the watu wa mungu (People of God) who attacked police stations in 1934 and were later prosecuted by the government. Of more lasting significance was the founding of a number of Kikuyu Independent Schools as an adjunct to the separatist churches. These schools attempted to perpetuate Kikuyu tradition and ideals while at the same time preparing students to function in the increasingly Westernized world of Kenya. Jomo Kenyatta in the days prior to Mau Mau was closely associated with the management of these schools. In this connection it should be noted that in the five years before Mau Mau a whole series of men claiming to be prophets appeared among the Kikuyu. These were both a symptom of the dissatisfaction with British rule and a warning for the future.

One should note a few sailent points from these few examples of separatist churches. First the movements were not localized. Separatist churches were found in all places where Christianity had made substantial gains from African religions. Secondly, almost all these churches attempted to accommodate Christian teachings with the religious and social practices of the African. The existence of these churches was a testimonial to the failure of white Christians, either through their missionaries or government authorities, to live up to the doctrines which were taught the African. Those factors which led large numbers of Africans to associate themselves with these churches were normally worldly rather than spiritual differences. Segregation, poor education, differential standards of opportunity and salary, combined with the urbanized African's feelings of loss of identity, caused these churches to flourish. These same factors encouraged the African to associate himself with embryo political parties and agitate for an end to colonial rule. The separatist churches early served the function of channeling the African's discontent with his lot normally in the direction of the other world. They also prepared the African later to demand of his masters a larger share of responsibility in governing himself and to restate the worth of his own particular culture.

Early political parties

European systems of rule in Africa north of the Limpopo River, however different from each other, had one feature in common. They were all authoritarian. Responsibility for all except the lowest level of decision making was retained by European officers appointed by the home government. Belgian and Portuguese rule did not provide any method by which Africans other than traditional rulers could become a part of the machinery of government. The French pursued a policy of assimilation which created a few well-educated Africans who could compete with their European counterparts for positions in the civil service. In Senegal the presence of the four communes gave Africans a chance to participate directly in municipal government, and after 1871 Senegal chose one representative to the French chamber of deputies. Elsewhere in French Africa it was more difficult for Africans to participate directly in political affairs. Nevertheless it was the practice to appoint Africans to the various advisory councils. The educated elite in French Africa were more involved with the power structure than their counterparts in British Africa. The British Colonial Office by the early 1920s had not only accepted the practical necessities of indirect rule, but its philosophic rationale as well. Thus there existed a deep-seated distrust of Africans who tried to imitate Europeans. Emphasis in all territories was placed upon what the British considered the traditional rulers, and the central administration tried to protect them from the inroads of the educated African. These educated, urban-based Africans, as one means of protesting their inferior status in some British territories, began to form political parties. Except for Senegal this type of protest was confined exclusively to British areas. Belgium and Portugal would not allow such activity and the French African elite were too satisfied with their positions to form political parties.

Africans of the four communes in Senegal had the right to elect one representative to the French chamber of deputies. Until 1914 this position as well as control over municipal politics had been dominated by the Creole population. In that year, however, Blaise Diagne, a black ex-customs official, was elected to the chamber of deputies. The political organization which he constructed gave him and his adherents control of the Senegalese politics until the 1930s. In 1917 Diagne became the undersecretary of state for colonies in the Clemenceau government. His example set the tone for later cooperation between the French African politicians and the metropole. Until the end of World War II politically conscious French Africans associated themselves with French political parties rather than forming their own organizations.

Even though the policy of assimilation worked to keep political parties from developing, it did not assume complete submissiveness of the African elite. In the 1930s many Africans joined the Socialist and Communist parties and thus were introduced to Marxism and its concepts relating to capitalism and imperialism. Perhaps as important for the future development of political parties was the uncomfortable feeling of many Africans who felt caught between two cultures. Léopold Sédar Senghor is perhaps the best example of this. He was given an excellent education in Senegal and Paris, and became the first African *aggrégé* qualified to teach in French secondary schools. He taught in French *lyceés* before the war, and in 1939 joined the army, later being captured by the Germans. Senghor was also a poet of merit and a nationalist. His poetry is filled with nostalgia and longing for Africa and stressed the importance of being African. Senghor and the French West Indian Aimé Césaire were responsible for creating the concept of *Négritude* which stressed the value of African culture distinct from any European taint. Later Senghor and another Senegalese, Alioune Diop, founded the magazine *Présence Africaine* to acquaint the world with these values. The duality between French and African culture so noticeable in Senghor was felt in varying degrees by every French African who later entered politics. This tension was in large part responsible for the course of nationalist development in French Africa in the 1950s.

In contrast to the French territories, nationalist evolvement in parts of British Africa resulted in the early development of African political parties. Political parties in British Africa generally shared certain common features. They were usually urban-based, and their programs were aimed at securing for a small African middle class some share in decision making. The colonial governments in the interwar period were hostile toward the leaders of these movements as well as toward the fundamental concept of African political parties. The urban politicians were accused of being an elite minority who could speak only for a few similar Africans and not the mass of the people who were governed by indirect rule. This official opposition to African political parties managed to restrict early politically organized activity to British West Africa and Kenya. Elsewhere there was not even rudimentary political organizations until after World War II.

Educated Fante in the Gold Coast had been encouraged before the Ashanti War of 1873 to work out differences between the various groups in order to create a Fante confederation. The coming of the war and subsequent imperial moves into the interior relegated the coastal elite to an ineffectual political position. The precedent remained, however, and in the 1920s the coastal elite who aspired to a stronger political voice found a spokesman in Joseph E. Casley-Hayford. He and his followers protested against the British plans to further strengthen the powers of the traditional rulers at the expense of the Western-educated minority. Casley-Hayford was one of the organizers of the National Congress of British West Africa and an important figure in the Pan African movement. He was not able to substantially affect British policy in the Gold Coast since he traditional rulers at the expense of the Western-educated minority. Casley-Hayford's opponents was Nana Ofori Atta, the powerful paramount chief of the Akim Abuakwa. He spoke for many when he argued that future political development had to depend upon cooperation with the British authorities and would be an evolvement of traditional practices. In 1927 Casley-Hayford won one of the three elected seats to the Legislative Council. This marked the end of real opposition in the Gold Coast to British concepts of rule. In the 1930s Joseph Danquah, a younger brother of Ofori Atta, formed the Gold Coast Youth Conference. This was primarily a coastal organization which believed in cooperation rather than opposition to the British authorities.

In the Gambia and Sierra Leone there were no early political parties, but there was a significant number of Africans who participated in political activities. In Sierra Leone the Creole population of the Freetown area, thoroughly Anglicized, formed the nucleus for later political parties. Due largely to the efforts of Sir Samuel Lewis, after 1893 Freetown was a self-governing municipality. Thus the politically active Creoles had some outlet for their desires to participate in government. British authorities ended this experiment in 1926 partially because of the lack of interest shown by the Creoles in participating and also because the authorities were concerned more with strengthening the traditional rulers than the educated Creoles. Political life in the colony area of the Gambia was restricted to a few educated Africans. Despite the efforts of men such as Edward Small, the Bathurst Creole or Aku population was never powerful enough to even create a political party. The protectorate was unrepresented on the Legislative Council until 1932 and even after that the British district officers and the many chiefs were the salient factors in the government of the Gambia.

Of the four British West African territories, only Nigeria had enough nationalist leaders in the interwar period to create significant political parties. Even there African political activity was concentrated in the cities and a large number of the nationalist leaders were West Indians. Early in the century such men as J. P. Jackson, editor of the *Lagos Weekly Record*, campaigned against British authoritarianism. Later Herbert Macaulay, a grandson of Bishop Samuel Crowther, became the most active opponent of Lugard's attempts at creating an efficient administration which, however, excluded the educated Nigerian from participation. He was the driving force behind the creation of the Nigerian National Democratic party (NNDP) in 1923 which won every election in Lagos to the Legislative Council from that date until 1938. Macaulay was involved in the dispute over the recognition and support of the eleko, the traditional ruler of Lagos. Macaulay's protestations over the deposition of the eleko by the British gained him a short prison term in 1928. His position was weakened since he did not represent all the factions of the educated in Nigeria. Men such as Sir Kitoyi Ajasa, owner of the *Nigerian Pioneer*, and Henry Carr, the resident of Lagos, represented and defended British policy and vehemently opposed Macaulay. Macaulay and other early nationalists were viewed by the authorities as dangerous subversives and their movements were carefully monitored and restricted. In 1923 Macaulay was given only seventy-two hours to leave Oyo Province and the ban upon his visiting the province was never lifted.

In 1934 nationalist protests against the quality of education at Yaba Higher College resulted in the formation of the Lagos Youth Movement. The organizers soon founded branches in many of the cities of southern Nigeria and the name was changed to the Nigerian Youth Movement (NYM). This organization gained the adherence of young men such as Samuel Akintola, Obafemi Awolowo, and H. O. Davies. In 1937 a new figure was introduced to the Nigerian political scene. This was Benjamin Nnamdi Azikiwe, educated in the United States, who was very active in politics. Through his newspaper, the *West African Pilot*, he began to preach a more radical nationalism, one that transcended the parochialism of the NNDP. With Azikiwe, an Ibo, the NYM could fairly claim to represent a large portion of the educated southern Nigerians. A quarrel between Azikiwe and other leaders led to the fragmentation of the NYM in 1941 and Azikiwe led most of the Ibo out of the party. In 1944 he formed a new movement called the National Council of Nigeria and the Cameroons (NCNC). Ostensibly a national party, it represented, in fact, the Westernized Ibo and eastern peoples of Nigeria.

All these early nationalists in British West Africa were thinking of limited advance for Africans. They did not demand independence, but instead they fought against the exclusiveness and racial bias in the crown colony system. They did not make radical demands, but they did wish to participate more fully in government. This can be clearly seen in the actions of the National Congress of British West Africa. Inspired by the activities of Du Bois and other Pan Africanists, Casley-Hayford and a few other nationalists created the organization in 1920. Its purpose was to bring together West African nationalists for periodic meetings to discuss common problems and to petition the British government for redress of grievances. The first meeting at Accra resulted in a memorial to the

Colonial Office which stressed four requests. These were for: (1) a legislative council for each area with one-half of the members being elected Africans, (2) control of taxation by the African members of the legislative council, (3) appointment and deposition of chiefs by the people, and (4) abolition of racial discrimination in the civil service.

Moderate as these statements appear now, they were considered revolutionary by the British. Lord Milner, the colonial secretary, dismissed the requests as representing the opinions of a small minority of Africans. The governor of Nigeria openly denounced the conference and the participants. At subsequent meetings at Freetown in 1923, Bathurst in 1925, and Lagos in 1929 the delegates restated the original resolutions and the British government continued to ignore the congress. Far ahead of its time, it expired after 1930 because of official apathy, the coming of the depression, and the death of Casley-Hayford, its most forceful member.

The only British dependent territory outside of West Africa which had any significant African political movements was Kenya. There the major question, particularly among the Kikuyu people, was land alienation. The Kikuyu maintained that Europeans could not claim the land since no Kikuyu was even authorized to sell it. The rapid growth of the African population in the two decades before World War II increased the tension between Europeans and Africans on this subject. There were other factors which disturbed the Kikuyu. One was the presence of large numbers of Indians in Kenya who occupied the lower echelon of the business and mercantile establishments. Thus the Kikuyu, the most Westernized of all Kenya's peoples, found their upward mobility in agriculture and government service blocked by Europeans, and by the Indians in trade. In response to their frustrations the Kikuyu in the 1920s joined a number of protest organizations. The first of these was the moderate Kikuyu Association formed by farmers of the Kiambu district. Its aim was to cooperate with the government to prevent further land alienation.

In 1921, Harry Thuku, a young Kikuyu civil servant, was the main organizer of the more militant Young Kikuyu Association. Thuku's organization soon had a large following and many times he spoke to thousands of Kikuyu at mass meetings near Nairobi. He urged direct action against the government's decision to raise the hut and capitation tax. Other complaints concerned a wage cut for African workers and the government requirement that all Africans carry a pass card. Underlying all of this was the Kikuyu feeling that the small politically dominant European population had stolen the land of the Kikuyu. In 1922 Thuku was arrested as a danger to the peace and security of Kenya, and without the benefit of a trial was exiled to the northern territories. Thuku's arrest triggered riots in Nairobi which resulted in the killing of over twenty Africans by the police. Without Thuku, the Young Kikuyu Association collapsed. A corollary organization, the Young Kavirondo Association in the Nyanza area, composed primarily of Luo was taken over by the missionaries in the following years. Thus it lost its potential as a protest movement.

In 1924 Joseph Kangethe and others formed a new organization, the

Kikuyu Central Association (KCA). Within a short period it had become a powerful force in Kikuyuland. The association appealed particularly to the young, better-educated Kikuyu. One of the young men early attracted to the organization was Jomo Kenyatta who was its secretary in 1928. The aims of the KCA were the same as Thuku's organization, but its leaders were milder in their expressions of dissatisfaction. In 1928 Kenyatta was sent to London to present the association's grievances to the Colonial Office about Kikuyu representation on the legislative council and land alienation. His mission unsuccessful, Kenyatta stayed in London as the KCA representative in Britain. There he attended the London School of Economics, did the research for his book, *Facing Mt. Kenya*, and avoided the struggles for power within the KCA. The association had gained more adherents with its opposition to government plans to end female circumcision. To Harry Thuku, released in 1930 and more conservative, the association seemed too radical, and he attempted to impose his ideas on the leadership. Failing in this, he broke with the KCA and formed the pro-government Kikuyu Provincial Association which was never popular with the bulk of the educated Kikuyu.

The KCA's stand on female circumcision resulted in a break between the educated Kikuyu and the missionaries. This led in the 1930s to the KCA and the various Kikuyu Associations creating and controlling their own schools which attempted to blend Western training with traditional Kikuyu values. In 1939 the Kenya Teacher Training College was opened. Within a decade the Kikuyu schools were an important factor in spurring on Kenyan nationalism. The failure of the prestigious Morris Carter Commission of the early 1930s to alter significantly the land settlement pattern in the highlands increased the alienation of the Kikuyu from the government. By 1940 when the government banned all political activity for the duration of the war, the KCA leaders had become the spokesmen of the younger, more radical Kikuyu rather than the British-supported chiefs. The groundwork for a violent protest against the white-oriented policy of the government had been laid.

In retrospect, early African political parties achieved few of the immediate goals of their founders. However, they provided a mechanism whereby Africans could protest against the authoritarian structure of European rule. They acted as training grounds for a new generation of African leaders. In some cases political parties such as the KCA and the NCNC were merely modified after World War II to confront the changed political environment. During the interwar period, in conjunction with the Pan African movement, they provided many Africans with hope for a better future.

Pan Africanism

A generation before viable African political parties were formed, Pan Africanism was being sponsored by black intellectuals as inevitable because of shared experiences of black men. The origin of the term Pan

Africanism is obscure. One of the first men to use it was Joseph Booth, the Baptist missionary to Nyasaland. His book, *Africa for the African,* and his actions in Central and South Africa underscored the theme of Africa for black men and an ultimate return to Africa of those whose ancestors had been taken away in slavery. In 1897, Booth, along with his Nyasa pupil, John Chilembwe, was responsible for the formation of one of the first African organizations dedicated to African unity—the African Christian Union.

However vague the origins of the term, its definition and use in the first half of the twentieth century is relatively precise. The ideal was supported by Western-educated blacks who resented their inferior status, and those who mourned their exile from Africa and had deep feelings of attachment for their theoretical homeland. Black writers and professional men, particularly in the United States, and the West Indies, reacting to white domination, saw a close parallel between their status and the lot of African peoples living under imperial control. The poets Countee Cullen and Langston Hughes found inspiration and solace in their kinship to Africans. Later the Senegalese poet Léopold Senghor and Aimé Césaire from Martinique coined the phrase *Négritude* to state the importance and uniqueness of blackness and the culture of Africa. The attitude expressed in the works of these and many other black writers was paralleled by the statements and actions of blacks in other professions. Typical were Dr. Edward Blyden, the West Indian-Liberian teacher and diplomat, Dr. Albert Thorne, West Indian founder of an African colonization scheme, and Reverend Charles Morris, Baptist missionary to South Africa. All of these intellectuals created, in their opposition to white control and customs, a hypothetical Africa which never was and a projection of a theoretical unity based upon the non-European nature of the African and his blackness. It is important to note that the driving force behind early Pan Africanism were non-Africans.

The man most responsible for taking the emotions related to Pan Africanism and transferring them into the arena of political action was W. E. B. Du Bois, a researcher and social scientist of great merit. In his many published works he had stressed the unity of the black world and the need for the ultimate freedom of blacks from white control. He assisted in the formation of the National Association for the Advancement of Colored People in the United States and was for many years the editor of its publication, *The Crisis.* In 1900 he attended the first Pan African Congress in London called by the Trinidad lawyer, H. Sylvester Williams. However little that was accomplished by this first meeting, it gave Du Bois the key for further concerted action by concerned black intelligentsia. Du Bois was the prime mover in convening four other Pan African conferences.

Black contributions to World War I and the subsequent problem of disposing of Germany's African empire presented Du Bois with a unique opportunity. In 1919 he proposed the convening of a conference to be held in Paris at the same time as the Versailles discussions. The conference was held despite the negative attitudes of most Allied statesmen because of the intervention of Blaise Diagne. Diagne was the most influential Senegalese politician and a member of the French ministry, and he persuaded Clemenceau to grant permission for the conference. It was attended by fifty-seven black representatives from all over the world, and they ultimately passed a lengthy resolution. This resolution was moderate, asking for such things as international laws to protect Africans, and the rights of Africans to participate in government as quickly as their development permitted. Nowhere did it demand the ultimate right of Africans to independence from European control. The representatives of the major powers ignored the conference and its resolution.

Du Bois was responsible for the convening of three other congresses. One called in 1921 was held in London and Brussels, the fourth Pan African congress met in London and Lisbon in 1923, and the fifth was held in New York in 1927. The resolutions of each of these congresses showed little advance over the Paris meeting of 1919. They asked for local self-government for "backward groups," interracial cooperation, and that "black folk be treated as men." The discussions and resolutions of all the congresses showed that despite the depth of their feelings, the black representatives were prisoners of their class and culture. Their demands were moderate and perhaps because of the lack of a popular base, they did not threaten. Thus the Pan African congresses of the 1920s had little effect upon the policies of the imperial powers. However, the conferences were not failures because they focused the attention of educated blacks, both African and non-African, upon the reality of one shared experience—control by whites. The congresses and the concomitant reporting of them in connection with continuing articles, novels, and poems by black authors conditioned the thinking of a new generation of educated Africans.

Although Marcus Garvey took no part in the Pan African congresses, he exercised a potent influence upon black attitudes and Pan Africanism. Garvey, a black Jamaican with a charismatic personality, built, by 1920, a large following in the northern United States. He stressed black exclusiveness and rejected Du Bois' ideas of cooperation with whites and ultimate black integration into white-dominated societies. His interest in Africa was largely conditioned by his hope of establishing a reverse migration of blacks from the Western Hemisphere to that continent. In 1920 he founded his "Negro Empire," called a black parliament which met in New York, and named himself Provisional President of Africa. Garvey organized a number of services, among them the Black Star Line to help expatriates return to Africa. His ideas foundered upon mismanagement of funds, hostility of European powers and the United States government, and the resistance of the New World blacks and African politicians to cooperate with his back-to-Africa schemes. Garvey was ultimately sentenced to prison, lost his large following, and died in 1940 in London without ever visiting Africa.

Garvey's influence did not depend upon the success or failure of his proposals but upon his writing and speeches of the early 1920s. This was also true of Du Bois and the others associated with the Pan African congresses. Pan Africanism never had a mass following in any African territory. It was always the concern of a very few educated Africans. These followed the developments of the congresses and extracted from the published works of Du Bois and Garvey those items which seemed to reflect their own problems or which dwelt upon conditions prevalent in their areas. Thus Kwame Nkrumah later could state that Marcus Garvey had been one of the most important influences upon his life and career.

World War II marked a dividing line between the older generation of Pan Africanism and the new African leadership. This is clearly seen in the fusion in Britain in 1944 of thirteen student and political organizations to form the Pan African Federation. The federation was responsible for calling the Sixth Pan African Congress which met at Manchester in 1945. Although Du Bois, aged seventy-three, was present, the meeting belonged to the young Africans. Such men as Kwame Nkrumah, Dr. Kuronkyi Taylor, and Joe Appiah of the Gold Coast, S. L. Akintola and H. O. Davies of Nigeria, and Jomo Kenyatta of Kenya, although then unknown, were the major forces within that congress. George Padmore, the West Indian ex-Communist, was also one of the organizers, and the South African novelist Peter Abrahams and the Togolese poet Raphael Aramttoe were present.

The conference marked the end of the patience of African elites with European imperialism. Its demand was for ultimate freedom for the African and independence from European rule. The conference resolution did not mention socialism, but stressed the protection of Africans from exploitation by the creation of what was termed economic democracy. The representatives at Manchester by implication rejected traditional African rule when they opted for the principle of one man–one vote. They agreed that the future of all African territories should be controlled by the Western educated and not left to the chiefs who had become tainted by acting as agents of the imperialists.

Thus a new strident note was added to Pan Africanism. The young Africans generally accepted Gandhi's ideas of nonviolence, but their statements foreshadowed active campaigns against the colonial powers which would result in confrontation. The Pan African movement after 1945 was controlled by African nationalists and they used its rhetoric to advance the cause of independence for their particular states. This led to an ambivalence not recognized by many observers in the 1950s. It became normal for political leaders such as Julius Nyerere and Jomo Kenyatta to speak of the inevitability of African unity but, nevertheless, to take part in the destruction of a potential Federation of East Africa. Almost all the French politicians supported Pan Africanism and yet accepted the dismemberment of the two large organizations—the French West African Federation and the French Equatorial African Federation.

African politicians in the 1950s were forced to assign priorities to their demands. Confronted with an ever-weakening European power structure, they chose the acceptance of colonial boundaries as the borders of independent states. Pan Africanism was used as a weapon against the Europeans in order to achieve national self-determination. The African ruling elites came to subscribe to the long-range hopes for African union, but considered this a secondary goal to independence and development of individual states. Once independence was achieved a host of new problems arose which took precedent over Pan Africanism. Thus while the Casablanca and Brazzaville groups still publicized their devotion to unity, the necessities of political life in the newly independent polities dictated policies which were hostile to Pan Africanism.

Glossary

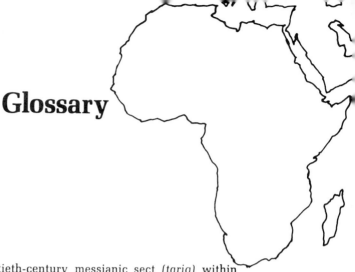

Ahmadiyah A twentieth-century messianic sect *(tariq)* within Islam. Founded by Mirza Ghulam Ahmad in the Punjab area of India. Ahmadiyah missionaries have been very active in the coastal parts of West Africa.

Aku Gambian term for Sierra Leone creoles who migrated to Bathurst.

Alafin Title of the ruler of Oyo empire.

Askaris African troops trained and armed in the European fashion by the Germans and Italians.

Assimilado A system by which Africans could gain rights equal to Portuguese citizens in Portugal's African territories.

Basorun The king's chief minister in the kingdom of Oyo.

Boer Dutch term for farmer, it came to be applied to all persons of Dutch descent in South Africa.

Cercle Name of the largest administrative unit within a colony of the AOF.

Chitimukulu Title of the paramount chief of the Bemba.

Commando A Boer military unit of varying size and composed of volunteers. Commandos were used with great effect in the unsettled areas of the eastern frontier of Cape Colony.

Contractos Laborers recruited and signed to contracts by the Portuguese to work on São Thomé.

Dash A gift or unofficial payment to a chief or official which enabled European traders to conduct business.

Destooling The act of removing Akan chiefs from office.

Drotsdy A large unit of local government in Cape Colony in the early nineteenth century.

Emir A title of nobility common to Islamic states. In northern Nigeria the emirs were rulers of city states subject only to the control of the sultan of Sokoto.

Eleko The hereditary ruler of Lagos.

Feld cornet In a Boer district in South Africa the feld cornet was the elected leader of commando operations.

Heemraaden In the early nineteenth century the elected legislative body of a drotsdy.

Hukimdar Egyptian title for the governor-general of the Sudan.

Imam A title which originally meant the leader of an entire Muslim community. In some places the term came to signify only a tribal leader.

Impi A regiment of Zulu or Matabele warriors.

Indaba Formal meeting of all responsible citizens in Swaziland.

Indigenas Portuguese term for the bulk of the African population of its territories.

Indigenat French system by which Africans could be punished without the formality of a trial.

Jihad A holy war or a war sanctioned by the religious authorities in Islamic states.

Kabaka Title of the ruler of Buganda.

Kaffir Originally the term meant a stranger. Afrikaners applied the term, sometimes in a perjorative sense, to all Bantu, but particularly to the Xosa.

Khalifa Arabic word for caliph or prophet. In Africa the term is generally associated with the career of Abdullah, one of the four khalifas appointed by the Mahdi.

Khedive Title meaning viceroy given to Muhammad Ali of Egypt by the Ottoman emperor in early nineteenth century. Later khedives were almost independent of Turkish control.

Khatmiyyah Most important Islamic sect (*tariq*) in the Sudan prior to the rise of Mahdism. It was founded by Ahmad ibn Idris in the early eighteenth century. Greatest teacher and missionary of this *tariq* was Muhammad al-Mirghani.

Kitwala Congolese name for the twentieth century Watchtower movement.

Landdrost Chief executive officer of a drotsdy, appointed by the central authorities at Cape Town.

Liqoqo Swazi aristocratic council whose composition was based on family ties.

Libandhla Swazi council where general populace was represented.

Litunga Title of the paramount ruler of the Luyi.

Loi Cadre An enabling act passed by French National Assembly in 1956 which was the first step toward a breakup of the two major federations—the AEF and AOF.

Lukiko Council of great nobles in Buganda.

Mahdi In certain sects of Islamic mysticism the Mahdi was the awaited prophet. In Africa the term is generally associated with Muhammad Ahmed, the Sudanese religious and political leader.

Mai The title of the ruler of Bornu.

Marabout An Islamic teacher of the Western Sudan. The name was also given to the puritanical reform movement which caused a series of wars in the Senegambia in the latter nineteenth century.

Mfecane Means the "time of crushing" and refers to the fifteen year period of internecine conflict between Bantu groups in southern Africa.

Mugabe Title of the ruler of the kingdom of Ankole.

Murdir Egyptian title for a governor of a province in the Sudan.

Mwami Title of the Watutsi ruler of Ruanda and of Burundi.

Mwato Kazembe Title of the paramount ruler of the Kazembe kingdom.

Mwato yamvo Title of the ruler of the Katanga Lunda.

Nilo-Hamitic Pastoral invaders of East Africa after the sixteenth century. Original home was probably the southern Sudan. Modern examples are the Nandi and Masai.

Nilotes Pastoral inhabitants of the upper Nile region and after the tenth century, invaders of East Africa. Modern examples are the Shilluk and Nuer.

Oyo mesi Major councilors of state and advisers to the alafin of Oyo.

Palmatario In Portuguese territories the punishment of beating the palms of the hands of Africans convicted of crimes.

Prazeros The owners of large interior land grants (prazos) made by Portugal in the eighteenth century. Intermarriage with the Bantu and isolation changed the prazeros. In nineteenth century Mozambique they were powerful enough to defy the central government.

Quadariyah An Islamic religious fraternity founded in Baghdad in the twelfth century. It is the most widespread Islamic sect in West Africa.

Ras Ethiopian title of nobility given to the great nobles who ranked just below the emperor in power and prestige.

Région Name of the largest administrative unit within a colony in the AEF.

Salihiyah A puritanical sect of Islam organized in the latter nineteenth century by Muhammad Salih. Very important in Somalia because of the efforts of the Mullah Muhammad Abdullah.

Sarkin Hausa title for a ruler of one of the city states before the jihad of Usuman dan Fodio.

Shibalo The system of compulsory labor practiced in Portuguese African territories.

Soninke The warrior class of a chief's retainers in the Gambia in the latter nineteenth century. They were the most committed opponents of the marabouts.

Tijaniyya A Muslim elitist order founded in North Africa which through the activities of Al Hajj Umar became one of the major Islamic sects in West Africa.

Vizier Normally the ruler's closest advisor and head of the bureaucracy in Islamic societies.

Watu wa mungu "The people of God," an anti-Western religious movement among the Kikuyu in the 1930s.

Selected Bibliography

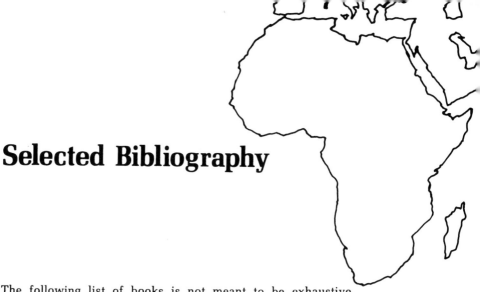

The following list of books is not meant to be exhaustive. Rather, it is a selection of books and articles which the author found most useful for reference for specific subdivisions of the book. Many of these can also be utilized by students who wish to do reading corollary with the text. Those which might prove most useful have been marked with an asterisk (*). Books available in paperback editions have been noted with a plus sign (+). A number of books, particularly general histories, have application to several topic areas covered in this textbook, although each work is cited only once under the most appropriate chapter heading.

Chapter One
WEST AFRICA BEFORE THE SCRAMBLE

ISLAMIC RESURGENCE

*Boahen, A. Adu. *Britain, the Sahara, and the Western Sudan, 1788–1861.* London: Oxford University Press, 1964.

Hodgkin, Thomas. "Uthman dan Fodio," *Nigeria Magazine,* October 1960.

Hunwick, J. O. "The Nineteenth Century Jihads" in J. F. Ade Ajayi and Ian Espie (eds.), *A Thousand Years of West African History.* New York: Humanities Press, 1965.

Ifemesia, C. C. "Bornu Under the Shehus" in Ajayi and Espie (eds.), *A Thousand Years of West African History.* New York: Humanities Press, 1965.

Johnston, H. A. S. *The Fulani Empire of Sokoto.* London: Oxford University Press, 1967.

*Kirk-Greene, A. H. M. *The Emirates of Northern Nigeria.* London: Oxford University Press, 1966.

Last, M. *The Sokoto Caliphate.* New York: Humanities Press, 1967.

*Trimingham, J. S. *A History of Islam in West Africa.* London: Oxford University Press, 1962.

EUROPEAN ATTITUDES

Coupland, Reginald. *Wilberforce*. Oxford: Clarendon Press, 1923.
*Curtin, Philip D. *The Image of Africa: British Ideas in Action, 1780–1850*. Madison, Wis.: University of Wisconsin Press, 1964.
Flint, J. E. "The Growth of European Influences in West Africa in the Nineteenth Century" in Ajayi and Espie (eds.), *A Thousand Years of West African History*. New York: Humanities Press, 1965.
*Hallet, Robin. "The European Approach to the Interior of Africa in the Eighteenth Century," *Journal of African History*, IV, 1963.
Hodgkin, Thomas. *Nigerian Perspectives*. London: Oxford University Press, 1960.
Martin, E. C. *The British West African Settlements 1750–1821*. London: Longmans, Green & Co., 1927.

EUROPEAN EXPLORATIONS

Baikie, William B. *Narrative of an Exploring Voyage up the Rivers Kwara and Binue . . . in 1854*. London: John Murray, 1856.
Barth, Heinrich. *Travels and Discoveries in Northern and Central Africa*, 5 vols. London: Longmans, 1857–1858.
Burton, Richard F. *A Mission to Gelele, King of Dahome*. London: Tinsley Bros., 1864.
Clapperton, Hugh. *Journal of a Second Expedition into the Interior of Africa from the Bight of Benin to Soccatoo*. London: John Murray, 1829.
Denham, Dixon, H. Clapperton, and W. Oudney. *Narrative of Travels and Discoveries in Northern and Central Africa in the Years 1822, 1823, 1824*. London: John Murray, 1862.
*Lander, Richard, and John Lander. *Journal of an Expedition to Explore the Course and Termination of the Niger*, 3 vols. London: John Murray, 1832.
Lupton, L. "The Death of Mungo Park at Bussa," *Nigeria Magazine*, March 1962, p. 58.
*Park, Mungo. *Journal of a Mission to the Interior of Africa in the Year 1805. . . .* Philadelphia: Edward Earle, 1815.

WEST AFRICAN NAVAL PATROLS AND THE SLAVE TRADE

*Coupland, Reginald. *The British Anti-Slavery Movement*. London: Thornton Butterworth, 1933.
Curtin, Philip D., and J. Vansina. "Sources of the Nineteenth-Century Atlantic Slave Trade," *Journal of African History*, V, 1964, p. 185.
Donnan, Elizabeth (ed.). *Documents Illustrative of the History of the Slave Trade to America*, 4 vols. Washington: Carnegie Institution, 1930–1939.

Duignan, Peter, and C. Clendenen. *The United States and the African Slave Trade 1619–1862.* Stanford: Stanford University Press, 1963.
Forde, Daryll (ed.). *Efik Traders of Old Calabar.* London: Oxford University Press, 1956.
*Lloyd, Christopher. *The Navy and the Slave Trade.* London: Longmans, Green & Co., 1949.

FREETOWN

*Fyfe, Christopher H. *A History of Sierra Leone.* London: Oxford University Press, 1962.
Gallagher, John. "Fowell Buxton and the New African Policy, 1838–1842," *Cambridge Historical Journal,* X, 1950, p. 36.
Haliburton, G. "The Nova Scotia Settlers of 1792," *Sierra Leone Studies,* No. 9, 1957, p. 16.
Kup, Peter. *A History of Sierra Leone, 1400–1789.* Cambridge: Cambridge University Press, 1961.
*Porter, Arthur T. *Creoledom: A Study of the Development of Freetown Society.* London: Oxford University Press, 1963.

LIBERIA

Boyd, Willis D. "The American Colonization Society and the Slave Recaptives of 1860–61: An Example of United States-African Relations," *The Journal of Negro History,* XLVII, 1962, p. 108.
*Hargreaves, John D. "African Colonization in the Nineteenth Century: Liberia and Sierra Leone," *Boston University Papers on African History,* I, 1964, p. 55.
Johnston, Harry H. *Liberia,* 2 vols. London: Hutchinson & Co., 1906.
Laughon, Samuel W. "Administrative Problems in Maryland and Liberia, 1836–1851," *The Journal of Negro History,* XXXVI, 1941, p. 325.
Lynch, Hollis R. "Sierra Leone and Liberia in the Nineteenth Century" in Ajayi and Espie (eds.), *A Thousand Years of West African History.* New York: Humanities Press, 1965.
*Staudenraus, P. J. *The African Colonization Movement, 1816–1865.* New York: Columbia University Press, 1961.

THE GOLD COAST

Amenumey, D. E. K. "The Extension of British Rule in Anlo (South-east Ghana), 1850–1890," *Journal of African History,* IX, No. 1, 1968.
Coombs, Douglas. *The Gold Coast, Britain and the Netherlands, 1850–1874.* London: Oxford University Press, 1963.
*Metcalfe, G. E. *Maclean of the Gold Coast: The Life and Times of George Maclean, 1801–1847.* London: Oxford University Press, 1962.
*Ward, William E. *Short History of Ghana.* New York: Humanities Press, 1966.

OYO AND THE YORUBA

*Ajayi, J. F. Ade. *Yoruba Warfare in the Nineteenth Century.* New York: Cambridge University Press, 1969.
*Akinjogbin, I. A. "Dahomey and Yoruba in the 19th Century" in Anene, Joseph, and B. Godfrey (eds.), *Africa in the Nineteenth and Twentieth Centuries.* New York: Humanities Press, 1967.
Biobaku, Saburi O. *The Egba and Their Neighbours.* New York: Oxford University Press, 1957.
+Bradbury, R. E. *The Benin Kingdom and the Edo-Speaking People of South-Western Nigeria.* London: International Affairs Institute, 1957.
+Forde, Daryll. *The Yoruba-Speaking Peoples of South-Western Nigeria.* London: International Affairs Institute, 1951.
Johnson, Samuel. *History of the Yorubas.* Lagos, Nigeria: C. M. S. Bookshops, 1960.
McIntyre, W. D. "Commander Glover and the Colony of Lagos, 1861–73," *Journal of African History,* IV, No. 1, 1963.
Phillips, Earl. "The Egba at Abeokuta: Acculturation and Political Change, 1830–1870," *Journal of African History,* X, No. 1, 1969, p. 67.

FRENCH ACTIVITIES TO 1870

Deschamps, Hubert J. *Le Senegal et la Gambie.* Paris: Presses Universitaires de France, 1964.
Faidherbe, Louis L. C. *Le Senegal: la France dans l'Afrique occidentale.* Paris: Hatchette, 1889.
O'Brien, Rita Cruise. "France in Senegal in the Nineteenth Century," *Tarikh,* II, No. 4, 1969, p. 21.
Quinn, Charlotte A. "Maba Diakhou Ba: Scholar-Warrior of the Senegambia," *Tarikh,* II, No. 3, 1968, p. 1.
Sabatie, Alexandre C. *Le Senegal: sa Conquête et son organisation, 1364–1925.* St. Louis, Senegal, 1926.
Schnapper, Bernard. *La Politique et le commerce Français dans le Golf de Guinée de 1838 à 1871.* Paris: Mouton, 1961.

Chapter Two
EAST AND CENTRAL AFRICA BEFORE THE SCRAMBLE

THE PEOPLES OF EAST AFRICA AND THE ARAB TRADERS

Beachey, R. W. "The East African Ivory Trade in the Nineteenth Century," *Journal of African History,* VIII, No. 2, 1967.
+Beidilmann, T. O. *The Matrilineal People of Eastern Tanzania.* London: International African Institute, 1967.
*Coupland, Reginald. *East Africa and Its Invaders.* London: Oxford University Press, 1961.
+Fallers, Margaret. *The Eastern Lacustrine Bantu.* London: International African Institute, 1960.

*Freeman-Grenville, G. S. P. "The Coast, 1498–1840" in Oliver, Roland, and G. Mathews (eds.), History of East Africa, I. London: Oxford University Press, 1963.

Gavin, R. J. "Sayyid Said," Tarikh, I, No. 1, 1965, p. 16.

Gray, Sir John M. History of Zanzibar. London: Oxford University Press, 1962.

*Gray, Sir John M. "Zanzibar and the Coastal Belt, 1840–84" in Oliver, Roland, and G. Mathews (eds.), History of East Africa, I. London: Oxford University Press, 1963.

*Low, D. A. "The Northern Interior, 1840–84" in Oliver, Roland, and G. Mathews (eds.), History of East Africa, I. London: Oxford University Press, 1963.

+Middleton, John, and Greet Kershaw. The Kikuyu and Kamba of Kenya. London: International African Institute, 1953.

+Middleton, John, and Jane Campbell. Zanzibar. London: Oxford University Press, 1967.

Oliver, Roland. "Discernible Developments in the Interior ca. 1500–1840" in Oliver, Roland, and G. Mathews (eds.), History of East Africa, I. London: Oxford University Press, 1963.

Posnansky, Merrick. Prelude to East African History. London: Oxford University Press, 1966.

Prins, A. H. J. The Swahili-Speaking Peoples of Zanzibar and the East African Coast. London: International African Institute, 1967.

Redmayne, Alison. "Mkwawa and the Hehe Wars," Journal of African History, IX, No. 3, 1968.

*Smith, Alison. "The Southern Section of the Interior, 1840–84" in Oliver, Roland, and G. Mathews (eds.), History of East Africa, I: London: Oxford University Press, 1963.

Trimingham, J. S. Islam in East Africa. London: Oxford University Press, 1964.

EUROPEAN EXPLORATIONS

Baker, Samuel W. Albert Nyanza, Great Basin of the Nile and Explorations of the Nile Sources, 2 vols. New York: Macmillan, 1866.

Burton, Richard F. The Lake Regions of Central Africa, 2 vols. London: Longmans, Green & Co., 1860.

*Coupland, Reginald. Livingstone's Last Journey. London: Collins, 1945.

*Farwell, Byron. Burton. New York: Avon, 1965.

Krapf, Ludwig. Travels, Researches and Missionary Labors during an Eighteen Year Residence in Eastern Africa. London: Trubner, 1860.

Livingstone, David. The Last Journals of David Livingstone in Central Africa, 2 vols. (ed. by Horace Waller). London: John Murray, 1880.

+*Moorehead, Alan. The White Nile. New York: Harper & Row, 1960.

Perham, Margery, and J. Simmons. African Discovery. London: Faber & Faber, 1949.

Speke, John Hanning. Journal of the Discovery of the Source of the Nile. London: Blackwood, 1863.

Stanley, Henry M. *Through the Dark Continent or the Sources of the Nile around the Great Lakes of Equatorial Africa*, 2 vols. New York: Harper & Brothers, 1878.

CONGO BASIN

+*Davidson, Basil. *A History of East and Central Africa*. New York: Anchor Books, 1969.
Vansina, Jan. "The Foundations of the Kingdom of Kasanje," *Journal of African History*, IV, 1963.
Vansina, Jan. *Kingdoms of the Savannah*. Madison, Wis.: University of Wisconsin Press, 1966.
Vansina, Jan. "More on the Invasions of Kongo and Angola by the Jaga and Lunda," *Journal of African History*, VII, 1966.
+*Willis, A. J. *The History of Central Africa*. London: Oxford University Press, 1964.

Chapter Three
SOUTHERN AFRICA TO 1872

Bond, John. *They Were South Africans*. London: Oxford University Press, 1956.
Gailey, Harry A. "John Philips' Role in Hottentot Emancipation," *Journal of African History*, III, No. 3, 1962.
Lye, William F. "The Difeqane: The Mfecane in the Southern Sotho Area, 1822–24," *Journal of African History*, VIII, No. 1, 1967.
Lye, William F. "The Ndebele Kingdom South of the Limpopo," *Journal of African History*, X, No. 1, 1969.
*Macmillan, William M. *Boer, Bantu and Briton*. Oxford: Clarendon Press, 1963.
Marais, J. S. *The Cape Coloured People, 1652–1937*. Johannesburg: Witwatersrand University Press, 1962.
Millar, Anthony K. *Plantagenet in South Africa: Lord Charles Somerset*. London: Oxford University Press, 1965.
*Morris, William. *The Washing of the Spears*. New York: Simon and Schuster, 1965.
Okoye, Felix N. C. "Dingane: A Reappraisal," *Journal of African History*, X, No. 2, 1969.
Rose, J. H., A. P. Newton and E. A. Benians (eds.). *The Cambridge History of the British Empire*, VIII, South Africa. Cambridge: Cambridge University Press, 1929.
Sanders, P. B. "Sekonyela and Moshweshwe: Failure and Success in the Aftermath of the Difeqane," *Journal of African History*, X, No. 3, 1969.
Theal, George McCall. *History of South Africa, 1795–1872*, 5 vols. London: George Allen & Unwin, 1908–1910.
Walker, Eric A. *A History of Southern Africa*. London: Longmans, Green & Co., 1957.
Walker, Eric A. *The Great Trek*. London: Adam and Charles Black, 1965.

Chapter Four
NORTHEASTERN AFRICA

THE EGYPTIAN PROBLEM

Baring, Evelyn (Lord Cromer). *Modern Egypt.* London: Macmillan, 1908.
Blunt, Wilfrid S. *Secret History of the British Occupations of Egypt.* London: Unwin, 1907.
Holt, P. M. *Egypt and the Fertile Crescent, 1516–1922.* Ithaca, N.Y.: Cornell University Press, 1966.
+Stevens, Georgiana G. *Egypt: Yesterday and Today.* New York: Holt, Rinehart and Winston, 1963.
*Tignor, R. L. *Modernization and British Control in Egypt, 1882–1914.* Princeton, N.J.: Princeton University Press, 1967.

EGYPT IN THE SUDAN TO 1885

Allen, Bernard M. *Gordon and the Sudan.* London: Macmillan, 1951.
Baker, Samuel. *Ismailia: A Narrative of the Expedition to Central Africa for the Suppression of the Slave Trade.* London: Macmillan, 1874.
Chaille-Long, Charles. *Three Prophets.* New York: Sampson Low, 1884.
*Collins, Robert O., and R. L. Tignor. *Egypt in the Sudan.* Englewood Cliffs, N.J.: Prentice-Hall, 1967.
Hill, Richard L. *Egypt in the Sudan, 1820–1881.* London: Oxford University Press, 1958.
Holt, P. M. *A Modern History of the Sudan.* New York: Praeger, 1963.
+*Moorehead, Alan. *The Blue Nile.* New York: Harper & Row, 1962.

ETHIOPIA THROUGH THE REIGN OF THEODORE

Abir, Modechai. *Ethiopia, The Era of Princes.* London: Longmans, Green & Co., 1968.
Abir, Modechai. "The Origins of the Ethiopian-Egyptian Border Problem in the Nineteenth Century," *Journal of African History,* VIII, No. 3, 1967.
Ceruli, Ernesta. *Peoples of South-West Ethiopia and Its Borderland.* London: International African Institute, 1956.
*Crummey, Donald. "Tewodros as Reformer and Modernizer," *Journal of African History,* X, No. 3, 1969.
Darkwah, Kofi. "Emperor Theodore II and the Kingdom of Shoa, 1855–65," *Journal of African History,* X, No. 1, 1969.
Darkwah, Kofi. "Shoa before the Reign of Menelik," *Tarikh,* II, No. 3, 1968.
Doresse, Jean. *Ethiopia.* New York: G. P. Putnam, 1959.
Hooker, J. R. "The Foreign Office and the Abyssinian Captives," *Journal of African History,* II, No. 2, 1961.
Huntingford, G. W. B. *The Galla of Ethiopia.* London: International African Institute, 1955.

+Jesman, Czeslaw. The Ethiopian Paradox. London: Oxford University Press, 1963.
*Mathew, David. Ethiopia, the Study of a Polity, 1540–1935. London: Eyre & Spottiswoodie, 1947.

ETHIOPIA AND THE SCRAMBLE TO 1945

Del Boca, Angelo. The Ethiopian War, 1935–1941. Chicago: University of Chicago Press, 1969.
Doresse, Jean. Ethiopia. London: Elek Books, 1959.
Greenfield, Richard T. Ethiopia—A New Political History. New York: Praeger, 1965.
Jones, A. H. M., and E. Monroe. A History of Ethiopia. London: Oxford University Press, 1960.
Marcus, Harold G. "Ethio-British Negotiations concerning the Western Border with Sudan 1896–1902," Journal of African History, IV, No. 1, 1963.
*Marcus, Harold G. "The Foreign Policy of the Emperor Menelik 1896–1898, a Rejoinder," Journal of African History, VII, No. 1, 1966.
Matthew, David. Ethiopia: The Study of a Polity, 1540–1935. London: Eyre and Spottiswoodie, 1947.
Mosley, Leonard. Haile Selassie, the Conquering Lion. London: Weidenfeld and Nicolson, 1964.
Pankhurst, E. S. Ethiopia: A Cultural History. Essex, England: Lalibela House, Woodford Green, 1955.
Pankhurst, Richard. "Italian Settlement Policy in Eritrea and Its Repercussions 1889–1896," Boston University Papers in African History, I, 1964.
Rubenson, Sven. "The Protectorate Paragraph of the Wichale Treaty," Journal of African History, V, No. 2, 1964.
*Sanderson, G. N. "The Foreign Policy of the Negus Menelik 1896–1898," Journal of African History, V, No. 1, 1964.
Toynbee, Arnold J. Survey of International Affairs, 1935: Abyssinia and Italy. London: Oxford University Press, 1936.
Ullendorf, E. The Ethiopians. London: Oxford University Press, 1965.

Chapter Five
THE SCRAMBLE FOR AFRICA

INTRODUCTION

Bodelsen, Carl A. G. Studies in Mid-Victorian Imperialism. Copenhagen: Gyldendalske Boghandel, 1924.
Brunschweg, Henri. Mythes et réalités de l'impérialisme colonial français 1871–1914. Paris: Librairie Armand Colin, 1960.
*Crowe, Sybil Eyre. The Berlin West African Conference, 1884–1885. London: Longmans, Green & Co., 1942.
Gallagher, John, and R. Robinson. "The Imperialism of Free Trade," The Economic History Review, VI, 1953, p. 1.
Gifford, Prosser, and W. R. Louis. Britain and Germany in Africa. New Haven, Conn.: Yale University Press, 1967.

*Hargreaves, John D. *Prelude to the Partition of West Africa.* London: Macmillan, 1963.

Keith, Arthur Berriedale. *The Belgian Congo and the Berlin Act.* London: Oxford University Press, 1919.

+*Langer, William. *The Diplomacy of Imperialism 1890–1902.* New York: Alfred Knopf, 1951.

Langer, William. *European Alliances and Alignments.* New York: Alfred Knopf, 1950.

Newbury, Colin W. "The Development of French Policy on the Lower and Upper Niger 1880–1898," *Journal of Modern History,* XXXI, 1959, p. 16.

Nowell, Charles E. "Portugal and the Partition of Africa," *Journal of Modern History,* XIX, 1947, p. 1.

Power, Thomas F. *Jules Ferry and the Renaissance of French Imperialism.* New York: King's Crown Press, 1944.

,Roberts, Stephen H. *History of French Colonial Policy, 1870–1925.* London: Frank Cass, 1963.

+*Robinson, Ronald, J. Gallagher, and A. Denny. *Africa and the Victorians.* New York: St. Martin's Press, 1961.

Townsend, Mary Evelyn. *Origins of Modern German Colonialism, 1871–1885.* New York: Columbia University Press, 1921.

WEST AFRICA

Ajayi, J. F. Ade. "The British Occupation of Lagos 1851–61," *Nigeria Magazine,* August 1961.

Alagoa, Ebiegberi Joe. *The Small Brave City-State: A History of Nembe-Brass in the Niger Delta.* Madison, Wis.: University of Wisconsin Press, 1964.

Anene, J. C. *Southern Nigeria in Transition 1885–1906.* Cambridge: Cambridge University Press, 1966.

+*Crowder, Michael. *A Short History of Nigeria.* New York: Praeger, 1966.

Flint, John E. *Sir George Goldie and the Making of Nigeria.* London: Oxford University Press, 1960.

Gailey, Harry A. "European Rivalry and Diplomacy in the Mellacourie 1879–1882," *Sierra Leone Studies,* No. 15, 1961, p. 135.

*Hargreaves, John D. "The Establishment of the Sierra Leone Protectorate and the Insurrection of 1898," *The Cambridge Historical Journal,* XII, 1956, p. 56.

Hargreaves, John D. "The French Occupation of the Mellacourie, 1865–67," *Sierra Leone Studies,* No. 9, 1957.

Idowu, H. O. "The Establishment of Elective Institutions in Senegal 1869–1880," *Journal of African History,* IX, No. 2, 1968.

O'Brien, Donal Cruise. "Toward an Islamic Policy in French West Africa 1854–1914," *Journal of African History,* VIII, No. 2, 1967.

Perham, Margery. *Lugard: The Years of Adventure 1858–1898.* London: Collins, 1956.

THE CONGO BASIN

+Abraham, R. G. *The Peoples of Greater Unyamwezi, Tanzania.* London: International African Institute, 1967.
Burton, Richard F. (ed. & trans.). *The Lands of Cazembe.* London: Royal Geographic Society, 1873.
Cookey, S. J. S. "Tippu Tib and the Decline of the Congo Arabs," *Tarikh,* I, No. 2, 1966, pp. 58–69.
+*Davidson, Basil. *A History of East and Central Africa.* New York: Doubleday, 1969.
Flint, Eric. "Trade and Politics in Barotseland during the Kalolo Period," *Journal of African History,* XI, No. 1, 1970, p. 71.
McCulloch, Merran. *The Southern Lunda and Related Peoples.* London: International African Institute, 1951.
Rotberg, Robert I. "Plymouth Brethren and the Occupation of Katanga 1886–1907," *Journal of African History,* V, No. 2, 1964.
Vansina, Jan. *Kingdoms of the Savannah.* Madison, Wis.: University of Wisconsin Press, 1966.
*Vansina, Jan. "Long-Distance Trade Routes in Central Africa," *Journal of African History,* III, No. 3, 1962.
Webster, J. B. "Mirambo and Nyamwezi Unification," *Tarikh,* I, No. 1, 1965, p. 64.
Whitely, Wilfred. *Bemba and Related Peoples of Northern Rhodesia.* London: International African Institute, 1950.

THE PORTUGUESE EMPIRE

Akinola, G. Akin. "The Mazrui of Mombasa," *Tarikh,* II, No. 3, 1968, pp. 26–40.
Boxer, Charles R. *Race Relations in the Portuguese Empire, 1415–1825.* London: Oxford University Press, 1963.
*Cunnison, Ian. "Kazembe and the Portuguese, 1798–1832," *Journal of African History,* II, No. 1, 1961, p. 61.
*Duffy, James. *A Question of Slavery.* London: Oxford University Press, 1967.
Liesegang, Gerhard. "Dingane's Attack on Lourenço Marques in 1833," *Journal of African History,* X, No. 4, 1969, p. 565.
+McCulloch, Merran. *The Ovimbundu of Angola.* London: International African Institute, 1952.
Newitt, M. D. D. "The Portuguese on the Zambesi: An Historical Interpretation of the Prazo System," *Journal of African History,* X, No. 1, 1969, p. 67.
*Newitt, M. D. D. and P. S. Gailake. "The Aringa at Massangano," *Journal of African History,* VIII, No. 1, 1967, p. 133.

EAST AFRICA

Coupland, Reginald. *Exploration of East Africa*. London: Faber & Faber, 1939.
*Flint, John. "The Wider Background to Partition and Colonial Occupation" in Oliver, Roland, and G. Mathews (eds.), *History of East Africa*, I. London: Oxford University Press, 1963.
*Freeman-Grenville, G. S. P. "The German Sphere, 1884–94" in Oliver, Roland, and G. Mathews (eds.), *History of East Africa*, I. London: Oxford University Press, 1963.
Hemphill, Marie de Kiewiet. "The British Sphere, 1884–94" in Oliver, Roland, and G. Mathews (eds.), *History of East Africa*, I. London: Oxford University Press, 1963.
Johnston, Henry Hamilton. *The Uganda Protectorate*, 2 vols. London: Hutchinson, 1902.
Lugard, Frederick D. *The Rise of Our East African Empire*, 2 vols. London: Blackwood, 1893.
Lugard, Frederick D. *The Story of the Uganda Protectorate*. London: Blackwood, 1901.

Chapter Six
CONSOLIDATION OF BRITISH POWER IN SOUTHERN AFRICA, 1872–1910

Bryce, James. *Impressions of South Africa*. New York: The Century Co., 1900.
Caplan, Gerald L. "Barotseland Scramble for Protection," *Journal of African History*, X, No. 2, 1969.
Cloete, Stuart. *Against These Three*. Boston: Houghton Mifflin Company, 1945.
Denoon, D. J. N. "The Transvaal Labour Crisis 1901–06," *Journal of African History*, VIII, No. 3, 1967.
French, Gerald. *Lord Chelmsford and the Zulu War*. London: Bodley Head, 1939.
Gandhi, M. K. *Satyagraha in South Africa* (trans. V. G. Desai). Stanford: Academic Reprints, 1954.
Gibb, Henry. *Background to Bitterness*. New York: Philosophical Library, 1955.
*Hanna, A. J. *The Story of the Rhodesias and Nyasaland*. London: Faber & Faber, 1965.
Marks, Shula. "Harriette Colenso and the Zulus, 1874–1913," *Journal of African History*, IV, No. 3, 1963.
Marquard, Leo. *The Story of South Africa*. New York: Ray Publishers, 1955.
Maurois, Andre. *Cecil Rhodes*. London: Collins, 1954.
Millin, Sarah Gertrude. *Rhodes*. Capetown: Central News Agency, 1952.
Ranger, T. O. *Revolt in Southern Rhodesia 1896–1897*. Evanston, Ill.: Northwestern University Press, 1968.

*Thompson, Leonard M. *The Unification of South Africa, 1902–1910.* Oxford: Clarendon Press, 1960.

Van der Poel, Jean. *The Jameson Raid.* London: Oxford University Press, 1951.

+*Williams, Basil. *Botha, Smuts and South Africa.* New York: Macmillan, 1948.

Williams, Basil. *Cecil Rhodes.* London: Constable, 1938.

Wills, A. J. *An Introduction to the History of Central Africa.* London: Oxford University Press, 1964.

Chapter Seven
EUROPEAN MECHANISMS OF CONTROL IN AFRICA

BRITISH AFRICA

Bourret, F. M. *Ghana, the Road to Independence.* Stanford: Stanford University Press, 1960.

*Ehrlich, Cyril. "Some Social and Economic Implications of Paternalism in Uganda," *Journal of African History,* IV, No. 2, 1963.

Gailey, Harry A. *A History of the Gambia.* London: Routledge & Kegan Paul, 1964.

*Gailey, Harry A. *The Road to Aba.* New York: New York University Press, 1970.

Huxley, Elspeth. *White Man's Country,* 2 vols. New York: Macmillan, 1935.

*Mungeam, G. H. "Masai and Kikuyu Responses to the Establishment of British Administration in the East Africa Protectorate," *Journal of African History,* XI, No. 1, 1970.

Ogot, Bethwell A. "British Administration in the Central Nyanza District of Kenya 1900–1960," *Journal of African History,* IV, No. 2, 1963.

Twaddle, Michael. "The Bakungu Chiefs of Buganda under British Colonial Rule 1900–1930," *Journal of African History,* X, No. 2, 1969.

Wight, Martin. *British Colonial Constitutions.* London: Oxford University Press, 1952.

Wylie, Kenneth C. "Innovation and Change in Mende Chieftaincy 1880–1896," *Journal of African History,* X, No. 2, 1969.

FRENCH AFRICA

*Cowan, L. Gray. *Local Government in West Africa.* New York: Columbia University Press, 1958.

Crowder, Michael. *Senegal, a Study in French Assimilation Policy.* New York: Barnes & Noble, 1967.

*Delavignette, R. *Freedom and Authority in French West Africa.* London: Frank Cass, 1968.

Johnson, G. Wesley. "Blaise Diagne: Master Politician of Senegal," *Tarikh,* I, No. 2, 1966.

Newbury, Colin W. "The Formation of the Government General of French West Africa," *Journal of African History*, I, No. 1, 1960.
Robinson, Kenneth E. "French West Africa," *African Affairs*, I, 1951.
Weinstein, Brian. "Felix Eboué and the Chiefs," *Journal of African History*, XI, No. 1, 1970.

BELGIAN AFRICA

*Anstey, Roger. *King Leopold's Legacy*. London: Oxford University Press, 1966.
*Brausch, George. *Belgian Administration in the Congo*. London: Oxford University Press, 1961.
Buell, R. L. *The Native Problem in Africa*, 2 vols. London: Frank Case, 1965.
Gravel, Pierre Bettez. "Life on the Manbi in Gisaka (Rwanda)," *Journal of African History*, VI, No. 3, 1965.
Ryckmans, Pierre. "Belgian Colonialism," *Foreign Affairs*, XXXIV, 1955.

PORTUGUESE AFRICA

+*Duffy, James. *Portugal in Africa*. Baltimore, Md.: Penguin, 1963.
Duffy, James. *Portuguese Africa*. Cambridge, Mass.: Harvard University Press, 1959.
Easton, Stewart C. *The Twilight of European Colonialism*. New York: Holt, Rinehart and Winston, 1960.
Egerton, F. Clement. *Angola in Perspective*. London: Routledge and Kegan Paul, 1957.

Chapter Eight
COLONIAL AFRICA—THE INTERWAR PERIOD

ECONOMIC DEVELOPMENT AND SOCIAL CHANGE

Blair, T. C. V. *Africa: A Market Profile*. New York: Praeger, 1965.
Cowan, L. Gray, James O'Connell and David G. Scanlon. *Education and Nation Building in Africa*. New York: Praeger, 1965.
Davis, Kingsley. *Economic Development and Cultural Change*. Chicago: University of Chicago Press, 1954.
Little, Kenneth. *West African Urbanization*. London: Cambridge University Press, 1965.
Marris, Peter. *Family and Social Change in an African City*. Evanston, Ill.: Northwestern University Press, 1962.
McCall, Daniel F. "Dynamics of Urbanization in Africa," *Annals of the American Academy of Political and Social Science*, No. 29, March 1955.
Munger, Edwin S. "Adam Smith in East Africa," *African Field Reports, 1952–1961*. New York: American Universities Field Staff, 1955.

SEPARATIST CHURCH MOVEMENTS

Hodgkin, Thomas. *Nationalism in Colonial Africa.* New York: New York University Press, 1957.
*Hooker, J. R. "Witnesses and Watchtower in the Rhodesias and Nyasaland," *Journal of African History,* VI, No. 1, 1965.
Lynch, Hollis R. "The Native Pastorate Controversy and Cultural Ethno-Centrism in Sierra Leone," *Journal of African History,* V, No. 3, 1964.
Rotberg, Robert I. *The Rise of Nationalism in Central Africa.* Cambridge, Mass.: Harvard University Press, 1965.
*Shepperson, George. *Independent Africans, John Chilembwe and the Origins,'Settling and Significance of the Nyasaland Native Revolt of 1915.* Edinburgh: Edinburgh University Press, 1958.
Shepperson, George. "The Politics of African Church Separatist Movements in British Central Africa, 1892–1916," *Africa,* XXIV, 1954.

EARLY POLITICAL PARTIES

+*Awolowo, Obafemi. *Awo.* London: Cambridge University Press, 1961.
+*Azikwe, Benjamin Nnamdi. *Zik.* London: Cambridge University Press, 1961.
Hargreaves, J. D. *Life of Sir Samuel Lewis.* London: Oxford University Press, 1958.
Leys, Norman. *Kenya.* London: Hogarth Press, 1925.
*Nkrumah, Kwame. *Ghana: the Autobiography of Kwame Nkrumah.* New York: Nelson, 1957.
Perham, Margery, and Elspeth Huxley. *Race and Politics in Kenya.* London: Faber & Faber, 1956.
Thomas, Issac B. *A Life History of Herbert Macaulay.* Lagos: N.P., 1946.

PAN AFRICANISM

Cronon, Edmund David. *Black Moses.* Madison, Wis.: University of Wisconsin Press, 1969.
Du Bois, W. E. B. *Color and Democracy.* New York: Harcourt, Brace & World, 1945.
Du Bois, W. E. B. *The World and Africa.* New York: Viking Press, 1946.
Hooker, James R. *Black Revolutionary.* New York: Praeger, 1970.
Hughes, Langston. *The Langston Hughes Reorder.* New York: Braziller, 1958.
+*Legum, Colin. *Pan Africanism.* New York: Praeger, 1965.
Lynch, Hollis R. *Edward Wilmot Blyden: Pan-Negro Patriot.* New York: Oxford University Press, 1970.
*Padmore, George (ed.). *History of the Pan-African Congress.* London: Hammersmith Bookshop, 1963.
Rudwick, Elliot M. *W. E. B. Du Bois.* Philadelphia: University of Pennsylvania Press, 1960.

Shepperson, George. "Notes on Negro American Influences on the Emergence of African Nationalism," *Journal of African History,* I, No. 2, 1960.

Index

COLLEGE OF MARIN LIBRARY

3 2555 00005724 5

117563

DT 20 .G3 1989
Gailey, Harry A.
History of Africa

V.2

	DATE DUE		
MAY 2 7 1992			
MAY 2 7 1994			

COLLEGE OF MARIN LIBRARY

KENTFIELD, CALIFORNIA

COM